教育部人文社会科学研究规划项目(13YJA740046)基金资助
中央高校基本科研业务费专项基金资助项目

功能语言学视角下责任情态的人际意义研究

On Interpersonal Meaning of Deontic Modality from the Perspective of Functional Linguistics

孙启耀　周薇薇　著
邓晓明　主审

HEUP 哈尔滨工程大学出版社

内 容 简 介

全书共分12章，以功能语言学为研究主线，系统介绍了责任情态人际意义的国内外研究动态，从新闻、政治、教育、广告、教学、性别和文化差异等方面对责任情态的人际意义展开系统的研究。

本书可供大学英语专业高年级本科生及研究生使用，也可供对情态及人际意义研究感兴趣的非英语专业研究生课外阅读参考。

图书在版编目(CIP)数据

功能语言学视角下责任情态的人际意义研究/孙启耀，周薇薇著. —哈尔滨：哈尔滨工程大学出版社，2014.7

ISBN 978-7-5661-0862-3

Ⅰ.①功… Ⅱ.①孙… ②周… Ⅲ.①功能(语言学)-研究 Ⅳ.①H0

中国版本图书馆CIP数据核字(2014)第172442号

出版发行 哈尔滨工程大学出版社
社　　址 哈尔滨市南岗区东大直街124号
邮政编码 150001
发行电话 0451-82519328
传　　真 0451-82519699
经　　销 新华书店
印　　刷 哈尔滨市石桥印务有限公司
开　　本 787mm×960mm 1/16
印　　张 14
字　　数 302千字
版　　次 2014年8月第1版
印　　次 2014年8月第1次印刷
定　　价 30.00元
http://www.hrbeupress.com
E-mail:heupress@hrbeu.edu.cn

前　言

PREFACE

韩礼德认为,语言具有三大功能:概念功能、语篇功能和人际功能。语言学界对前两个功能研究得比较透彻,成果也较为丰硕。而第三个功能——人际功能——则没有引起学界相当的重视。相对来说,人际功能研究得比较少,成果也相对弱一些。时至21世纪初,李战子以敏锐的目光观察到了人际功能没有得以充分研究的事实,率先对话语的人际意义展开了研究,取得了一系列的成果。受李战子研究的启发,我们注意到语篇中责任情态的研究还鲜为人知,语篇责任情态的人际意义更是无人涉足。本书作者不揣鄙陋,以语篇责任情态的人际意义为研究出发点,冀望能开辟一点新的研究天地。

全书共分12章,以功能语言学为研究主线,系统介绍了责任情态人际意义的国内外研究动态,从新闻、政治、教育、广告、教学、性别和文化差异等方面对责任情态的人际意义展开系统的研究。本书可供大学英语专业高年级本科生及研究生使用,也可供对情态及人际意义研究感兴趣的非英语专业研究生课外阅读参考。

本书最后一章尝试研究了责任型情态研究中的一个重要概念——责任型情态的表达度。责任型情态的表达度主要体现在情态量值和情态取向两个方面,其中倾向性责任型情态的表达度通常被认为和量值对应,义务性责任型情态的表达度一般被认为与取向对应。通过对不同语料进行责任情态的人际意义研究,我们发现,责任型情态的实现手段具有鲜明的特征。英语话语倾向使用限定性情态操作词和谓语的扩展式来表达责任型情态,并且前者的使用频率要远远高于后者。语篇中限定性情态词的使用能够使说话者的观点和评论更客观,进而更容易为听众所接受,同时也有助于说话者委婉地表达出自己的态度和看法,避免承担绝对的责任。在情态量值方面,当说话者想要表达承诺和期望的时候,他们倾向使用中量值的责任型情态;在陈述和阐明责任和义务时,则倾向使用高量值的责任型情态。在情态取向方面,主观隐性占据主要地位,客观隐性时有出现。就情态意义而言,倾向性责任型情态表达出现的频率高于义务性责任型情态的表达。

作者在编写过程中参阅了国内外有关学者的研究成果,追踪了相关领域研究的最新发展动态。在学习过程中,作者也受益匪浅。要加以说明的是,本书所用材料是作者在不同阶段针对不同的目的收集的不同材料,稍有重复还请谅解。在本书成稿之际,笔者要感谢那些对责任情态研究的发展做出贡献的研究人员,包括作者本人的研究生董欣蓉、刘源、韩蕾、嵩贺、费钰芜、宋鹏飞以及李美婷等。同时感谢所有关心、支持本书的机构和个人。感谢哈尔滨工程大学研究生精品课的部分资助。本书1,2,5,7,9章由周薇薇撰写,约13万字,3,4,6,8,10,11,12章由孙启耀撰写,约17万字,最后由孙启耀统稿,邓晓明教授主审。

作者希望本书能引起更多人对责任情态研究的关注。由于水平有限,不当之处在所难免,诚挚地希望广大师生和读者提出批评和建议。

著　者

2014年3月于哈尔滨

目　录
CONTENTS

CONTENTS

CONTENTS

Chapter 1 Literature Review

It has been over 2,000 years since the term of "modality" is introduced to classic philosophy by Aristotle. During the development of science typically linguistics, in the West, modality has been under the discussion from the perspective of modal logic. Afterwards, some branches in linguistics like traditional grammar, semantics, semiotics, cognitive linguistics, psycho-linguistics and systemic functional linguistics probe into the study of modality respectively. Presently, scholars transit their study of modality from modal verbs to modal meanings, and come into the field of discourse gradually.

1.1 Basic Concepts and Classifications

In the theory of Systemic Functional Linguistics (SFL), the definition of modality is closely associated with Lyons. He believes that modality expresses speakers' views and attitudes on sentences and their descriptions. Modality cannot be limited only to modal verbs, but some other words like *frankly*, *fortunately*, *possibly*, *wisely*, etc. (Lyons, 1977:451) The definition of modality is later modified in Halliday (1985) as referring to "intermediate degrees, between the positive and negative poles" and realizing "the speaker's judgment of the probabilities, or the obligations, involved in what he is saying" (1994:75).

Affected by Lyons et al, Bussmann, the editor of *Dictionaries of Language and Linguistics* also provides a definition of modality: Modality signifies the attitude of speakers on utterance contents (2000). It is about the mood in forms, ranging from indicative mood to subjunctive and imperative mood. It may be different sentence patterns like declarative sentences, interrogative sentences, and imperative sentences. Bussmann indicates modality can be realized by a series of ways: (a) tone of verbs; (b) vocabularies like *hopefully* and *maybe*, and modals like *can* and *may*; (c) syntax, like using the explanation structure made by *would* and *have to*. (Bussmann, 2000:308)

In the general sense of understanding, modality can be seen as a speaker's cognitive and emotional attitude towards a state. (Asher, 1995) The understanding of modality in linguistics derives from modal logic, that is, a subject's effectiveness and relativity to a series of possible worlds. (Bybee, 1995:4) The only modality in traditional logic is linked with necessity and possibility. The modality in the logic is based on necessity and possibility. Here the possibility means a subject is real at least in a possible world. The essence of modality is related effectiveness of the meaning of a sentence to a series of possible world.

Due to different perspectives held by linguistic schools, there has never been an anonymous classification of modality. Lyons (1997:793) divides modality into two parts, that is, epistemic modality and deontic modality. Epistemic modality is about knowledge and belief while deontic modality is about possibility and necessity of morally responsible main body's behavior. This is dichotomy from the perspective of logic. Besides, in traditional grammar, modality is the meaning that a series of modal auxiliary verbs express. Grammarians hold the idea that modality is equivalent to modal expressions syntactically and from the perspective of morpheme. Every sentence consists of two parts, that is, *dictum* (the expressed content) and *modus* (how to express the content). The main task of linguistics is to distinguish the modality part from the content part. When modality is expressed by a high-level rhyme, it is easy to distinguish them; while the modality itself is only one part of a simple sentence, and the distinction becomes complicated. In this situation, the modal expression has many forms, such as adverbs, modal verbs, or marks on the verbs (mood, tense) etc. Palmer has took it as a general classification in sense of meaning. He further divided modality into propositional modality and event modality. The former is composed of epistemic and evidential modality; the latter is classified into deontic and dynamic modality. Deontic modality consists of three sub-categories—permissive, obligative and commissive (Palmer, 1979:22). However, Palmer's study on deontic modality is confined to modal auxiliary, and numerous expressions except for modal auxiliary contain deontic meanings, which could be regarded as deontic modality.

Modality can be classified from different perspectives. "According to the distinction between propositions ('information', i. e. statements and questions) and proposals ('goods-&-services', i. e. offers and commands), Halliday classified modality into two types: modalization and modulation" (Fan Wenfang, 2001:97). The former one refers to the degree of probability and usuality. Generally speaking, it means that modality is used to express the speaker's opinion or a request for the listener's opinion. However, modulation refers to obligation, inclination and willingness. In the communication, people need to exchange goods and services with others. They use modality to show that they wish to do something or request someone else to do something. At this time, modality expresses strong interpersonal meaning.

The classification is thought to be wrong, because two sub-categories of modality seem to be corresponding to epistemic modality and deontic modality, which cannot be mentioned in the same breath, according to Bybee (1994). He equals deontic modality with root modality, where epistemic modality develops from (qtd. in Li Zhanzi, 2002:76). Besides, Givon holds that deontic modality is marked, while epistemic is unmarked because no responsibility is loaded in epistemic modality. He classified modality into epistemic and evaluative modality, and maintained that deontic modality is only a part of the latter (Givon, 1995:121). A more elaborate classification was made by Simpson who classifies modality into four categories, namely, deontic system, boulomaic system, the epistemic system, with the subsystem of perception modality (Fan Wenfang, 2001:79).

Additionally, linguists give different classifications based on different semantic types, modality orientation and typology category. For instance, Halliday (1985) classifies modality as high-modality value (*must*, *ought to*, *need*, *has to*, *is to*), median-modality value (*will*, *would*, *shall*, *should*) and low-modality value (*may*, *might*, *can*, *could*). The three modality values are frequently used in the study of meaning of discourse and utterance, so as to discuss the interpersonal function of writers and readers, and speakers and listeners.

Scholars at home and abroad have paid increasing attention to interpersonal meanings expressed by modality in specific discourse. In this book, the authors aim at analyzing interpersonal meanings expressed by deontic modality from different perspectives, including political speeches, advertisements, verbal language, education language, female language, etc.

1.2 Studies on Modality

1.2.1 Studies on Modality Abroad

It is said that modality is both an old and a young topic. Since the proposal of modal theory by Greek philosopher Aristotle, more than two thousand years have witnessed the study of modality. However, lots of problems concerning modality haven't been convincingly resolved or explained. No matter in the field of logistics or linguistics, owning to the complexity of modality and the close relationship between human beings' cognition and modality, the study of modality can be called the ivy of the study in those two fields.

The research of modality is primarily performed in philosophical category. Linguistic research of modality developed from the study results of modal logic. Aristotle's modal logic put forward and defined four modal operators: *necessary*, *contingent*, *possible* and *impossible*. Moreover, he discussed the modal propositions that consist of these four modal operators. The modal logic is to study the alethic modalities of the "possibility" and "impossibility". The traditional modal logic represented by Aristotle mainly researched modal syllogistic, modal judgment and certain analysis of modality and so on.

At the early twentieth century, Lewis did a more systemic study of modals from the aspect of mathematical logic. It marked the establishment of the modern modal logic. In 1950's, Von Wright, Anderson and other researchers pointed out the similarity between deontic logic and alethic modal logic and hold the view that those deontic concepts such as: *obligatory*, *permitted*, *forbidden* can also be taken as a kind of modality which are closely linked with the alethic modality. Moreover, those researchers have done rigorous logical analysis about it. Von Wright divided modal into four modes: alethic modal, epistemic modal, deontic modal and existential modal. (Von Wright, 1951: 213) He admitted that existential modal concerns with quantification theory. Although it isn't usually considered as a branch of modal logic, it has basic similarity with other modals which can be seen from the table below.

Table 1.1 Basic Similarities of Modals

alethic modal	epistemic	deontic	existential
necessary	verified	obligatory	universal
possible	permitted	existing	
contingent	undecided	indifferent	
impossible	falsified	forbidden	empty

Von Wright (1951) listed these modal logic categories in order to explore their formal structures, just as qualification theory does. His classification of modality significantly influenced general modal logic and linguistic research of modality. Especially, he classified epistemic and deontic modality which has a direct impact on the study of modality and this kind of classification has been used in linguistic study of modal.

Modal logic in general refers to alethic modal logic; narrowly speaking, it also includes deontic logic, tense logic, intuitionistic logic etc.

From logical aspect, Rescher identified eight kinds of modal including: ① alethic modal concerning "possible" and "necessary"; ② epistemic modal connected with knowledge and belief; ③ temporal modal which related to time concept; ④ boulomaic modal expressing hope, desire and other notions; ⑤ deontic modal which concerned with obligation, permission, and forbiddance etc. ;⑥ evaluative modal concerning good or bad and so on;⑦ causal modal about cause and effect;⑧ likelihood modal conveying possibility. (qtd. from Perkins,1983:9).

Rescher (1968) takes modality as a concept which is relative to proposition, that is to say, a complete and independent sentence expresses a true or false proposition, and when this proposition is modified by the restricted component and turns into another proposition, and the restricted component is the so called modality of the former proposition. Therefore, Rescher studied modality from the broad sense and identified some types of modality, for instance, causal modality which is not regarded as a kind of modality by the later researchers.

The analysis of modal forms in logic is different from actual natural language. But the research results of modal logic significantly guided the study of modality in linguistics and shed great lights on it.

Of course, just as Palmer said, the viewpoint of concern of modality is different between linguists and logicians (1986). Logicians explore the formal structures of modal according to alethic table while linguists mainly investigate the types of modality which can be clearly identified and the system manifesting these kinds of modal. Moreover, logicians mainly concern alethic modality which is unimportant in everyday language and cannot be distinguished from epistemic modal by the users of languages.

The modality in natural language widely attracts linguists. In western countries, many linguistic schools including those of traditional grammar, semantics, transformational-generative grammar, pragmatics, systemic functional grammar and cognitive grammar have researched modal and achieved considerable results. In 1960s and 1970s those linguists who mainly studied western languages especially English have began to analyze modality in languages especially from the aspect of semantics. By analysis, we learned that there are some modal meanings including: *possibility*, *contigency*, *obligation* and *permission*. They were divided into two major types: *epistemic modality* and *deontic modality* (Lyons, 1997: 452). Moreover, researchers have explored the relationship between them.

Lyons has earlier systemically observed the modality in English (Lyons, 1997: 17). He attempted to define modality and discussed necessity and possibility in epistemic modality and deontic modality. He also analyzed the relation between epistemic modality and factivity and probed into the relation between tense and modality. In addition, he proposed the concept of modality. With the great influences, his researches on modality provided a starting point and foundation and specified the direction of later studies.

Palmer (1979) did a systemic analysis of meanings and forms of modal verbs. He defined modal verbs according to Lyons' definition and classification. He pointed out that modal verbs in

English have special syntactic and lexical features. According to the meanings expressed by English modal verbs, he classified modality into epistemic modality, deontic modality and dynamic modality and each includes possibility and necessity. Palmer (2007) primarily systematically analyzed the meaning of modal verbs which is the main carrier of English modality and provided a sample for the later studies on English modal verbs and modality in other languages.

Perkins examined various kinds of modality meanings (Perkins, 1983: 32). His examining objects are not only limited to modal verbs, but also include other modal expressions. Moreover, he tried to interpret those expressions comprehensively. He also studied the relationship between modal expressions and politeness and researched the modal expressions in children's language. He defined modality from the aspect of possible world and divided modality into epistemic modality, deontic modality and dynamic modality. These three categories of modality are constrained respectively by three kinds of rules: rational rules, institutional rules and nature rules. Perkins' study brought us into realizing the varieties of modality expressions in natural language and showed us the complexity of expressing modality; at the same time his study broadened the views of modality study.

Based on corpus, Coates analyzed the syntactic context in which modality appears (Coates, 1983: 83). She particularly analyzed how the context influences the expressed meanings of modal verbs. She classified modality into epistemic modality and non-epistemic modality and pointed out that most of the modal verbs have the indeterminacy between these two kinds of modality. Moreover, the indeterminacy is manifested by gradience, ambiguity or merger. She investigated the syntax environment which can eliminate the indeterminacy and held the view that the agentivity of the main verb in the sentence, the futurity of the time, the factivity of the proposition, the past tense form of the modality and the stress and tone etc. All play roles in defining the meaning of the modal verbs. Coates' study manifested that the modal category is not isolated but intrinsically linked with other categories.

In 1986, Palmer attempted to define modality as a general grammatical category and established a frame system to describe the modality system of various languages. He analyzed different means of expressions of epistemic modality, deontic modality in different languages and explored the modality meaning concerns complement clauses and oblique clauses and discussed the relationship between modality and tense, negation, and person. Palmer believed that modality expresses the attitude of the speaker and is a sub-branch of semantics.

Papafragou (2003: 186) studied how English modal verbs express their meanings as to illustrate the interaction between lexical meaning and pragmatic meaning. Based on meta representation theory and relevance theory, he discussed the role played by contexts in transmission of modal verbs' lexical meanings. Her basic point is that the semantic coding of modal verbs largely underdetermines the explanation of these verbs in discourse comprehension. Therefore, she believed that English modal verbs have unitary lexical meanings which combine with different pragmatic meanings and produce a series of different context decoding. Her researches deepened the interpretation of modality into pragmatic level and provided more aspects for studying and interpreting of modality.

Based on the study in 1986, Palmer reconstructed modality system and researched epistemic modality, evidential modality, deontic modality and dynamic modality under two major categories: prepositional modality and event modality. Moreover, Palmer profoundly discussed mood such as indicative and subjunctive which is relevant to modality and studied some concepts concerned mood such as realis and irrealis. From the linguistic typology aspect, Palmer (2007) summarized the generality in modality semantic system of human beings' languages and the individuality in the methods of expressing modality. It deepens the study of composition and the methods of expressing of modality semantic system.

1.2.2 Studies on Modality at Home

Although there are rich means of expression of modality in modern Chinese, Chinese linguists haven't focused on the study of modality yet. The specific study of modality was probably from 1989 when Liao Qiuzhong translated *Mood and Modality* written by Palmer. Until the 12th seminar on Modern Chinese Grammar held in Changsha, Hu'nan in April 2004, modality was indentified as one of the themes of the meeting. Before this, the study of Chinese modality expressions such as auxiliaries, modality adverbs, modal particles etc. was put on syntactic features or on the semantic description or analysis and never consciously put on the study of modality in human beings' languages.

Wang Li (1984: 74) had described mood adverbs and modal adverbs as the expressing methods of mood. However, he didn't analyze them systematically and only considered these adverbs as the expressions of emotions. That is to say, he didn't explore the essence of the meaning of mood adverbs and modal adverbs.

Later researchers began to consciously pay attention to modality such as He Yang (1992), Qi Huyang (2002), Lu Chuan (2003), Cui Xiliang (2003) and other researchers all attempted to overall study modern Chinese' modality system. Except the studies on "mood", Qi Huyang also differentiated "mood" from "implication" and holds the view that "implication" should not be included in "mood". He shares the similar ideas with He Yang. However, he classified the mood system from the more generalized aspect. From his point of view, the mood system consists of two sub-ones: the functional classification and the intentional classification. They studied modal auxiliaries, modal adverbs, mood particles, sentence categories, interjections and so on. We can see that although they both applied the word "mood", the so called "mood" they researched is the modality we refer to.

The main idea of Lu Chuan is that there are two kinds of subjective information in language: ① subjective factors; ② subjective markers. Subjective markers express the speaker's intention, emotion and attitudes by mood markers and modality markers. "Mood" reflects the communication intention of the speaker while "modality" performs the attitude of the speaker to the listener based on the inherent subjective knowledge. Although he didn't point it out clearly, we can get from his point of view that "mood" is expressed by sentences and mood auxiliaries while "modality" is expressed by adverbs (especially modal adverbs) and modal auxiliaries.

In essence, Lu Chuan's "mood" is roughly equivalent to the "function mood" He Yang and Qi Huyang refer to. The "modality" here refers to He Yang and Qi Huyang's volitional modality. The only difference is Lu Chuan believed that "mood" and "modality" should be differentiated and both belong to subjective markers while He Yang and Qi Huyang regarded them both as "mood". It is meaningless to discuss these terms. Although Lu Chuan's understandings and expressions are more thorough, to this category, in essence, He Yang and Qi Huyang share the same viewpoint. It goes as follows:

Table 1.2 Modality Classifications of Some Chinese Researchers

Lu Chuan(2003)		He Yang(1992) Qi Huyang(2002)	
subjective mark	mood	functional mood	mood
	modality	power, judgment, emotional mood	

Their researches have both progress and drawbacks: they have explicitly realized that meanings expressed by mood auxiliaries, modal adverbs, modal auxiliaries etc. all belong to a major category and tried to construct it systematically; the drawbacks lie in their understandings to different categories of sentences (declarative, interrogative, imperative and exclamative).

"Modality" in Cui Xiliang's study is the same as Palmer defined. He broadens the implication of modality to every event and situations concerning complex verbs. From his point of view, the modal meaning conveyed by mood auxiliaries and modal adverbs in Chinese is speaker-oriented modality while those expressed by modal auxiliaries are all illocutionary modality.

Actually, there are two problems: one is that modal auxiliaries not only deliver dynamic modality and deontic modality, but also convey epistemic modality; the other is that not all the modal meanings expressed by modal auxiliaries are illocutionary modality. As a matter of fact, only dynamic modality is a kind of illocutionary modality while epistemic modality and deontic modality are speaker-oriented modality.

The studies by the researchers we mentioned above are all from the theoretical aspect of modality and attempt to systematically study the modality system in modern Chinese from the aspect of modality meaning. However, some of their explanations for modality system need further researches. For example they didn't specify the roles played by various expressions in modality system.

Although the domestic study and studies abroad of modality is not comprehensive and thorough, it could play a significant role in our discussions.

1.2.3 Studies on Modality in Different Fields of Linguistics

In general sense of understanding, modality can be seen as a speaker's cognitive and emotional attitude towards a state. The understanding of modality in linguistics derives from modal logic, that is, a subject's effectiveness and relativity to a series of possible worlds. The only modality in traditional logic is linked with necessity and possibility. The modality in the logic is based on necessity and possibility. Here the possibility means a subject is real at least in a possible world. "The essence of modality is relativized effectiveness of the meaning of a sentence to a series of possible world." (Li Zhanzi, 2002:74).

Besides, in traditional grammar, modality is the meaning that a series of modal auxiliary verbs express. Grammarians hold the idea that modality is equivalent to modal expressions syntactically and from the perspective of morpheme; every sentence consists of two parts, that is, dictum (the expressed content) and modus (how to express the content). The main task of linguistics is to distinguish the modality part from the content part. When modality is expressed by a high-level rhyme, it is easy to distinguish them; while the modality itself is only one part of a simple sentence. The distinction becomes complicated. In this situation, the modal expression has many forms, such as adverbs, modal verbs, or marks on the verbs (mood, tense) etc.

In Halliday's functional linguistics, language has three functions, that is, ideographic function, interpersonal function and textual functions (Li Zhanzi, 2002:74). The interpersonal function concerns the interactive relationship between the author and the targeted readers, i. e. the speaker uses languages to express his/her attitude towards what is said or written as well as to influence listeners' attitude and behavior. And modality acts as the main semantic sector of this interpersonal function, which makes itself obtain a very important position beyond logic and the traditional grammar.

The study of modality in discourse can help us understand how people make meanings about interpersonal dimensions such as the power or solidarity, their status and social roles, and their attitude and judgments.

Different linguistic domains have made studies on modality, involving traditional grammar, semantic, transformational-generative grammar, pragmatics, and systematic functional grammar, etc.

(1) Modality in traditional grammar

Traditional grammar considers modality as auxiliaries. From the perspective of syntax, traditional grammar divides auxiliaries into three types: basic auxiliaries, modals, and semi-auxiliaries, mainly discussing the change of words when modals are used as auxiliaries, their place in interrogative sentences, affirmative sentences and negative sentences, their relationships with other compositions and particularity of modals. From the perspective of meaning, traditional grammar also divides modals into three types: permission and probability, obligation and necessity, and willingness and prospect.

The studies on modality on the perspective of traditional grammar could be summarized as two aspects. On the one hand, many researchers hold the view that they should continue to study modality with the methodology as the predecessors did. Palmer (1974, 1979) analyzed the semantics meanings of the modal verbs systematically. Quirk (1972) proposed the criterions on determiners. For example, *may* and *might* both convey the meanings of "permission" or "request", or the unsure supposition; it expressed a meaning of "wish" when *may* is put at the head of a sentence, such as "May God bless you!" and "He might be at home". When *might* conveys a meaning of supposition, it doesn't present the tense. *may* and *might* could also convey the meanings of possibility, and the mood of *might* is more indirect.

Modality study in terms of traditional perspective mainly discusses the changes of the word form of modal verbs (mainly auxiliary verbs such as *can*, *could*, *may*, *might*, *shall*, *should*, *will*, *would* and *must*) which exist in interrogative sentences, positive sentences and negative sentences. For example, "The young girl can manage it." and "The old lady might recognize it." From the above two sentences we could observe that although the modal auxiliary verbs convey different functions in the sentence, one point should be agreed that the modal auxiliary verbs follow the infinite verbs, and verbs in original form follow it forever. If we want to change the positive sentence into interrogative sentence, the modal auxiliary verbs should be put ahead of the sentence, plus a *not* behind them when a negative sentence is needed.

On the other hand, some researchers think that the studies on modality on the traditional perspective focus on more about the problems of form, logic and concept, etc., which results in ignoring the study on language itself (Sweester, 1990). Thus, many researchers such as Coats (1983), Lyons (1977), Perkins (1980, 1983), Sweester (1982, 1984) and Halliday (1985, 2000), started to focus more on the study of modality on many perspectives such as semantics, pragmatics, and functional grammar, which injected new blood to the modality research field. Geoffrey Leech (1971) gave a detailed discussion on modal auxiliary verbs. He divided the modal auxiliary verbs into seven types: conception meaning, associative meaning, social meaning, emotional meaning, reflection meaning, collocation meaning, theme meaning, which conveys the different modality meanings. For example, Palmer (1979) made a figure that showed the different meaning conveyed by the modal auxiliary verb *can*.

We admit a fact that the study on modality on traditional perspective has both advantages and disadvantages. The advantage is that it provides a clear framework of modality, and it is helpful for those fresh language learners. However, we have to say that the study on modality on traditional grammar perspective have a big limitation that the study is only about modal auxiliary, departing from the context.

(2) Modality in semantics

Studies of modality in semantics mainly focus on modal logic, concerning necessity and probability. Common semantics concentrates the study of modality on epistemic modality and deontic modality.

In modal logic, modality is considered as functional words, making complicated sentences with those sentences without modals, for example, "it is impossible that" and "Kate can be here early" can make one sentence "It is impossible that Kate can be here early."

Most studies place emphasis on alethic modality, i. e., one proposition's effectiveness mapping on a series of true and false values in the probable world. The probable world is consistent with the real world, and if the sentence statement is a true incident, we would comment it in the context of the true world; however, if this statement exists in the non-real world, like fables and non-fictions, it may be a probable world. *Thought* can be a probable world, and "we may regard the real world as one part of the probable world, and in this way, the context explained by sentences can be the congregation of the probable world or one subset of it." (Jiang Yan et al., 1998: 361-362)

Additionally, there are three viewpoints on modals in traditional semantics (Papafragou, 1998). Firstly, modals are ambiguous. There may be two explanations for one modal, i. e., cognitive modality and deontic modality, and both of these two meanings have no relationships.

Secondly, modals have multi-meanings, which is the main viewpoint and reflects the variations of people's sentiment. Lastly, modals are univocal. They believe modals have one core meaning, and this core meaning gives rise to all other real meanings.

(3) Modality in transformational-generative grammar

Being affected by traditional grammar, transformational-generative grammar solely limits modality to modals. People firstly touch upon modality when talking about verbs. Owing to the fact that modals do not have the form of past participles, gerunds and the third person singulars, while verbs have those transforms, the three forms become the distinctions of modals and verbs (Radford, 1988:59). Meanwhile, this also serves as the test standard for verbs, since modals must be followed by verbs.

(4) Modality in pragmatics

Though it concerns most about utterance and context, pragmatics takes certain interest in modality. Modality in pragmatics is mainly about the study of implicature and presupposition. As Verschueren (1999:129) points out: "Modality is an inherently pragmatic phenomenon. It involves many ways in which attitudes can be expressed towards the 'pure' reference-and-predication content of an utterance." The pragmatic perspective on language use targets the very nature of everyday linguistic action, seen in terms of its users, the uses which language serves, and the dialectal synergies which arise between these elements and the ever-shifting social, cultural and ideational contexts in which language users act and exist. Many aspects of our lives are oriented towards convincing a colleague to approach a task in a new way, trying to eradicate one of our own prejudices. Some of us, even, are involved professionally in the business of changing minds: the therapist who affects his patient's self-concept; the teacher who introduces students to new ways of thinking about a familiar topic; the salesperson or advertiser who convinces consumers to switch brands.

(5) Modality in systematic functional grammar

Systematic functional grammar has made significant contribution to the study of modality. It proposes that modality is one crucial part of interpersonal function, displaying language users' estimation and uncertainty on the cognition of things. (Halliday, 1994) Halliday connects modality and polarity into one, holding the opinion that modality refers to the medium statement of "YES" and "NO", i. e., the area between positive meaning and negative meaning. He also classifies modality into two types: modalization and modulation. Both of them are correspondent to proposition and proposal. Modalization has two subsets: probability and frequency, which are realized by modal operation words like *will*, modal adjuncts like *probably* or *usually*, or the integration of modal operation words and modal adjuncts in the way of "that will probably be

John"; modulation can be divided into obligation and willingness, mainly being completed by modal operation words and the development of predicates (Hu Zhuanglin, 1994: 120-121). Moreover, Halliday puts forward the concept of metaphors of modality, and regarding it as one part of interpersonal metaphor. In this way, Halliday points out that modal functions are not only embodied by modals, but by nouns, adjectives, adverbs, prepositional phrases and some related structures like short sentences (Hu Zhuanglin, 1989: 123). These viewpoints are thought to be great breakthrough and contribution of systematic functional grammar to the study of modality.

Functional linguists do their researches on modality from a new perspective. They propose that language has three metafunctions: conceptual, interpersonal and textual. The interpersonal function is concerned with the co-relationship between the speaker and the hearer, that is, the speaker expresses his/her idea or attitude, and influences the hearer's attitude and behavior. Thompson (2000) claims that people use language to communicate with others and to maintain social relationships, at the same time, people use language to express their viewpoints about the world, even use language to change the world.

Functional linguists define modality as the speaker's judgment for the effectiveness and significance of the proposition he/she gives, or the obligations that he/she asks for in the command, or the will he/she wants to express in the proposition. As modality covers the intermediate meaning between yes and no, and the speaker's assessment and uncertainty about the things, it will result in the fact that the speaker's expression contains possibility and desirability. However, this possibility and desirability shows the trace of modality expressions. Fowler also believes that modality expresses the speaker's evaluation or attitude.

For some reasons and certain purposes, sometimes the speaker doesn't express his/her viewpoint in a direct way, but he/she wavers in the intermediate meaning between positive and negative polarity, so the proposition can be more or less likely, more or less desirable. Linguists generally agree that there are a variety of ways to express modality meaning. The ways can be verbal, for example, the unconscious word "Ah", "Uh" or can be the conscious words to express modality meaning, such as modality, auxiliary, adjective, or other ways like adverbial and tones etc. The ways can be non-verbal as well; modality meanings can be expressed by facial expressions and gestures. To sum up, by analyzing the modality in the language, we can find out the thinking patterns of the speaker.

(6) Modality in cognitive linguistics

In cognitive linguistics, more attention is focused on the study of modality. The researchers attach importance to both synchronic phenomenon and periodical evolution, and put emphasis on the effect of cognition of speakers' mind on language meaning, which provides novel thoughts to the study of modality.

The first linguist to open up the study of modality in cognitive science is Talmy (Talmy, 1988). He employed the theory of force schemas to explain deontic modality and cognitive modality. The theory indicates that when basic schema acts on certain object as the external force, the object would move forward along the direction of the force, which is named forced action. The other two related topics are blockage and removal of resistance. Blockage appears when the external force encounters resistance. The force would make the turn and the obstacles would go forward along the direction of force. Removal of resistance means that the force would go forward along the given direction when obstacles are removed. Talmy believes the deontic meaning of modals may be explained by the force and blockage schema mentioned above (Saeed, 1998:317). For example, the meaning of *may* is an obstacle of force in people's mind, or the removal of the potential obstacle that never appears.

Being affected by Talmy, Sweetser made studies from the perspective of cognition, and expanded the study into a wider field (Sweetser, 1990:49-51). She believes modality in language is the reflection of the real world domain on rational world and speech act domain, which also means the semantic extention of root modality. Root modality refers to the modality involved the real world, for instance, obligation, permission or capability; cognitive modality means the necessity, probability and possibility of the rational world. The reason of the reflection we frequently apply the language in the external world as well as in the internal psychological world, and this application shows certain metaphorical structure paralleled with the external world, based on the force schema.

Langacker (1991) proposed his unique ideal cognitive model—dynamic evolutionary model. His model includes two important parts: the first is the structured world model, i. e., the world is structured in a particular way. In this way, something and some state may exist, while others are evacuated. The particular structure of the world tends to the happening of some things but to stop that of other things, which is so called "normal development". Some incidences never take place, because they are not consistent with the structured world. The second is the cognitive model correspondent to evolution of objective reality. For certain conceptual activists, only a limited part of reality is known. These concepts with the concept of dynamic force are called dynamic evolution model (DEM).

1.3 Studies of Interpersonal Meaning

Interpersonal meaning has been considered as an important part in Systemic Functional

Grammar for a long time, and has been studied by many researchers both abroad and at home. As the core parameter of modality, deontic modality is a concept which is closely related to interpersonal meaning. The appropriate manipulation of deontic modality has a corresponding effect on the embodiment of interpersonal meaning. Halliday (2000:342) defines interpersonal meaning as to serve to establish and maintain social relations: for the expression of social roles, which include the communication roles created by language itself, for example, the role of questioner or respondent, which we take on by asking or answering a question; and also for getting things done, by means of their interaction between one person and another. Halliday also describes interpersonal meaning from the perspective of exchange. He claims that interpersonal meaning represents speaker's own attitude and judgment, and it expresses the role relationships seeking to influence the attitude and behavior of others. According to Halliday's model of interpersonal meaning, it mainly includes two types—interactional one which is realized by mood, and attitudinal one by modality. However, mood and modality are not in a paralleled position though the model seems to suggest that. Givon (1995) modifies the model of interpersonal meaning as "epistemic", "evaluative" and "interactive". Martin (2005) claims that the study of interpersonal meaning by the approach of systematic grammar is not comprehensive, and he proposes Appraisal Theory to enrich the content of interpersonal meaning. Martin points out that, apart from grammatical methods, lexical aspect can also go on and on with new exploration. Li Zhanzi (2002) holds that, as the core concept of interpersonal metafunction at discourse level which carries a heavy semantic load, modality goes beyond its logical and grammatical notion.

1.3.1 Studies of Interpersonal Meaning Abroad

A long time ago, interpersonal meaning caught the eyes of many linguists even if it was not termed as such. In 1929, Bakhtin held that the meaning does not exist in the word or in the soul of the speaker or the listener. It is the response of interaction between the speaker and the listener by the material of a particular sound complex. In Bakhtin's point of view, only the current of verbal interaction confers more meanings on a word.

Eggins (1997) considers interpersonal meaning as the meaning of rotes and relationship, which is represented by status, intimacy contact and sharing between interactants.

Burton and Dimbleby (1997) argue that interpersonal meaning incorporates four main components: exchange of communication, specific social background, how they perceive themselves and how they wish to express themselves.

Halliday (2000:187) holds that interpersonal meaning concerns how the language realizes the dynamic meaning of the language to establish and to maintain the social relationship between the speaker and the hearer, and how the language is used to express one's own attitude or to influence the attitude and the behavior of others. According to Halliday (2000), interpersonal meaning is realized by mood system, which consists of two sub-systems: the mood system and the modality system. He also holds that other components also embody interpersonal meaning, such as the person system, the attitudinal type of epithet, the connotative meanings of lexical items functioning in the group, and prosodic features.

Linguists give the interpersonal meaning many explanations. Thompson provides a comprehensive definition for the interpersonal meaning. He definitely perceives interpersonal meaning as the meaning contained in the language to be used to communicate with other people, to show their points and to affect their behavior and attitude. On this basis, people can set relations and keep in contact with others (Thompson, 2000). Our research adopts the interpersonal meaning that Thompson gives clear and elaborated explanation about his definition of interpersonal meaning. He also discusses evaluation, claiming that "evaluation is the central part of the meaning of any text and any analysis of the interpersonal meaning of a text must be taken into account" (Thompson, 2000: 155).

Martin developed a new system of interpersonal meaning—Appraisal Theory from the perspective of semantics. "Appraisal Theory is concerned with the language of evaluation, attitude and emotion and with a set of resources that explicitly position a text's propositions interpersonally" (Martin and Rose, 2003: 22). Generally speaking, it studies how the speakers use appraisal resource to maintain their social relationships.

Eggins and Slade (1997) discuss the interpersonal meaning of casual conversation. They talk about the criteria for analyzing casual conversation, particularly some useful grammatical resources for judgment, such as choices for identifying different roles and role relations between speakers. Through examining the use of mood and modality system in actual interaction, they find that "the speaker makes meaning about such interpersonal dimensions as: the power and solidarity of their relationship; the extent of the intimacy; the level of their familiarity with each other; their attitudes and judgments" (Eggins, 1997: 193)

1.3.2 Studies of Interpersonal Meaning at Home

In China, Li Zhanzi (2002), Huang Guowen (2001) and Zhu Yongsheng (2001) have made some efforts on the study of interpersonal meaning. Li Zhanzi (2001) claims that "interpersonal meaning should not be investigated on the grammatical hierarchy. It should be investigated from the perspective of social interaction, that is, the micro-social hierarchy and macro-social hierarchy". Li Zhanzi also studies the use of epidemic modality and she finds that epidemic modality plays an important role in expressing interpersonal meanings in academic discourse. She also extends Halliday's interpersonal system, and puts forward three types of interpersonal meaning, namely: cognitive, evaluative and interactive. Li Zhanzi points out: "The interpersonal metafunction of language serves to describe the information between people. In other words, it expresses the speaker's identity, status, attitude, motivation and his inference of matters" (Li Zhanzi, 2002: 59). The interpersonal metafunction of language is a very important concept for discussing the interpersonal meanings. The concept of the interpersonal meaning has come to prominence as a result of general linguistics moving from concentrating on isolated sentences and isolated speakers to a holistic view of the communicative event that takes into account, among other things, how interaction between participants is being managed.

Huang Guowen (2002) analyzes the interpersonal meaning of six translation versions of a Chinese poem Qingming. He studies from the four aspects of interpersonal meaning: *clause types*, *speech roles*, *vocatives* and *interactants*. By analyzing, he presents us a deeper understanding of the translation.

To sum up, all these theories have helped the author to do research on interpersonal meaning. Each of the theories has its merits as well as defects. Then the author will use the relevant theories to analyze the language use in business negotiation English.

1.3.3 Related Studies of Interpersonal Meaning on Modality

Modality plays an important role in realizing interpersonal meaning. In human language, modality is an essential way to express people's thoughts and feelings in communication. Dating back to the ancient Greek times, modality began to be realized as a logical concept. Aristotle proposed the notions of "impossibility", "possibility", "necessity" and studied the relations between them, and provided the basis for modal logic, which is one of the branches of logic. Then researchers approach it from different angles. Logicians, philosophers, and linguists took into the study of modality. However, at that time, the researchers only focused on the study of modal auxiliary, and other parts didn't get the deserved attention. With the development of functional linguistics, more modal expressions did not get much attention.

In sum, since modality is an important branch of interpersonal meaning from Halliday's Functional Grammar, the study of deontic modality helps us understand how people express interpersonal meaning such as power or solidarity in relationships, social roles, judgments or attitudes. Therefore, proper configuration of deontic modality is considered to be an important means to realize interpersonal functions. By perceiving interpersonal meaning of deontic modality, values and ideologies encoded in utterances are to be unveiled.

1.4 Studies on Deontic Modality

1.4.1 Main Expressions of Deontic Modality

In the framework of Systemic Functional Grammar, modality expressions have been expanded from modal operators in traditional grammar to a broader scope. To be more specific, Halliday (2000) believes that there are altogether four ways to express modality: finite modal operators, modal adjuncts, expansion of the predicators and modality metaphors. And according to Thompson (2008), who once made a further classification of modality to distinguish positive modality from negative modality as well as neutral modality meaning that there is no modality in the statement. Deontic modality as one of the major modalities is positive and is usually realized by many evaluation adjectives and adverbs as well as perception verbs rather than words of estrangement.

Deontic modality expresses need, behavior or obligation that the speaker feels or is allowed to perform and it is divided into inclination (or intention) and obligation. In addition, there are mainly two ways to express obligation and inclination or willingness of deontic modality, that is, finite modal operators (namely *may*, *might*, *can*, *could*, *must*, *shall*, *should*, *will*, *would*, *ought to*, *have to*, *dare* and *need*) and expansion of the predicators (including adjective phrases and passive verb phrases). Furthermore, finite modal operators are often thought of as subjective implicit in the expression of modal meanings of deontic modality in Systemic Functional Grammar and they are attributed to different modal values. Speaking of predicator expansions, there are such adjective phrases as *be willing to*, *be happy to* and *be pleased to* which display the speakers' inclination and willingness. And there are such passive verb phrases as *be obliged to*, *be expected to* and *be allowed to* which show the speakers' demand, request and suggestion. All these expressions of predicator expansions are very effective in emphasizing objectivity and stating the facts for they usually leave the listeners the impression that the pressure and obligation don't come from the speaker himself/herself but from other aspects like regulations or conventions.

1.4.2 Values of Deontic Modality

As mentioned above, modality has degrees and scales, so values of deontic modality concern the degree to which the speaker commits him/herself to the validity of his/her utterance (Li Wenmei & Wang Wen, 2008: 25). The higher value the speakers use, the more certain the utterances are. As for the values of deontic modality, Halliday (2000) has listed three scales respectively as follows:

Table 1.3 Three Values of Deontic Modality (Halliday, 2000:358)

value \ deontic modality	obligation	inclination
high	required	determined
median	supposed	keen
low	allowed	willing

Table 1.4 The Values of Finite Modal Operators(Halliday, 2000:362)

modal meaning	obligation	inclination/willingness	probability
finite modal operators	must, ought to, need, have to	will, would, shall, should, is to	can, may, could, might
value	high	median	low

1.4.3 Previous Studies on Deontic Modality

Modality has attracted the linguists' attention for a very long time, while deontic modality has only got attention in late few years despite of the fact that it had been put forward a long time ago. It was Lyons (1977) who systematically observed English modality from the semantic level in the early time and discussed necessity and possibility in epistemic modality and deontic modality. Lyons' research makes a big difference to later modality study. To be more specific, his research has provided a starting point, laid the foundation and pointed out the research direction for later studies.

At present, the most widely accepted definition of modality is that it refers to "the speaker's or writer's attitude toward the exchanged information in cognition, emotion and willingness" (Asher, 1994:255), which also means that the language user is uncertain about the exchanged message. According to Halliday (2000), "modality was connected with polarity, which covers precisely the meaning between yes and no, the intermediate degrees between positive and negative polarity, where the speaker can present his/her proposition as more or less likely, more or less desirable" (Halliday, 2000:356). Halliday also makes distinction between two basic types of modality, that is, modalization and modulation. Modulation, also called deontic modality, means that if the commodity is goods-and-services, the modality relates to how confident the speaker can appear to be in the eventual success of the exchange. In commands, this concerns the degree of obligation on the other person to carry out the command; whereas in offers it concerns the degree of willingness or inclination of the speaker to fulfill the offer.

Deontic modality also refers to the attitude toward the things that possibly happen from the moral and convention aspects, which expresses the speaker's opinion or attitude toward the possibility and necessity of the event to be true and deals with permission and commitment and the like. More specifically speaking, deontic modality focuses on the necessity and possibility of the responsible agent to do some action. It describes the following event after the offered action is done rather than the action proposition itself. Besides, deontic modality often has a source or source of cause which may come from the authoritative individual or organization, or maybe from morality and law rules or some intrinsic motivation. According to Palmer (2001), deontic modality relates to obligation or permission, emanating from an external source.

However, although deontic modality stems from some kind of external authority such as rules or the laws, typically and frequently the authority is the actual speaker, who gives permission to or lays an obligation on the listener. It is for this reason that Searle (1983: 166) speaks of "directives" which he defines as "where we try to get others to do things". Directives are the most common types of deontic modality. They are permissive and obligative and expressed by may and must. Apart from the two typological categories of deontic modality, "permissive" and "obligative", there is another category, "commissive", which is defined by Searle (1983) as "where we commit ourselves to do things (166)". They are signaled by the modal verb *shall*. They can usually be seen either as promises or as threats; the only difference between these seeming to be whether what the speaker undertakes to do is or is not welcome to the listener. Furthermore, deontic modality has an intrinsic connection with future time.

Since Halliday put forward the three language meta-functions, the interpersonal function has been widely realized and there appear a lot of studies about discourse interpersonal function and meaning. Halliday (1994) holds that "interpersonal meaning concern shows the dynamic meaning of the language is realized to establish and maintain the social relationship between the speaker and the hearer, and how the language is used to express one's own attitude or to influence the attitude and behavior of the others" (187). Eggins and Slade (1997) discuss the interpersonal meaning of casual conversation. After that, Thompson (2008) introduces evaluation into the analysis of the interpersonal meaning of a text. He claims that "evaluation is a central part of the meaning of any text and that any analysis of the interpersonal meanings of a text must take it into account" (65). Later on Martin (2008) develops a new system of interpersonal meaning from the semantic aspect, e. g. the appraisal theory.

Von Wright (1989) makes a further creative study on modality both in philosophy and the later linguistics. He has discussed three types of modality: alethic modality, deontic modality, and combined modality between epistemic modality and existential modality in his book *An Essay in Modal Logic*. Among them, most researchers have made a study on and accepted epistemic modality and deontic modality. Lyons gives a clear definition of modality and he points out that the meanings of modality are related to people's attitudes and opinions. And the expressing forms of modality are merely limited to modal verbs. There are many other forms to express modal meanings, such as *frankly, fortunately, possibly and wisely*. Meanwhile, those words also make a real difference in terms of the comprehension in language subjectivity and discourse modality. He also classifies two types of modality on according to Von Wright' framework, that is, "epistemic modality is concerned with matters of information, knowledge, belief and opinion, while deontic modality is concerned with the necessity or possibility of acts performed by morally responsible agents" (793-823). To a great extent, modality is also regarded as the speaker's cognitive, emotive and volitive attitude to a state of affairs. We may still see an incongruous name in Halliday's modal. There seem existing two branches of the general modality called "epistemic modalization" and "deontic modulation". Therefore, because of more than one modal meaning that some modal verbs may indicate, this kind of classification inevitably leads to a polysemy problem.

While Bybee (1995) considers that there isn't a general modality that evolves into epistemic modalization and deontic modulation. He points out that the deontic modality should be regarded as the root modality that often develops into epistemic meanings. He also conducts a change process in the classification of modality as follows: agent-oriented modality, speaker-oriented modality and epistemic modality. Agent-oriented modality includes all modal meanings that predicate conditions on an agent with regard to the completion of an action referred to by the main predicate, such as obligations, desire and so on (qtd. in Palmer 20). With discussing so many different definitions and types of modality above, we find that epistemic modality and deontic modality are the most fundamental recognizable types of modality that are attractive in modern linguistics studies. We always explain these two types of modality in formal semantics and in standard modal. The fact that epistemic and deontic modality merge with one another diachronically and are often indistinguishable synchronically confirms the view that they are rightly classified under the same term "modality" (Lyons 334). At the same time, many researchers are concerned with making a distinction between these two types of modality, so that the process can promote the research on "deontic modality". In Lyon's book *Semantics II* (1977), he makes another achievement about the subjectivity of the discourse.

From another perspective, we can generalize that "deontic modality" means deontic modality in accordance with another concept. Halliday hasn't explicitly explained that term and he just mentions this concept in his research and his works. While Thompson makes a detailed discussion and study on "deontic modality", he gives it a definition as "how far the speaker overtly accepts responsibility for the attitude being expressed" (2000:60). According to Halliday's framework but with slight difference, Thompson conducts four main features on the scale of "deontic modality", that is, to some extent the speaker openly accepts responsibility for the subjective assessments.

Peter Collins (2009) has examined the meanings of the English modal auxiliaries, and a set of semantically-related quasi-modals, in three paroled corpora representing BrE, AmE, and AusE. A tripartite classification scheme was adopted, distinguishing between epistemic, deontic and dynamic modality. Also addressed was the interaction between modal expressions and negation, and between modal expressions and temporality in his book *Modals and Quasi-modals in English*.

In China, Huang Guowen (2002), Li Zhanzi (2002), Hu Zhuanglin and Zhu Yongsheng (2005) have made great contributions to the study of interpersonal meaning. In 2002, Li Zhanzi published her book named *Interpersonal Meaning in Discourse* and Huang Guowen studied the interpersonal meanings of the English version of a Chinese poem.

Therefore, there is no doubt that English modality, as one of the important semantic carriers in discourse for interpersonal function, has also been studied a lot. For instance, Yang Haihong (2010) makes an analysis of interpersonal meaning of modality in public service advertisements. Ying Qiaojun (2010) conducts a study on interpersonal meanings of modality in presidential inaugural addresses during the cold war and Li Feng (2011) writes a paper about the analysis of interpersonal function of mood and modality in political speeches. All these studies are about the analysis of interpersonal meaning of modality in different types of discourse without getting into further division of modality.

In terms of deontic modality, there are also a few researches about its interpersonal function and meanings in different types of discourse. Under the framework of Systemic Functional Grammar, Li Kuo (2007) writes a thesis about the study on deontic modality in English. He talks about the history of the study on modality, mood and modal system with reference to basic semantic concepts and theories. Meanwhile he makes a thorough study on the deontic modality in English language and analyzes deontic modal expressions in different styles of English texts. Besides, Liu Yuan (2011) writes a paper on the study of the interpersonal meaning of deontic modality metaphor in business negotiation English. He mainly analyzes the use of deontic modality metaphor and the interpersonal meaning conveyed by it in business negotiations as well as the reasons why deontic modality metaphor can be used in business English from the perspectives of the characteristics of business English, the function of deontic modality metaphor and social culture.

Apart from the studies on the interpersonal function or meaning of deontic modality based on a certain kind of discourse, many researches on the contrastive analysis about interpersonal meaning of deontic modality between Chinese and English discourses have also been conducted. For example, He Jianghai (2011) makes a contrastive study on modality in American and Chinese TV interviews and finds out that the modality systems in the two groups of interviews have both similarities and disparities. Specifically speaking, modal realizations are similar in the two groups while the distribution of modal expressions is quite different from each other in them. Apart from that, Liu Li (2011) conducts a contrastive analysis of modality in Chinese and American news personal commentary with the aim to explore and explain the microcosmic differences in the use of modality between Chinese and American news personal commentary and try to synthesize the native use of modality to provide some clue to English classroom of modality teaching. Furthermore, Sun Qiyao and Song He (2012) make comparisons between interpersonal meaning of the deontic modality in Chinese and English advertisements, which goes to further specific aspect of modality, deontic modality, with the findings that there exists a different realization form of deontic modality and a different modality orientation in Chinese and English ads as well as the different cultural value systems reflected by the use of deontic modality.

1.5 Prospect and Reflections

Previous studies in China reflect comprehensive and intensive discussions and studies of modality from different perspectives, with abundant achievements and results. However, a series of problems also exist in the current study. First and foremost, too many repeated results were presented, showing researches' shortage of status quo of modality, and little innovations and significant findings could be seen, either. For example, some studies about metaphorical modality and cognitive modality in academic discourse have been made comprehensively in the past ten years. However, some researchers investigated modality from these aspects as well. This phenomenon gives rise to the fact that the cultivation of graduates and postgraduates is not quite satisfactory. Therefore, to summarize and reflect upon the studies from the perspective of interpersonal meaning may reduce investigators' blindness and enlighten their research.

Secondly, it is quite imperative to broaden and update research points. Currently, the study about interpersonal meaning in China involves much less coverage. Compared to abundant studies on written discourse, those on spoken discourse are rather deficient, among which studies on spoken discourse of teachers and students, parents and children, husband and wife, doctors and patients, seniors and juniors at work, etc., deserve more attention, especially the interpersonal meaning expressed by the modality in these discourse. Sweetser (1990) makes an explanation on root modality, which is regarded as a brave attempt to extend modal meaning to the cognitive field. He classifies deontic modality into the field of root modality, while cognitive modality is the result of metaphor of deontic modality, i. e., the switch of two metaphorically paralleled domains from the outside world to the psychological one. How to explain the construction of interpersonal meaning of modality from the point of cognition and extend it from static state to dynamic state? This is a new question to consider and investigate.

Thirdly, the lack of study on interpersonal meaning of deontic modality deserves people's attention. Lyons classifies modality into cognitive modality and deontic modality, where cognitive modality concerns about knowledge and belief, and deontic modality is about probability and necessity of deontic subject behavior involving morality (Li Zhanzi, 2002: 74). At present, some researchers have carried out studies on interpersonal meaning of cognitive modality, whereas, very few studies on that of deontic modality has been performed. Therefore, the focus of deontic modality, especially its interpersonal meaning, would open up a new realm for pragmatic strategy and cognition of discourse.

Fourthly, the study on cross-culture differences of interpersonal meaning of modality is disregarded and needs more concern. Language and culture depends on each other and influences interactively. Each unique pattern of culture in different minorities determines the existence of variable thoughts and language expressions. Thus, cross-culture differences are also displayed by the expression and construction of interpersonal meaning of modality in China and the West. However, not too many researchers pay attention to the comparison of interpersonal meaning of modality.

The authors choose the present topic mainly due to the following reasons: firstly, interpersonal meaning plays an important role in human communication, and having a good command of interpersonal meaning will help the speaker keep a relative relationship with the partner. In addition, modality metaphor has been widely used in various discourses, and has caught some researchers' attention. However, the present researches are limited, not to mention the deontic modality metaphor. Deontic modality metaphor as a special language structure contains many kinds of interpersonal meanings in various discourses, especially in persuasive discourses. But few researchers have done researches on it. Secondly, in view of theoretical development, the study of the deontic modality can offer a new perspective to the development of systemic functional theories.

Modality study is thriving. The ascendancy of the central modal auxiliaries is now being challenged by the more widespread use of semi-modals and speaker preference for suppletive forms, often involving the emergence of new forms. Of course, where research is grounded in syntactic theory (Barbiers et al., 2002) or concerned with establishing typological categories (Palmer, 2001), a narrower focus on the verbal carriers of modal meanings and their interaction with other grammatical categories, such as negation and interrogation, is to be expected and is indeed necessary. However, more recent researches which seeks to investigate the phenomenon of modality would ideally cast a wider net. At least, in a pragmatic perspective, modality needs to be examined in its contexts of use where modal synergies evolve and are purposefully adapted by speakers in accordance with their communicative needs, as these change with contexts of use. Thus, the study of deontic modality is to explore how and when modal expressions combine in discourse, why they do, why speakers exploit the modal system the way they do, and what the underlying cognitive mechanisms and motivations are for their choices of words. All in all, there have been significant advances made in our knowledge of how mood and modality operate in English and cross-linguistically. The findings of recent studies need to find their way into applications and practical use of modality.

Chapter 2 Deontic Modality from the Perspective of Functional Linguistics

Halliday's Systemic Functional Grammar deals with language not only on language itself, but also on the social environment of language. It emphasizes the practical use of language and the dynamic meaning of language according to the actual process that people use language to communicate and build social cultural reality. It is highly theoretical and practical.

Based on Halliday's Systemic Functional Grammar, this book makes an analysis of the deontic modality. Among Halliday's three metafunctions, the interpersonal function as a theoretical support can help the authors understand interpersonal meaning in the discourse. Then the values of modality and the four orientations are all closely related to deontic modality metaphor, especially explicit subjective orientation and explicit objective orientation.

2.1 Halliday's Systemic Functional Grammar

2.1.1 Halliday's Three Metafunctions Theory

Halliday (2000) proposed three metafunction theories: ideational function, interpersonal function and textual function. Among them, interpersonal function focuses on the study of various interpersonal meanings that are realized by the selection of language structures. The different structures can express the same meaning, which is the category of grammatical metaphor. In the following section, the author will elaborate the three metafunctions, and the content of interpersonal grammatical metaphor.

The ideational function refers to the content of language, that is, to use language to express people's experience about the world, to describe events, to give information, and etc. It consists of transitivity, voice and polarity.

The interpersonal function serves to establish and maintain social relationships between people. People use language to express his opinions and attitude towards other people or the things around them, and influence others' behaviors as well. It includes mood, modality, and intonation.

The textual function is to use language to organize messages in ways which indicate how they fit in with the other messages around them and with the wider context in which the speaker and the writer are talking and writing. It consists of thematic structure, information structure and cohesion.

As the purpose of this section is to seek for the interpersonal meaning of deontic modality metaphor in the discourse of business negotiations, the author will focus the attention on the interpersonal function.

2.1.2 Halliday's Systemic Functional Framework about Mood and Modality

2.1.2.1 Mood Structures

Halliday defines mood as "the selection by the speaker of a particular role in the speech situation, and his determination of the choice of roles for the addressee" (2000:33). Thompson identifies mood as a component of a clause that expresses the entity that the speaker wants to act as to be responsible for the validity for the proposition being advanced in the clause (2000:45). Therefore, mood is one of various decisive factors for deontic modality. As Thompson's model about "deontic modality" has been mentioned in the last chapter, what we attempt to do next is to provide a relatively complete system for deontic modality.

Halliday holds that the most fundamental types of speech role, which lies behind any exchange, are giving (which means "inviting to receive" at the same time) and demanding (which means "inviting to give" at the same time). The commodity being given and demanded (that is, being exchanged) can be divided into two categories: goods-&-services and information. He also explains two general mood types, that is, indicative (which includes declarative and interrogative) and imperative (2000:68). As indicative is the most common clause in both Chinese and English, there is no need to give more details. As for imperative, it has a different person system from the indicative. In English, imperative clause usually begins with verbs while the subject of the imperative is "you" or "me"; still, the use of "let's" indicates the inclusion of "you".

Except for the basic four mood structures, passive structure can also be a way to realize deontic modality. When Halliday discusses the special significance of having subject and finite in English clause, he indicates that the subject supplies the rest of what it takes to form a proposition, in other words, it is the one that is being held responsible—responsible for the functioning of the clause as an interactive event. It is perhaps easier to see this principle of responsibility in a proposal (a "goods-&-services" clause), where the subject specifies the one that is actually responsible for realizing (i. e., in this case, for carrying out) the offer or command (2000:76). Thompson identifies that the use of passive forms such as "be supposed to" or "be obliged to", with a separate non-modal finite, to express deontic modality. For example,

(1) You're supposed to be doing your practice.

(2) You ought to be doing your practice.

In the examples above, there is a difference in the degree to which the speaker seems to be taking responsibility for the pressure on the other person. It makes one feel the pressure comes from other sources, not directly from the speaker. Similarly, there is a potential contrast between *must* and *have to*; the former could be no more than a suggestion or an invitation. The latter suggests that there is some compelling reason which is not the speaker's intention, thus the speaker takes no responsibility for the obligation.

2.1.2.2 Modality

Following Halliday, Thompson further studies the value of modality, which is considered as the third variable for modality framework.

1. Values of Modality

According to Halliday, modality is connected with polarity. Polarity refers to the choice between positive and negative. "Modality covers the meaning between yes and no, the intermediate degrees between positive and negative polarity, where the speaker can present his proposition as more or less likely, more or less desirable" (Halliday 85). Take probability for example.

yes certainly probably possibly no

Figure 2.1 The scale of the value of probability

Thus, Halliday (1994) established three basic modality values: high, median and low. It means that the speaker can control the degree of certainty about the validity of a proposition or the degree of the obligation and inclination by choice of words or sentence patterns. For instance, *certainly* has the highest value, *possibly* has the lowest value and *probably* is in the median. Modality metaphor also has different degree of values. For example,

(3) I believe he has gone.

(4) I think he has gone.

(5) I guess he has gone.

Among the three sentences, sentence (3) has the highest value, and expresses the speaker's assertion about the sentence. However, sentence (5) just expresses the speaker's supposition, and has the lowest value. In modality metaphor expression, the highest value always signals a higher degree in which the speaker commits himself to the validity of what he is saying in a proposition, or the extent to which he appears to be putting pressure on the listener to carry out a command in a proposal. For the lower value, the speaker uses it to disguise the responsibility for him to take for what he is saying.

In our study of deontic modality, we will take this variable concerning modal operators into account because the degree of the modal operators can also show how deontic modality serves to help the addresser voice his/her opinion and influence others. According to the scale of modal value, Halliday (2000) classifies English modal operators which are illustrated in the following table:

Table 2.1 Modal Operators in English (2000:76)

	low	median	high
positive	can, may, could, might, (dare)	will, would, should, is/was to	must, ought to, need, has/had to
negative	needn't, doesn't/didn't + need to, have to	won't, wouldn't, shouldn't, (isn't/wasn't to)	mustn't, oughtn't to, can't, couldn't, (mayn't/mightn't, hasn't/hadn't to)

Peng Xuanwei (2000) notes that Chinese volitives are called modal verbs as well. However, it is different from English modal verbs because English modal verbs change its form along with tense whereas Chinese volitive bear no grammatical feature like this. Therefore, the contrastive analysis is limited to semantic functions.

2. Orientations of Modality

Halliday points out that the basic distinction that determines how each type of modality will be expressed is orientation. When the speaker expresses his/her opinion in the way of his/her own subjective point of view, it is subjective orientation. But if he/she chooses the way of expressing objectively, the orientation is objective. "There are two other modal expressions, implicitness and explicitness. Implicitness is usually realized when the modality is expressed in the same clause as the main proposition, while explicitness is used when it is expressed in a projecting clause" (Halliday, 2000:353).

In human communication, sometimes the speaker expresses his/her opinion in a direct, subjective way, while sometimes in order to achieve certain interpersonal function, he/she uses objective expressions as if it is not his/her opinion at all. Each type of modality is realized by the modality orientation. Speakers express their attitudes towards something either subjectively or objectively. Halliday (1994) elaborates that "The term 'implicit' is used when the modality is expressed in the same clause as the main proposition, while 'explicit' is used when it is expressed in a separate clause" (355). Therefore, the modality orientations also include another two types of implicitness and explicitness.

Halliday (2000) points out that each type of modality is realized in accordance with orientations. Meanwhile, Thompson calls the orientations as "deontic modality" in his book *An Introduction to Functional Grammar*. He provides a comprehensive table to explain the realization of modality.

Table 2.2 System of Modality

type		subjective explicit	subjective implicit	objective explicit	objective implicit
modalization	probability	I think/ in my opinion/ John knows	John will know	It's likely that John knows	John probably knows
	usuality	Mary 'll sit quiet	It's usual for Mary to sit quiet	Mary usually sits quiet	
modulation	obligation	I want Jean to go	Jean should go	It's expected that Jean goes	Jean's supposed to go
	inclination		Brown'll help		Brown's keen to help

A. Explicit Subjective Orientation

Subjective explicit orientation is realized by the usage of minor clause and modal words. It is metaphorical. In subjective explicit orientation, the personal pronoun is the realization of interpersonal meanings in addition to modal verbs. Projecting clauses with the present tense of the first person are usually considered as the metaphorical modality, and place emphasis on the speaker's deontic modality to the propositions. Subjective explicit orientation is an effective way to make the speaker's attitude clear and subjective.

By expressing in explicit subjective orientation, the author expresses that the opinion is from his own opinion instead of a set fact. When the speaker wants to illustrate his/her own viewpoint in a strong subjective way, this kind of orientation is a good choice. Projecting clause is considered as the most typical modal expression employed in this orientation. For example,

(6) I think he is right.

(7) He believes that it will rain.

(8) We admit that we are wrong.

All of these sentences are explicit subjective orientation. The projecting clauses are composed by explicit pronouns *I*, *he*, and *we* and verbs. By expressing in explicit subjective orientation, the speaker emphasizes the subjective nature of the opinion. For modal responsibility, in this kind of expression, the extent for the speaker to accept the responsibility for what he/she said is the highest.

B. Explicit Objective Orientation

Objective explicit orientation is realized by the minor clause and nominal modal expressing forms. It makes the information more objective in an explicit way. The minor clause that embodies the modal meanings expresses a relation process to hide the speaker's deontic modality.

For this kind of orientation, projecting clause also plays an important role in realizing modal meaning. For example,

(9) It is likely that he is right.

(10) It is obvious that it will rain.

The two projecting clauses show explicit objective in a verbal process. In addition, nouns can also express modality in explicit objective orientation. For example,

(11) There is possibility of raining this afternoon.

(12) It is obligation for students to go to school.

From these four sentences, we can find out that the projecting clause and nominalization often express modality in explicit objective orientation, that is to say, modality metaphor often expresses in explicit objective orientation, especially in persuasive texts, so as to make his opinion to be objective. By using explicit objective orientation, the speaker aims to disguise the source of the opinion, and the opinion seems to come from the fact instead of his own assertion, and make it easy for the hearer or the partner to agree with him or her.

C. Implicit Subjective Orientation

Subjective implicit orientation is realized by the modal verbs and comment adjuncts. It is also metaphorical. The speakers express their attitude or opinions to a proposition just like the fact without obvious subjectivity. Thompson maintains that the representative modal expressing forms are comment adjuncts and modal auxiliary verbs (2000:61).

In this kind of modal orientation, modal expressions are realized by modal verbs. As far as Thompson is concerned, "modal operators exploit the finite slot and thus are firmly rooted in the interpersonal, subjective meanings of the clause" (61). For example, she will be ill. In this sentence, the orientation is expressed by modal verb will.

D. Implicit Objective Orientation

Objective implicit orientation is realized by modal adjuncts, modal words and passive voice. Meanwhile, the modal adjuncts hold a leading position in objective implicit orientation. Almost all mood adjuncts indicate the objectivity of a proposition in an implicit way.

In this kind of orientation, mood adjuncts play an important role. In Halliday's opinion, nearly all the mood adjuncts are used to indicate the objectivity of a proposition in an implicit way. Besides, the passive verb predicators are used to indicate implicit objective modal orientation. For example: you are supposed to go abroad. It seems that the pressure comes from other sources, not from the speaker. Compared with explicit objective orientation, implicit objective orientation shortens the distance between the speaker and the hearer, implying that the speaker is standing in the position of the hearer.

To sum up, explicit orientations both subjective and objective are realized by modality metaphor. The so called explicit subjective orientations are the modal expressions that are encoded in a metaphorical clause in order to show the speaker's subjective opinion. On the other hand, the speaker can use explicit objective orientation to disguise his own opinion, give this opinion an objective sentence pattern, so that it looks like the fact itself instead of his opinion. According to the degree of modal responsibilities the speaker takes in the discourse, Thompson (2000) orders subjective, objective, explicit, and implicit these four orientations. Among them, explicit subjective orientation expresses the speaker's willingness to be responsible for what he said, and it is the way of maximizing modal responsibility. Then the implicit subjective and implicit objective follows. The last one is explicit objective orientation. From the theories, we can conclude that once the speaker uses implicit objective orientation, it means either the speaker is unwilling to take responsibility for the proposition, or the speaker wants to disguise responsibility. The following table can prove the relationship between modal orientations and modal expressions.

Table 2.3 The Relations between Modal Orientations and Modal Expressions

modal orientation		modal expression
explicit	subjective	projecting clause, modal lexical verb
	objective	projecting clause, nominal modal expression
implicit	subjective	finite modal operator; comment adjunct
	objective	modal lexical verb; mood adjunct

2.2 Martin's Appraisal Theory

Appraisal Theory proposed by Martin is developed within the framework of Systemic Functional Linguistics. This is concerned more particularly with the language of evaluation, attitude and emotion, and with a set of resources that explicitly position a text's propositions interpersonally (Martin & Rose, 2003:22). It is a particular approach to explore, describe and explain the way language is used to evaluate, to adopt stances, to construct textual personas and to manipulate interpersonal positioning and relationships. To sum up, it investigates how writers/speakers position such evaluation and how to engage with other voices and alternative positions as they construct for their current communicative context. This theory is concerned with three independent yet closely related domains: attitude, engagement and graduation which will be introduced in the following sections.

2.2.1 Attitude

Attitude associates with our feelings, including emotional reactions, judgments of behaviors and evaluation of things (Martin, 1997:42). As the main system in Appraisal Theory, it involves three semantic regions covering what is traditionally referred to as *emotion*, *ethics* and *aesthetics* which are corresponding to its three sub-systems: *affect*, *judgment* and *appreciation*. Martin (1997) defines *affect* as evaluation by means of the writer/speaker indicating how they are emotionally disposed to person, thing, happening or state of affairs. It can be realized through adjectives, verbs (mental processes), emotion-loaded nouns and adverbs. *Affect* is concerned with positive and negative values such as un/happiness, in/security, dis/satisfaction. They refer to "affairs of the heart" (such as happiness, love, hate and sadness), "ecosocial well-being" (such as anxiety, fear, confidence and trust), and telos (the pursuit of goals)—ennui, displeasure, interest and pleasure (Martin, 1997:42-51).

Judgment is concerned with the meaning construing our attitudes to people and the way they behave. In general terms, *judgment* can be divided into those dealing with "social esteem" and those oriented to "social sanction", both of which have a positive and negative pole. Social esteem involves assessment about how normal, capable or brave someone is, such as lucky/unlucky, fortunate/unfortunate, competent/incompetent, and brave/cowardly, while social sanction includes two aspects: veracity (how truthful someone is) such as credible/incredible, honest/deceitful, and propriety (how ethical someone is) such as ethical/unethical, moral/immoral (Martin, 1997:52).

Appreciation is concerned with meaning construing our evaluations of "things", especially things we make and performances we give, but also including natural phenomena. Similar to *affect* and *judgment*, *appreciation* has both a positive and negative dimension. There are three variables under appreciation: reaction (Do they catch our attention? or Do they please us?), composition (balance and complexity) and valuation (how innovative, authentic, timely etc.) (Martin, 1997:56).

2.2.2 Engagement

Alongside with *attitude* in Appraisal System, *engagement* is concerned with the linguistic resources by which speakers/writers adopt a stance towards the value positions being referenced by the text and with respect to those they address. The *engagement* resources provide the means which allows the speaker/writer to convey the degree of his or her commitment to the opinion being presented. In fact, *engagement* is informed by Bakhtin's /Voloshinov's now widely influential notions of dialogism and heteroglossia under which all verbal communication, whether written or spoken, is "dialogic" (Martin, 1997: 92). And the stance the writer/speaker adopts closely associates with the responsibility he/she would like to assume. Moreover, some cultural values and ideologies can be revealed by observing interpersonal meaning that writer/speaker attempts to construct through modal methods. *Engagement* is basically classified into the monoglossic and heteroglossic. The former is realized by bare assertions while the latter is construed by resources which can be grouped into two broad categories according to whether they are "dialogically expansive" or "dialogically contractive" in their intersubjective functionality. The distinction turns on the degree to which an utterance, by dint of one or more of these locutions, actively makes allowances for dialogically alternative positions and voices (dialogic expansion), or alternatively, acts to challenge, fend off or restrict the scope of such (dialogic contraction) (Martin, 1997:102-104).

To conclude, *engagement* resources are further classified into the following headings in terms of its functionality: ①*entertain*—those words by which the authorial voice indicates that its position is one of a number of possible positions, to greater or lesser degree, make dialogic space for those possibilities. ② *attribute*—those formulations which dissociate the proposition from the text's internal authorial voice by attributing it to some external source. Attribute resources can be further divided into "acknowledge" and "distance". ③*disclaim*—those formulations by which some prior utterance or some alternative position is invoked as to be directly rejected, replaced or held to be unsustainable. It includes "deny" and "counter". ④*proclaim*—acting to limit the scope dialogistic alternatives in the ongoing colloquy, rather than directly rejecting or overruling a contrary position. Its subtypes include "concur", "pronounce" and "endorsement".

2.2.3 Graduation

Graduation operates across two axes of scalability—that of grading according to intensity of amount and that of grading according to prototypicality and the preciseness by which category boundaries are drawn (Martin, 1997: 137). In other words, *graduation* is concerned with the gradability of the attitude and engagement values. Its subdivisions *include* force and *focus*. The first dimension of scaling with respect to intensity is labeled as *force*, while the scaling in terms of the sharpness or softness is labeled values of *focus*. The adverbs of intensification such as *slightly*, *rather*, *really*, *very*, *completely* are generally considered as the typically expressions to realize the *force* (Martin, 1997: 140). In fact, the realizations of *force* also include comparative and superlative morphology, repetition and various other intensified words (Martin, 1997: 137). Martin proposes a system of resources of *force* under which intensification and quantification are classified. Intensification refers to the scaling of qualities and processes, while quantification is concerned with imprecise measuring of number and imprecise measuring of the presence or mass of entities and imprecise of reckonings of extent in time and space. *Force* adjusts gradable items by means of raising or lowering whereas focus makes non-gradable words gradable by means of sharpening or softening. And writers/speakers graduate the *focus* of their semantic categorizations of people and things through words such as *about/exactly or real/sort of/kind of* (Martin 152).

2.3 Study of Interpersonal Meaning from Systemic Functional Grammar Perspective

Li Zhanzi (2002) points out that "interpersonal meaning" originates from the interpersonal function in the functional grammar. She explains that "the interpersonal metafunction is concerned with communication between the writer and reader in the discourse and the writer's attitude to what he writes or speaks about" (2002:2).

As is known, the interpersonal meaning is an important part in communications. Halliday (1985) points out, "a language, then, is a system for making meanings; a semantic system, with other systems for encoding the meanings it produces", thus with the growing awareness people have paid more and more attention to making a study on the interpersonal and negotiable meaning in the language. Therefore, the study on the interpersonal meaning is also becoming urgent and reasonable.

Halliday (1985) and Thompson (2000) pave the way for the theory of Systemic Functional

Grammar. On the basis of their theoretical framework, researchers and linguists of the functional grammar conducted many studies on the interpersonal meanings and explored the realizations of the interpersonal meaning in their works (Halliday, 1985; Sinclair & Coulthard, 1975; Martin, 1992).

Some interesting and practical genres or the texts divert many other researchers' focus just like the casual conversations and advertisements. Eggins and Slade (1997) make an analysis on the casual conversation, especially some useful grammar resources for judgment, for instance, people will choose different mood to make an interaction with others and identify the different roles between them in their published book *Analyzing Casual Conversation*. Leech (1966), Bex (1996) and Cook (1992) pay their attention to the discourse of advertisement, which bring some interesting insights into the research on the advertising texts.

As is known, the systemic functional grammar is one of the most important theories that have great effect on the academic field in China. Many well-known researchers are devoted to this domain (Hu Zhuanglin (2008), Huang Guowen (2001), Zhang Delu (1998), Zhu Yongsheng (2001) and Li Zhanzi (2002)). Among them, Li Zhanzi is one of the few in China who have made great contributions in exploring the realization of the interpersonal meaning. In 2000, she published her doctoral dissertation concerned with the study of interpersonal meaning in autobiography. This book concentrates on the analysis of the interpersonal meanings by advancing and enriching Halliday's theories, which is the main contribution of this book. In other words, it is proved in her book that the pronoun system and the direct quotation are the effective approaches to realizing the interpersonal meaning. In 2002, she published a new book titled *Interpersonal Meaning in Discourse*. On the basis of her former book, the new book has brought in many new items, such as a comprehensive analysis on modality, tense, personal pronouns, direct discourse and reflexive expressing forms. Furthermore, she added the dimension of "appraisement" to make a research on the interpersonal meaning and analyzed the combination of interpersonal meaning with ideational and discourse meaning. From the perspective of stylistics, Liu Shisheng (1998) conducts the research on different ways to realize the interpersonal comment in literary dialogue and literary narration. Consequently, the analysis on literary discourse is revealed. In a word, all these research findings have laid a foundation for exploring the interpersonal meaning.

In recent years, more and more researchers (Li Zhanzi, 2001; Zhou Dajun, 2003; Miao Xinwei, 2004; Zheng Yuanhui, 2005) have begun to focus more on this domain and many postgraduates (Li Fang, 2003; Zhang Shanshan, 2004; Chen Jieyan, 2005) have made the relevant researches on this topic, but there are still few papers concerning with the research on interpersonal meaning. At the same time, the study on the comparison about the interpersonal meaning is even much fewer. However, Xu Yulong (2002) has maintained that the contrastive study is not only a fundamental way to make the research on things but also a basic method to explore the linguistics. Therefore, it is no doubt to make a study on the inter language for using the contrastive research method. Taking these factors into account, the present study attempts to conduct a relatively comprehensive and systematic research through using the contrastive method to make a study on the interpersonal meaning.

This chapter is devoted to the extension of theoretical framework for the present study. According to the definition of deontic modality given by Thompson, we recollect other potential factors such as mood structures, subject and deixis, and some of which have been hinted by modern linguists to enrich the framework at Systemic Functional level. With the common concern of deontic modality and Appraisal Theory in mind, we extend the framework to an Appraisal Theoretic level to ensure the comprehensiveness and appropriateness of the whole analytical framework. In the following chapters, we will make an in-depth contrastive analysis of deontic modality in different fields.

Deontic modality has got attention until Lyons (1977) clearly divides modality into deontic modality and epistemic modality which are also the widely accepted classification of modality in modern linguistics. According to Lyons, deontic modality expresses the view or attitude of the speaker about the possibility and necessity of the acts performed by morally responsible agents, concerning with permission and obligation (793). In other words, with deontic modality, the speaker can decide the development of an event by making use of controlling power or authority to influence the partner's action.

Deontic modality is quite delicate and complex to explore since there are too many linguistic means to realize it, explicitly or implicitly. The analysis of deontic modality in the context where exist two different values and ideologies is more challenging. Therefore, following Thompson's study about deontic modality, it is not enough to extend its interpersonal elements just based on Halliday's Systemic Functional Framework which generally covers mood and modality. With concern of the definition of deontic modality in mind, it is more comprehensive to integrate Martin's Appraisal Theory in present analytical framework due to the fact that it deals with "the kind of attitudes that are negotiated in a text, the strength of the feeling involved and the way by which values are sourced and readers aligned" (Martin and Rose, 2008: 22). Engagement and graduation in particularly, closely associate with the concern of deontic modality. In addition, Appraisal Theory is of great significance to explore the deeper level, in this respect, it provides us more complete perspectives for the extent to which the speaker openly accepts responsibility for the subjective assessments being expressed. Furthermore, when we make contrastive analysis of deontic modality in political speeches of different countries, we should take social context into account.

Chapter 3 Interpersonal Meaning of Deontic Modality in News

3.1 Introduction

Modality is kind of subjective judgment, and a way to express people's viewpoints, too. Language is used to communicate with the purpose of building interpersonal relationship, influencing other people's behavior, revealing the view of the world, and arousing others' response. In functional grammar, Halliday defines the value of modality. News covers all the fields in life and provides people with immediate information, with the result of affecting people's interest and comment on accidents and affairs. The study of news inevitably becomes one important part of linguistic analysis. The use of modality, especially deontic modality shows precisely the communication purpose and context of news. This part will study the features of deontic modality in news and how it affects the interpersonal functions by using systemic functional linguistic theories.

With functional linguistic theory embodied in English news as a breakthrough point, this section focuses on the writer's measure of modal responsibility and interpersonal interests he/she represents, especially that of editorials. Multi-perspective discussion is developed centering on the strategic application of modal responsibility in English news. Finally, it comes to the conclusion that further research on deontic modality is expected to be conducted as a branch of functional linguistic theory, and different values of deontic modality embodied in news report have its social power which exerts a profound influence upon public opinions.

3.2 Modality in News

Systemic functional linguists have considered modality, a sub-part of mood system which deeply expresses interpersonal meaning, as a tool of realizing interpersonal function of language. Fowler (1979:85) pointed out that modality might show "appraisal" or "attitude" of authors or speakers. Halliday (1994:356-357) classified modality and polarity into a whole, and he believed modality was referred to as the mediate state between "yes" and "no", i. e., the area between positive meaning and negative meaning, which were also modality and attitude, which brought the concept of deontic modality into people's eyes. Thompson (1997) discussed deontic modality in details, and defined it as "the degree of responsibility that speakers could get publicly". In fact, deontic modality is a subject with great significance. Out of different reasons, writers or speakers may take various kinds of ways to cover their responsibility, so as to alleviate subjectivity of their sayings (Thompson, 1996:60-63). And according to White (qtd. in Zhang Keding, 2007:498), news report was the media with intense value and consciousness. It deeply influences and changes people's belief and attitude to the real world. Theoretically speaking, news reports are supposed to be neutral, just and objective. They are journalists' accumulation of facts, in which viewpoints evidently are of parties involved in the affair, not of journalists. Therefore, if modality exists in news reports, it mainly points out the source. (Thompson, 1996:64) Sometimes, some people with great power would make use of modality to reinforce their willingness to be accepted by other people (Fowler, 1979:203). So, writers of the news usually make the advantages of modality to instruct readers to have a look at the problem from the objective perspective, not from their own points. Thus, the study on deontic modality in terms of news is quite essential.

In recent years, with the growing study of grammatical metaphor, people have found the strategy of grammatical metaphor was to upgrade interpersonal appraisal from phrases to short sentences. Halliday (1994:342) put forward that characterization of grammatical metaphor showed that metaphor was revealed in structure organization. In this way, it was metaphor that led to the extension of meaning: systemic category of interpersonal meaning may be extended through the newly generated patterns. Based on this idea, some expressions like *I think/expect/believe/reckon that...* are obtained by coding modal metaphor into an explicit subjective clause. Structures like these usually show probable interpersonal meaning, and are regarded as subjective comment of speakers. Martin (1997:68) held that this way to show interpersonal meaning was explicitly subjective, and enabled speakers to realize their responsibility. The part of subject is considered to be responsible. For instance, in *I will...*, the one taking responsibility is *I*. However, *he* takes responsibility in *He says that I will...*. But in *It is supposed that I will...*, *it* becomes virtual responsibility taker. In news, to study deontic modality is quite significant. Clear objective orientation may enable speakers to be free from modal responsibility, and explicit subjective orientation highlights that of the speakers'. Taking news editorial as an example, the best way to objectify writers' opinions is to use objective modals in order to dissemble responsibility. For example:

(1) Military or not, it's likely that the capability of Chinese space program will place space-faring nations like the United States and Russia on notice that they cannot rest on their laurels.

This editorial was written by an American journalist about successful emission of Shenzhou VI. The writer employed explicit objective modality to lesson the personal view since the first sentence "It is likely that...". The whole sentence added objective certainty to the personal view and the viewpoints based on interests of the country or the group, which was beyond people's doubt. In the editorial, some explicit subjective modality expressions like "I think/doubt..." are frequently used on purpose to emphasize speakers' idea or uncertainty of judges. For example,

(2) I don't think any of us has ever really appreciated how important looking good is to Singaporeans, show organizer Gillian Loh said in a statement.

Sometimes, the explicit subjective modality orientation may reflect closeness between speakers and listeners, and social interpersonal meaning. Therefore, in news, writers can use explicit subjective modality like *I will*, *we will* to show their politeness and respect to readers. In this way, deontic modality with higher degree covered by first personifications would show more politeness and appeal. For example,

(3) The bitterness and self-delusion evident in Gore Vidal's essay is saddening.... But we did make progress in the intervening years, and we will continue to make progress in the future. (Newsweek, Feb. 2, 1993)

With regard to the vital social value of news, socialists have been making explorations on news English, ranging from classification, rhetoric, grammatical metaphor to other theories in functional linguistics. All of the studies have provided broad platform for deontic modality study in English news.

Halliday (2000) puts forward four variations in modality, i.e., classification, modality value, orientation and positivity. Classification studies differences between "statement" and "suggestion". Speakers could associate language with language status and virtual judgment. According to different purposes, modality can be divided into modalization and ideology. Modalization can be realized by modals and auxiliaries. Modals indicate the state of a verb or views of certain incident of writers/speakers. Auxiliaries express speakers' judgment of information relevance. Ideology includes the degree of responsibility in orders or intensity of willingness. Responsibility can be realized by modals or passive forms of verbs. Willingness is usually expressed by modals and modal adjectives. Halliday (2000) also believes modalization can be divided into possibility and frequency. Possibility means "yes" or "no". It involves different probabilities. Frequency means "yes" and "no". It is about variable frequency. For example:

(4) Experts in Japan and the United States said that the releases from nuclear plants could go on for weeks or months.

(5) Marquette and Kentucky are probably sick of playing each other in the N. C. A. A. tournament, but this year, they probably would not mind another meeting.

(6) If someone did discover the original script, it probably would not have much effect on Shakespeare studies.

The three sentences explain the application of possibility in modality in terms of modals, modal adjuncts, and the combination of these two. Evidently, modal verbs take the predominant position in expressing possibility, and become the major component in the process of modals realization. Using modal verbs makes it possible to use and understand language better. Since news readers come from all walks of life, the use of modal verbs makes news report easier to comprehend.

Modal value studies the degree of certainty of propositions or the degree of pressure when listeners are subjective to orders. Modal and modal values are closely connected. According to Thompson (2000), owing to modal's enclosure of degree and grades, people could endow certainty of a proposition a higher or lower value, or gift the pressure higher or lower ranks when asking others to execute commands. Halliday classifies modal value into three ranks: high, median, and low. Among them, median has a major position. Generally speaking, news reports are required to be just, and writers tend to avoid higher or lower modal values to influence readers' viewpoints. For example:

(7) Younger patients would be more likely than older ones to get the best kidneys under a proposal being considered by the nation's organ transplant network.

The most common median modal value is *would*. News writers choose *would* instead of *will* to describe what people have done or said. *Would* is the past tense of *will*. Most reports took place in the past, and *would* is more likely to express possibility than *will*. In these ways, news writers use median modal value to prevent news going to extreme, and make news be with more verity.

Orientation determines basic characterizations of modals realization. It mainly studies how speakers express their willingness. Halliday (2000:357) points out that each type of modality is realized in accordance with orientation and that orientation is "the distinction between subjective and objective modality, and between explicit and implicit variants". He attributes the orientation of modality to four kinds: subjective, objective, implicit and explicit. Subjective orientation is the basic feature of modality. Objective orientation is expressing subjectivity in an indirect way. When switching subjectivity to objectivity, speakers can realize the communicative purpose of shifting responsibility, covering fact and saving face. On the contrary, they can achieve the goal of expressing stance and attitude. Sometimes when speakers are reluctant to express their opinions clearly for politeness or other reasons, they may adopt indirect expressions to make their utterance more objective and reasonable. There are still other occasions on which speakers also employ subjective orientation to emphasize their opinions. The explicit orientation will be adopted when the speakers want to express their attitudes explicitly. For example, "I think that he will come" and "it is likely that he will come". In the end, the implicit orientation is in line with modal verbs or adverbs. Examples of the combination of the four orientations and deontic modality types are shown as follows:

Table 3.1 System of Types of Orientation on Deontic Modality (Halliday, 2000: 358)

orientations / type of deontic modality	subjective explicit	subjective implicit	objective implicit	objective explicit
modulation obligation	I want John to go	John should go	John is supposed to go	It is expected that John goes
modulation inclination		Jane will help	Jane is keen to help	

Generally speaking, subjective explicit orientation is realized by projecting clauses and modal verbs. It is usually employed to highlight the speakers' responsibility or personal opinions to the proposition. Besides, the subjective explicit orientation is an effective way to express speakers' attitudes clearly and obviously.

In terms of subjective implicit orientation, it is realized by modal operators and comment adjuncts. Modal operators are frequently used because they are "firmly rooted in the interpersonal and subjective meanings of the clause" (Thompson, 2000: 63). At the same time, "comment adjuncts are basically perceived subjective" (Biber, 1999: 126). By adopting subjective implicit orientation, the speakers intend to objectify their viewpoints and attitudes toward the proposition. Objective explicit orientation is mainly realized by the projecting clauses which make the proposition more objective in an explicit way. By applying the objective explicit orientation, to some extent, the speakers can conceal their responsibility and objectify their point of view by making their utterance appear to be the fact, thus convincing the audience to believe and accept them.

Objective implicit orientation is often realized by modal adjuncts, modal operator and passive verb phrases. Among them, modal adjuncts are the most commonly used. In the framework of Systemic Functional Grammar, almost all the modal adjuncts seem to convey the objectivity of a proposition in an implicit way.

Objective implicitness is related to the lowest modal value in all orientation expressions, and realized by modal additives or passive voice. Modal additives take the lead to realize objective implicitness orientation. Prospective readers of news come from all kinds of ranks in different areas, so writers would use common modal additives to make objective implicitness orientation come true. For example:

(8) Sheriff Baca, the only law enforcement official invited to testify, said he worked regularly with the CAIR chapter in his area and pushed back.

(9) While homes may be more affordable, many buyers are still having trouble getting mortgages to buy them.

(10) The success of Republican propaganda machine obviously is part of the reason.

In the three modal additives, extreme modal additives come out with more frequency than time additives and tone additives, mainly because modals show the medium degree of positive and negative levels. Therefore, positive additives and modal additives are more frequently used than others.

Activeness studies the middle part between positive and negative forms, in which negativity includes direct negativity and transitional negativity. Usually, activeness is expressed by restrictive components, and each restrictive verb has two forms: positive and negative. Negative ones are more important in English news. However, in negativity, direct negativity is mostly used than transitional negativity. News writers tend to use positive expressions to bring encouraging reports to readers. When one accident has not been confirmed by the officials and it is not the proper time for readers to know about, and writers would choose not to report, for if there are mistakes in news, great inconvenience would be taken to readers. News writers have responsibility to ensure truth and certainty of news reports. For example:

(11) Japan reeled from a rapidly unfolding disaster of epic scale on Sunday, pummeled by the death toll, destruction and homelessness caused by the earthquake and tsunami and new hazards from damaged nuclear reactors that were leaking radiation.

The example above shows that news writers try to describe things around us. Although the reports are about disasters, news writers give descriptions from the optimistic point, because no negative structure has been used in the report. In view of this, news writers do good to bring positive influence to the society.

3.3 Features of Modals in English News

This part attempts to analyze the distribution and usage characteristics of the key model verbs in English political news texts with 200 pieces of English political news as data from the perspective of Systemic Functional Grammar and Critical Discourse Analysis. The data were collected from *Time*, *the Times*, *the New York Times*, *the Washington Post*, *the Associated Press*, *Reuters* and *Agency France-Press* on the internet and quantitative analyses have been made. The results show that among the key model verbs, the median-value model verbs *would* and *will* occur most frequently in English political news texts and reveal its hidden ideological implication.

Authors searched and counted showing times and frequencies of 9 modal verbs, and found *would* and *will* appear with the highest frequency. *Might*, *must*, and *shall* are rarely used, which is about only 5.9%. Some other words like *could*, *can*, *may* and *should* cover the proportion of 35.5%. *Would* and *will* appear 628 and 568 times respectively. In English news, *would* and *will* mostly express willingness, determination and wishes. For example,

(12) Morrell also noted the release as scheduled would come as thousands of new U S troops head into Afghanistan's volatile south. (*The Times*, *Obama Wants Detainee Photos Blocked*, May 13, 2009)

(13) On the floor of the Democratic National Convention last summer, Newsom told *The Times* that he hoped to run in 2010—but first he wanted to see if voters would embrace Obama's campaign focus on youth and generational change. (*The Times*, *California's Big Race to Succeed Schwarzenegger*, Feb 16, 2009)

(14) He projected that government spending would reach 49% of national output this year. (*The Times*, *Greens vow to stamp out corruption*, Mar 8, 2009)

People's choice of words are related to ideology and social environment. In speeches, writers/speakers' opinions and attitudes are displayed by vocabulary and grammar in discourse. For different language types, ways to express opinions and attitudes are also different. *Would* and *will* intensely show great probability. They appear with the highest frequency and also can be found in indirect speeches. Fairclough (1995: 37) ever said public media is inclined to using indirect speech, so as to mix boundary of speakers'utterance and writers' utterance. In this way, opinions in the news can be naturally accepted and understood. Reports using direct speech are likely to be regarded as convincing language with frequency of modal verbs. Reporters employ direct speech to assure readers the truth of news, justice and accuracy of language, viewpoints without individual emotion. Using indirect speech enables reporters to show their opinions sufficiently. Even reports with direct speech cannot be totally just, for the reason that it is the reports to determine interviewees, and composing words. Because of this, reporters tend to mix their own opinions and attitudes into reports subconsciously. The phenomenon comes into being that reports take the leading role and readers are in a passive position. At the same time, *will* and *would* express involving more uncertainty, so reporters would like to use them to leave some space for them to return, which can guarantee benefits and interests of authority and reporters themselves.

3.4 Deontic Modality in Appraisal Theory

P. R. White's doctoral dissertation (1998) Telling media stories: The news as rhetoric has supplied the study of news discourse with a detailed theoretical structure. The appraisal theory in systemic functional linguistics endows discourse analysis of news a significant status. It is considered to be a newly-developed vocabulary grammatical frame during the study of interpersonal meaning in systemic functional linguistics, which attaches importance to various kinds of negotiable attitudes. Martin (1997) classified the appraisal system into *attitude*, *engagement*, and *graduation*. In this part, we would take *attitude* and *engagement* which are closely associated with deontic modality, to intensively analyze deontic modality in English news.

3.4.1 Deontic Modality in Attitude System

Martin divided "attitude" into *affect*, *judgment*, and *appreciation*, where, the latter two were closely related to deontic modality, deserving our attention. *Judgment* and *appreciation* are two kinds of systematized affect, and cover the attitude of writers of English news and social editorials. According to White (1999), there were explicit and implicit judgments. Explicit judgment can be realized by modifiers, property, environmental components of expressions and attitude vocabularies, while implicit judgments mainly refer to markers. Comparatively, explicit judgments are likely to be identified. For example:

(15) Rice signs with talent agency. (*China Daily*, January 24, 2009)

This is a news report that Rice signed with a famous agent company in Hollywood. Under the condition of not hurting interests of countries and groups, and not violating ethics and morals, solely positive judgment will not put obstacles to news writers. But negative news frequently came out. News writers usually mediate deontic modality when the affairs are not involved with interests of countries, governments and individuals. At this time, they use markers to express judgment meaning, to arouse readers reaction together with other appraisal tools in certain cultural context and consciousness background. For instance, when the writers judge with explicit judgment to say the government is "incompetent", they also can use the implicit judgment "the government did not lay the foundations for sustainable development." instead. (qtd. Zhang Keding, 2007: 234) Let's look at another example:

(16) Phone game mocks Japan's 'drowsy' ex-finance minister. (*China Daily*, Feb. 25, 2009)

This is a report about the former financial minister of Japan, who was drunk and became the leading role of mobile games. Here the writer seemed to make a joke with the former financial minister, but not to highlight his drunk state. This is a good way of showing lower deontic modality. That is to say, the markers above degrade responsibility to the lowest point. Obviously, in realizing *judgment*, English news mainly depends on *attitude* vocabularies which are more indirect and implicit. At most times, the writers themselves would be in the backstage, with the purpose of providing readers more blanks to interpret language expressed by *judgment* in accordance with their own cultural background and consciousness. In fact, in one cultural context, writers and readers have judgment standard in common, and appropriate deontic modality also will lead readers to unconsciously make similar judgment with writers.

Vocabulary metaphor serves as the tool to realize *appreciation*. Vocabularies in English news usually express implicit objective deontic modality. We intend to mainly talk about nominalization metaphor. In terms of appraisal, if descriptions are nominalized as nouns or noun phrases, sources of appraisal can be concealed and get to be objective, and further appraisal of the noun phrases also can be made. Martin and White (2005: 64) also illustrated that *attitude* meaning cannot only be expressed by *attitude* vocabularies, but by some vocabularies with concept meaning. From these perspectives, English news can not only make descriptions more objective, but exerts influences on readers' attitude as well. For example:

(17) That agenda will include philanthropic efforts involving classical music and college educations for disadvantaged students, as well as initiatives to help US children become global citizens. (*China Daily*, January 24, 2009)

To be more specific, the sentence can be *People make a philanthropic effort on agenda including classical music... as well as initiatives to help US children become global citizens.* In comparison, the distinctions are found that the process and participators disappear, and the degree that writers would like to accept deontic modality arrives at the best. So, nominalization metaphor is referred to as higher deontic modality by implicit objective expressions. Some other regular metaphor such as... *Prices skyrocketed* in English news may intensify mood. These expressions without deontic modals or grammatical characterization are not the facts only describing inflation, but to upgrade publicly accepted subjective judgment into a higher degree. Lower deontic modality can also get readers and writers closer through *appreciation*. For example:

(18) The war is un-American. This Administration and this war are not typical of the US. They are exceptions to the rule. Today's Washington has not only broken from the different strands of wisdom which have guided the US since its birth, but from the model that has shaped American foreign policy since 1945. (qtd. in Hu Zhuanglin, 2000: 332)

This is a report of Iraqi War written by the journalist of *The Guardian*. Readers have difficulty appreciating the interpersonal power of those boldface words, largely because the writer has employed some implicit objective lower deontic modality. The readers who firstly get to know Iraqi War may find it hard to get the real intention of the writer. On the other hand, it can leave more room for people to imagine. Even though readers are unwilling to agree with the writer, they won't feel unexpected. Therefore, deontic modality acts as the mitigator for readers to appreciate.

3.4.2 Deontic Modality in Engagement System

In news discourse, writers are likely to be subjective if they directly intervene the utterance information. The study shows that writers in news reports and editorials mostly act as participators. And they give approval to information, and ensure trustworthy of the information. Martin (2008) believes deontic modality explicitly displays subjective opinions of the speakers, but there also exist abundant viewpoints, so deontic modality is thought to be heterogloss. In news reports, typical heterogloss expressions like... *demonstrated that*..., ... *is claiming that*... are widely spread. These are with higher deontic modality, because speakers take the responsibilities of the news contents. In addition, news writers use other tools involving modals like *might*, *may*, *could*, *must*, etc., modal adverbs like *perhaps*, *probably*, *definitely*, etc., modality attributive clauses like *it's likely that*..., *it's possible that*... and psychological mapping verbs like *I suspect that*..., *I think that*..., *I believe*, *I'm convinced that*..., *I doubt*, etc.". Halliday (1994: 254) puts forward that the tools above fall into the categorizations of modals non-experienced or non-informational from the perspective of interpersonal role. The Appraisal Theory (Martin, 1997: 98) illustrates that *X claims that*, *it rumors that* can be categorized into subset: distance, which clearly explains the distance between speakers and propositions, and lower deontic modality appears. Actually, when writers make heterogloss appraisal, they have already begun the first filter of the original materials, so that the value of deontic modality is conducted to the degree they would like to intervene. At the same time, readers may get writers opinions involved in their own thinking space based on different value of deontic modality so that individual appraisal comes into being.

In conclusion, semantic connotations of deontic modality could be extended by the application of the appraisal theory and grammatical metaphor in English news. Vocabularies, grammar and other relevant sentences expressing deontic modality are considerably important semantic carrier. The appraisal in short sentences exerts more influences on readers. Also, the realization of a considerable number of appraisals largely depends on moderate performance of deontic modality. In other words, deontic modality system in English can abbreviate various types of appraisal expressions to reflect thinking ways of writers and their interest groups.

3.5 Summary

This part analyzes the features of modal verbs in English news based on systemic linguistics and appraisal theory, and discovers highly-used modal verbs and those with low value. The result shows modal verbs with median value like *would* and *will* are frequently used; modal verbs with low value are sometime used, while those with high values rarely appear. In this way, reporters would make news more objective, just and accurate, and at the same time ensure the interests of power authority, and protect themselves. The study of deontic modality may enhance readers' critic consciousness, impose their awareness of power and ideology, and improve their analysis capacity.

Chapter 4 Interpersonal Meaning of Deontic Modality in Politics

4.1 Introduction

To make a comprehensive analysis on interpersonal meanings implied by modality in discourse, deontic modality should be paid enough attention. Though contribution to the development of deontic modality has been made, studies are constrained in deontic modality metaphor (Sun Qiyao, 2010) and modal auxiliary (Palmer, 1989), and registers of study are limited in business discourse and certain formal speeches. News reports are supposed to reflect facts to maximum extent, but in reality, what journalists report is far from objective (Huang Fang, 2010: 145). As one of the most accessible methods to learn about current affairs, ideas implied in newspaper exert a remarkable influence on its reader. The significant role of political news in daily life and politics makes it worthwhile to explore interpersonal meanings of deontic modality.

Two purposes are to be completed in this chapter, namely, to find out the inclination of reporters in using deontic modality by comparing distribution of three sub-categories of deontic modality and to reveal underlying interpersonal meanings in political news. The study might provide a wilder space for study of deontic modality, interpersonal meaning and political discourse and help news reports readers recognize some individual opinions applied in so-called objective news reports.

Political discourse includes political speech, political news reporting, and political documents, etc. In this paper, political discourse refers to political news report. Corpus consists of 50 political hard news including 25 domestic news and 25 diplomatic news. Domestic news involves in news of elections, government announcements, parties and politics; diplomatic news refers to international negotiations, etc.

4.2 Deontic Modality in Political Discourse

As talked above, modulation, as a sub-class of modality, is thought to be corresponding to deontic modality. It "relates to how confident the speaker can appear to be in the eventual success of the exchange of goods-and-services" and consists of obligation and inclination (Thompson, 2000:67).

The author has found in corpus that there is another type with deontic meaning, *agreement*, which holds no position in Halliday's classification of modality; *permission* which belongs to obligation sometimes expresses meanings of inclination; *attempt*, which is excluded, could also express meaning of inclination, a sub-category of modulation. In this paper, deontic modality is classified into three categories, namely, obligation, agreement and willingness.

These three categories are distributed differently in corpus: obligation takes up 38.53%, permission 9.52% and willingness 51.94%, which shows that journalists prefer willingness in expressing deontic interpersonal meaning. The author is going to discuss how three aspects of deontic modality are realized and distributed in the political discourse like this domestically and diplomatically, and give reasons from perspective of value.

4.2.1 Obligation in Political Discourse

In demanded goods-and-services, modality concerns the degree of obligation on the other person to carry out the command and its scale includes permissible/advisable/obligatory (Thompson, 2000:67). Here, modality of obligatory is not only concerned with "the other person" but also the speaker. Thus, in political discourse, modality of obligation can be further divided into suggestion, responsibility, blaming, commanding and appealing.

Table 4.1 Distribution of Modality of Obligation in Corpus

modality of obligation	(percentage in modality of obligation/in deontic modality) in domestic news	(percentage in modality of obligation/in deontic modality) in diplomatic news
suggestion	2.64%/1.03%	2.20%/0.84%
responsibility	15.64%/6.19%	14.98%/5.76%
blaming	5.07%/1.98%	3.08%/1.20%

Table 4.1(continued)

modality of obligation	(percentage in modality of obligation/in deontic modality) in domestic news	(percentage in modality of obligation/in deontic modality) in diplomatic news
commanding	28.41%/11.08%	23.13%/8.93%
appealing	4.41%/1.72%	2.86%/1.12%
total	56.17%/21.91%	43.83%/17.09%

As shown in table 4.1, obligation is applied more frequently in domestic news than in diplomatic news. Among these five classifications of obligation, modality of commanding plays the top role in both two kinds of news. Commanding is often related with words such as *order*, *urge*, *require*, *force* and so on, which imply the urgency of a response and the determination of the speaker.

According to the results, modality of obligation with low, median and high values are distributed almost equally in corpus, accounting for 34.35%, 31.54% and 33.87% respectively. However, slight difference lies between two kinds of news: high and median valued modality is employed more frequently in diplomatic news while in domestic news modality with low value often appears. For example,

(1) Democrats argue that this is unfair, fearing tax cuts would require cutting even more from government programs that primarily aid the poor.

(2) The memo asked the United States for "direct intervention in conveying a strong, urgent and direct message" to the military, demanding that it end its "brinkmanship".

Sentences (1) and (2) are excerpted from domestic and diplomatic news respectively and the underlining words are modality of commanding. In the first sentence, the speaker makes a supposition of potential consequences brought by tax cuts. In order to be objective, he resorts to using a low valued modality *require*. In the second example, reporter creates an atmosphere of emergency and points out the severity of the situation by using high valued modality *demand*, because the memo related with Osama bin Laten is of great concern with safety of Americans.

4.2.2 Agreement in Political Discourse

Permission can be seen as the lowest degree of pressure, opening the possibility for the other person to do the action but leaving the decision to them (Thompson, 2000:69). Agreement shares some commons with permission. When the agent of agreement is addressee, it implies the meaning of obligation. When the agent is the addresser, it expresses willingness. In view of its specialty, agreement is included into neither obligation nor willingness. Here, agreement is divided into permission and admittance.

Table 4.2 Distribution of Modality of Agreement in Corpus

modality of agreement	(percentage in modality of permission/in deontic modality) In domestic news	(percentage in modality of permission/in deontic modality) In diplomatic news
permission	40.91%/4.12%	54.55% /5.15%
admittance	1.82%/0.17%	2.73% /0.26%
total	42.73%/4.04%	57.27% /5.41%

Table 4.2 shows that permission takes a dominant place in this category, referring to giving permission or forbiddance but the proportion of modality of agreement in deontic modality, which is less than 10%, implicates that interpersonal meaning of giving permission seldom appears in political news. Giving permission implies the unbalanced power of two parties in a conversation. In most cases, two parties deal with political issues by negotiation instead of asking permission, which leads to low frequency of permission.

Modality of agreement is usually expressed by low valued modality, which accounts for 39.42%. Similarly, speaker or reporter prefers low value in domestic news while high value in diplomatic news. For example,

(3) "We cannot put America's safety in jeopardy by virtue of the failure of this committee and the failure of his leadership", Mr. Romney said.

(4) Mr. Keeb also said he would insist that the International Criminal Court, which has issued a warrant for Mr. Qaddafi's arrest for crimes against humanity, allow Libya to try him first.

Sentence (3) and (4) are extracted from domestic and diplomatic news respectively. The first sentence means that the failure of this committee and its leadership may threaten the safety of the United States, and Americans will not allow that occurring. This paraphrased sentence is more explicit than sentence (3) in expressing permission, because of the use of low valued modality *cannot* in sentence (3). Besides, the speaker employs *we* to resonate with readers. As talked above, permission is concerned with power. It is not always the case. In sentence (4), the leader of Libya degrades his country to ask permission of a prior persecution of Qaddafi from International Criminal Court by employing high valued modality *allow*. It is a strategy of ensuring the efficiency of negotiation, namely, showing respect to the other.

4.2.3 Willingness in Political Discourse

According to Thompson, in offered goods-and-services, modality "concerns the degree of willingness or inclination of the speaker to fulfill the offer (the speaker may signal: ability/willingness/determination)" (2000:67). It is found that in political discourse acceptance and attempt also show inclination of the speaker to commit him/herself to the validity of what he/she said. From the perspective of deontic modality, willingness can be divided into willingness, acceptance, attempt, determination and promise.

Table 4.3 Distribution of Modality of Willingness in Corpus

classification of willingness	(percentage in modality of willingness/in deontic modality) in domestic news	(percentage in modality of willingness/in deontic modality) in diplomatic news
willingness	11.83% /6.09%	25.00% /12.89%
acceptance	11.33% /5.84%	10.83% /5.58%
attempt	4.83% /2.49%	5.83% /3.01%
determination	3.17% /1.63%	2.67% /1.37%
promise	7.00% /3.87%	8.67% /4.47%
total	38.67% /19.93%	61.33% /31.62%

Unlike the other two categories, modality of inclination is used mainly in diplomatic news, and it plays a dominant role in deontic modality, as shown in Table 4.3. Among these five sub-categories, willingness appears most frequently in corpus, especially in diplomatic news. Compared to modality of obligation, willingness is more polite when the speaker asks other to do something, and thus the urgency and severity of issue is weakened.

Data have shown that when a speaker or reporter expresses willingness, he or she intends to use low valued one in both two kinds of news, taking up 21.42% and 34.32% respectively. For example,

(5)...both said they hoped the mix of cuts could be changed to reduce the effect on the military.

(6) "Otherwise, we will move a petition in the Supreme Court for taking action", Mr. Sharif warned at a rally of thousands of his supporters in Faisalabad, in Punjab Province.

In sentence (5), as an explicit subjective expression, *they hoped* reveals that speakers would like to take certain responsibility on what they have said, but the responsibility is reduced by the low valued verb, *hope*. Besides, passive voice in this sentence makes it unclear who is the actor to change the mix of cuts, which also contributes to the weakened responsibility. *Will* in sentence (6) has a meaning of threatening or warning. Speaker employs a low valued modality of willingness to express interpersonal meaning of high valued modality of obligation, which enables him to avoid appearing too compelling and arousing the antipathy from the supporters.

4.3 Interpersonal Meanings of Deontic Modality in Political Discourse

4.3.1 Politeness

Language as a tool of communication is used not only to give information or express emotions but also to establish or develop interpersonal relationship by speakers. Due to variability of social activities and complication of interpersonal relationship, we need to provide or ask for information directly, but sometimes we are required to fuzz our attitudes or ideas by means of euphemism or indirect words (Li Jie, 2005:9). In political communication, power of two parties is usually unbalanced. In order to ensure one party's interest being maximized, its idea must be acceptable and negotiable to the other. Therefore, the strategy of politeness or euphemism is employed by party in the inferior position to show its respect and by party in the superior position to avoid being offensive. The appropriate employment of deontic modality is an efficient approach in dealing with political issue smoothly. For example,

(7) Daniel Stecich, a trader with TJM Institutional Services in Chicago, said he blamed both parties for putting the economy at risk by not reaching a compromise that included both spending cuts and tax increases. "They better do something to make this market calm down", he said.

That two parties of America failed to make a census on deficit reduction has aroused attention of most Americans, and the decreasing frequency of meeting among Congressional Committee which charged with reducing the deficit has made people, especially traders, frightened, most of whom had lost hope in its ability of carrying out "a plan to get the country back in the black". The interviewee used the deontic modality with median value, *better do*, instead of high valued *must*, to show his politeness. Though he blamed both parties according to the reporter, he controlled himself, which may also be influenced by his social role of being a trader who lacks of power and needs supports from the government meantime.

Level of politeness is influenced by many elements, such as familiarity of relationship between speakers, power and solidarity and social statues, etc. However, on certain occasions, degree of modality exerts great effects in the level of politeness (Li Jie, 2005: 12). In political news discourse, interpersonal meaning of politeness is often given by interviewees in direct speech and indirect speech, and usually realized by modality of low and median value. In domestic news, it is employed by the underprivileged, such as protesters, demonstrators and citizens. In diplomatic news, however, it is one of a communicative strategies though the user, as a party of the international negotiation, is more powerful than the other.

4.3.2 Self-protection

Self-protection can be regarded as one reason of being polite to others because the speaker is trying to get rid of being criticized. It is wise not to be absolute or extreme and to leave negotiable space between the both, which saves face of the speaker when his or her opinion is unacceptable to the other.

(8) And Mark Mellman, a Democratic pollster who is not connected to the Obama campaign, said, "There is a clear sense that the president has reached out and tried to work with Republicans, and there is an equally clear sense that they have not tried to reach out and work with him.

After a failed attempt of reaching an agreement on deficit reduction, Mr. Obama implied "Republicans will never agree to raise taxes on the wealthy to balance any spending cuts, so let the voters decide", to which the Republicans argued that the failure should be attributed not to Republicans but Obama. Mark Mellman used explicit objective expressions, *there is a clear sense that*, trying to minimize subjective degree of his own opinion on this issue. This expression has hidden the origin of information and transformed speaker's own idea into an unsusceptible fact, which enables the reader or hearer to accept this argument more easily (Chang Chenguang, 2001). Besides, the objective expression can protect the speaker from being attacked when his or her idea turns out to be wrong.

Interpersonal meaning of protecting oneself is not held only by interviewees, namely, speakers in direct and indirect speeches. Example (9) will be analyzed from perspective of reporter.

(9) But though all the political leaders called for elections to begin on schedule next week, a growing number acknowledged privately that the violence was likely to force their delay—potentially adding to the unrest.

The cabinet handed over power to transitional military rulers after security forces suppressed street protests in Egypt. Two dozen political parties met together to comfort protesters and talk about the oncoming election. Though there is possibility of election, the reporter still doubts whether it could be held as scheduled, concerning the severe problem of "how the military might begin to hand over power". The uncertainty makes the reporter to use modality with low value, *likely* and *potentially*, to avoid of losing face resulted from a wrong supposition.

It is known to us that as a source of current affairs, newspaper reporters are supposed to report what has happened honestly. To win support of more readers, they make every effort to get rid of initiating dissatisfaction of both common people and officials. Political issues have always been sensitive, and reporters have to be careful in choosing words when reporting in case of getting somebody powerful offended.

4.3.3 Position-declaration

In domestic news, interpersonal meaning of declaring one's stance occurs in dealing with controversial issues or running for president between Republicans and Democrats or between their supporters. In diplomatic news, it occurs when the interest of the speaker's country is threatened or when the speaker expresses attitude to an international affair or issue. Examples (10) and (11) are excerpted from domestic and diplomatic news corpus respectively.

(10) Republicans wasted no time trying to fan the idea of a leadership deficit in the White House, even before the committee made its failure official Monday. "He's done nothing", said Mitt Romney, the former Massachusetts governor who is seen by the Obama circle as the candidate most likely to be the Republican presidential nominee. "It's another example of failed leadership."

(11) Earlier on Friday, Mr. Wen had pushed back against the United States, saying that "outside forces should not, under any pretext" interfere in a regional fight over the control of the South China Sea.

Example (10) shares the same background with example (9). The word *nothing* belongs to mood adjunct or polarity in Halliday's modality system, or denial, a sub-class of contradiction in Martin's appraisal system (Martin, 2005: 103-118), which shows the speaker holding an opposite position. We can clearly sense from the quotation that Mitt Romney is making a refutation to the Obama's blame and as a member of opposite party he is trying to criticize the action of party in power and to attribute the failure to the latter.

Example (11) has taken place when "that the United States is refocusing to the booming Asia-Pacific region after a decade of preoccupation with wars in Iraq and Afghanistan", which increases the intension between China and America. As prime minister of China, Wen Jiabao declares his position of criticizing intention of America to interfere regional affairs through median valued modality of obligation, *should not*, which also implies politeness of Mr. Wen. Then he uses mood adjunct *any* to strengthen his determination to protect South China Sea from being controlled by the U. S.

4.3.4 Social Statues

The choice of using modal expressions with strong deontic modality, for example, *it's necessary that*, made by speaker, reveals that the speaker may hold a superior statue with power and influence in society, and vice versa (qtd. in Martin, 1992: 523-535). In political news discourse, however, it is not always the case.

It is discovered that words of demonstrators or protesters are usually sharp and direct, that is, they intend to use modality with high value or interrogative sentence to express their strong emotions, such as to show urgency of their requirement, anger or disappointment, and ultimately to draw attention of society, especially the government. Officials, as interviewees, have the tendency to employ modality with median or low value to comfort the protesters for fear that situation is worsened or they become the focus of being criticized. For example,

(12) But a delay would be sure to set off an even bigger insurrection. The Muslim Brotherhood warned in a statement on Sunday that "we, along with our well-informed people, will not allow the cancellation or delay in the elections no matter what the price is."

This declaration was given by Islamist Muslim Brotherhood of Egypt to "call for an accelerated end to military rule before the drafting of a constitution". There was only one week left before parliamentary election. Military and security forces seemed to have no intention to secure the polls according to many protestors, and representatives of Muslim Brotherhood employed the modality of obligation with high value, *warn*, to declare its stand, that is, to prevent the military from "encouraging the strife as a pretext for postponing the election of a more legitimate body" firmly. Besides, they also use the modality of agreement (declination) with median value, *not allow*, to strengthen their determination. However, as a civilian party, Muslim Brotherhood has no power to ban military action, and what it can do is to appeal people to protest, which could be an explanation of the use of median value, *not allow*.

4.3.5 Objectiveness and Credibility of News

Objectiveness and credibility are two basic features of news-reporting. Direct speech and indirect speech are the most commonly and frequently employed approach in realization of these two basic features in news discourse. By quoting what witnesses and authorities have said, reporters intend to express his or her own stance and opinion and compel indirectly readers to accept (Chen

Zhi'an & Jiang Yuhong, 2003:82). In addition to direct and indirect speeches, other methods, such as nomination, quotations, passive voice, etc. are also used to ensure objectiveness and credibility.

(13) And how the behind-the-scenes dealings of an obscure group of lawmakers in Washington will read after being retold by spin doctors in both parties is anyone's guess. A Quinnipiac University poll released Monday found that American voters blame Republicans in Congress more than they do President Obama and Congressional Democrats by 44 percent to 38 percent, with a similar spread among independent voters.

This example has taken place under the same situation of example: fear and disgust has widespread through Americans from all walks of life due to the failure of super committee in coming up with deficit reduction plan. The subject of the first sentence is a how-clause, which is more objective than the expression of *anyone is guessing how*.... The second sentence indicates the source of investigating result, which is credible for readers for it is not the speculation of the reporter.

Low or median valued deontic modality is used to make speculations and implicit and explicit objectiveness is employed to objectify those speculations. In pursuit of credibility, reporters usually resort to median and high valued modality to emphasize the authority of reports.

4.3.6 Ironic Effect and Propaganda

According to Fowler (1993), journalists reflect stance, ideas and attitudes of newspapers or themselves through words choice and conversion even in an obviously neutral news report. News reports offer not only facts but also opinions (White, 1998).

Irony is one of the most common methods when journalists report. In news discourse, irony refers that journalist employs cynicism or sarcasm to criticize or negate some social phenomena, in purpose of expressing stance, opinions or emotions of journalist. The ultimate goal of reporter lies in propaganda as expected in advance (Yang Yan, 1990:20). Let's look at example (10) again.

The journalist has employed words like *waste no time*, *trying to fan the idea of*, and *even before*, to describe the action of Republicans. We can feel clearly that the reporter is supporting Obama while criticizing Republicans' buck-passing: what Republicans have done these days is to stir up people to blame Obama and Democrats instead of making efforts to discuss deficit reduction. The reporter later proved the wrongness and irrationality of Republicans by quoting "This president has done exactly that. He put forward a detailed, balanced, 3 trillion deficit reduction plan, and overwhelming majorities of Americans support his approach". The employment of mood adjunct *no* and *even* in *waste no time* and *even before* increases the ironic effect.

4.4 Summary

At the beginning of this chapter, the author gave a brief introduction to the background studies on interpersonal meaning of deontic modality. Then the author introduced achievements on interpersonal meaning and deontic modality at home and abroad, followed by the significance of this study.

The author discussed deontic modality in political news discourse domestically and diplomatically and interpersonal meanings of deontic modality. Three categories of deontic modality, namely, obligation, agreement and willingness, are distributed distinctly in corpus—modality of willingness accounts for more than 50% while agreement less than 10%—which shows speakers or reporter's inclination of interpersonal meaning. The author also talked about the influence of value on distribution of deontic modality: obligation is usually high and median valued in diplomatic news while low valued in domestic news; agreement is usually expressed by low valued modality domestically and high valued modality diplomatically; in both kinds of news, low valued modality of willingness is frequently employed. Six interpersonal meanings of deontic modality have been found, namely, politeness, self-protection, position-declaring, implication of social role, pursuit of objectiveness and credibility of news reports and realization of propaganda by irony. The first two interpersonal meanings and pursuit of objectiveness are usually realized by modality with low or median value and explicit or implicit objective expressions; purposes of declaring position and ensuring credibility of news are realized by means of high or median values.

Chapter 5 Interpersonal Meaning of Deontic Modality in English Education

5.1 Introduction

As a main device for realizing the interpersonal meaning of languages, modality system is catching more and more attention of researchers both from home and abroad. Actually, modality has always been a central topic in linguistics, philosophy and logics. In the field of linguistics, linguists of systemic-functional grammar have shown their particular interests in the modality system.

Former research of modality system mainly focuses upon the system itself, such as the classification of modality and different expressions of modality system. With an increase in the numbers of linguists who are concerned about modality system, their studies begin to associate modality with certain kinds of discourse, such as advertisements, English news, scientific reports, etc., on the purpose of analyzing the interpersonal meaning expressed by modality system.

However, these previous studies are mostly about epistemic modality, which means that deontic modality has not received as much attention as epistemic one has, not to mention deontic modality that occurs in the compositions written by non-English majors.

Halliday has proposed that any language has three meta-functions: the ideational function, the interpersonal function and the textual function (Hu Zhuanglin, 2000: 10). As more and more researchers are carrying out various kinds of research on these meta-functions of languages, the interpersonal meaning, which received relatively less attention during the past years, has really caught an increasing amount of attention from relevant researchers.

Undoubtedly, both Halliday and Thompson have made outstanding contributions and laid solid foundations for further research of interpersonal meaning of languages. Thompson (2000: 28), provides us a relatively comprehensive definition of interpersonal meaning. According to his viewpoint, as a kind of meaning expressed by languages, the interpersonal meaning enables us to interact with others, so that we can develop and maintain certain kinds of relationships with them.

Moreover, it also enables us to influence or even change the attitudes or judgments pertaining to a certain issue of other people when we try to voice our own attitudes or judgments. In this case, the interpersonal meaning is of great significance in our social activities. In addition, as to the devices used for the realizations of interpersonal meaning, Halliday carries out his own study from the perspective of mood and modality system respectively (Hu Zhuanglin 2000:313).

Despite these achievements by systemic functional linguists, their theories of interpersonal meaning of languages are usually used to describe verbal communications in the same linguistic community under the same cultural background (Zheng Yuanhui, 2000: 26). In other words, systemic functional linguists, to a great extent, ignore certain kinds of influence resulting from different types of cultures.

Domestically, Zheng Yuanhui has done some research of interpersonal meaning of languages by associating it with translation. Better still, he (2009:26-27) points out that communicators from different cultures possess their unique social standards and value systems, which will have great influence upon their understandings and opinions of certain issues. Obviously, his theory provides us with some inspirations when we try to give a better explanation about the preferences for different values and orientations of deontic modality of these non-English majors.

In this instance, this part selects 50 compositions written by non-English majors and tries to carry out a study on the interpersonal meaning of deontic modality in these compositions to fill this gap and hopefully provide some valuable information for further investigations.

From the perspective of functional linguistics, modality refers to "the area of meaning that lies between yes and no or the intermediate ground between positive and negative polarity" (Halliday 2000:335). With the intention to offer a clearer explanation of modality, Halliday (2000:89) has classified it into two types, that is, modalization and modulation, which also can be named as epistemic modality and deontic modality respectively in functional grammar.

Generally speaking, epistemic modality concerns about the speaker's judgments on the possibility of a proposition. It includes scale of probability, such as *perhaps*, *probably* and *possibly*, and scale of usuality, such as *sometimes*, *usually* and *always*. When it comes to deontic modality, it refers to the speaker's degree of confidence on ultimate success of the exchange of a proposition. Similarly, deontic modality consists of scale of obligation, such as *allowed*, *supposed* and *required*, and scale of inclination, such as *willing*, *keen* and *determined* (Yang Shu, 2006: 131). In other words, deontic modality expresses what people should do when they are facing certain situations.

With deeper study on modality system, Halliday endows it with various kinds of values, namely, high, median and low values, which can be used to specify the degree of probability or willingness.

Normally, different values of modality can convey different degrees of authority identity of people towards certain issues. Both Martin J. R. (1992:26) and Zhang Delu (1998:45) have pointed out that in normal conditions, people with higher status in a society are more likely to use modal expressions of high value, such as *must*, to demonstrate their decisiveness and authority, while those of lower class prefer to express themselves through expressions of median value or even low value, such as *can* and *may*, to show their proper respect and politeness to others.

Moreover, when it comes to the interpersonal meaning expressed by the modality system, Zheng Yuanhui (2009:91-97) explains it from three aspects. First of all, modal expressions can indicate the speaker's attitude or modal commitment pertaining to certain issues. Secondly, when the speaker tries to express his/her personal viewpoints, he/she has already realized that the readers may or may not agree with his/her opinions. In this instance, modality serves as a device of showing politeness to readers. Finally, he also believes that modality is a way to show unequal status of the communicators in a society, and his opinion is similar to the viewpoints of Martin J. R. and Zhang Delu.

In this case, it is necessary for us to explore different frequencies of three modal values of modality system in the compositions, so that we are able to find out the potential kinds of interpersonal meaning expressed by these non-English majors. Undoubtedly, when we are exploring the interpersonal meaning in these compositions, we should take the traditional culture of China into consideration, for it has such significant impacts upon Chinese people.

In general, if the writer wants to emphasize that the opinion is his/her personal viewpoint, he/she will definitely choose the subjective orientation, and the explicit subjective one in particular. In contrast, through objective expressions, especially explicit objective orientation, the writer will objectivize his/her point of view, thus making it sound more real and objective (Li Jie, 2002:178). Although Li Jie has given differences among the four sub-types of orientations, he doesn't point out certain kinds of interpersonal meaning expressed by these orientations. As a result, we will move on and explore the interpersonal meaning demonstrated by different orientations in the compositions on the basis of the general information given by him.

5.2 Methodology

Fifty compositions written by sophomore students of Harbin Engineering University, who are non-English majors, are collected in this section for the purpose of analyzing the interpersonal meaning of deontic modality. Relevant analyses will be conducted from the perspective of main kinds of realizations, different values and orientations, and the interpersonal meaning of deontic modality respectively.

In addition, these compositions share the same topic: Do you think Chinese people are united? Obviously, this writing assignment falls into the categorization of argumentative writing. According to the requirements, the writer needs to state his/her own opinion clearly with at least 200 words.

5.2.1 Deontic Modality in the Compositions

5.2.1.1 Main Kinds of Realizations of Deontic Modality

In systemic functional linguistics, Halliday(2000:76) has suggested that the modality system can be realized through the following possible ways, such as the use of modal verbs, modal adverbs, adjectival predictors, prepositional phrases, nominalizations and modal clauses, etc. Therefore, we will try our best to find out different expressions of deontic modality used by the sophomores in their compositions.

Generally speaking, there exist five main kinds of expressions of deontic modality in these 50 compositions, which are used by the writers to convey their own viewpoints. In order to present the usage of these expressions more directly, this paper works out a table (Table 5.1) pertaining to the frequencies of these different expressions.

Table 5.1 Frequencies of Different Expressions of Deontic Modality

expressions / statistics	modal auxiliaries	modal clause	predicator constituents	verbs/ phrases	adjectives
number	177	3	6	20	10
percentage	81.94%	1.39%	2.78%	9.26%	4.63%

From the table above, we will detect that the use of modal auxiliaries serves as the commonest device to express deontic modality. In these compositions, modal auxiliaries, such as *must*, *can*, *can't*, *could*, *may*, *should*, *will*, *need* and *dare*, are commonly used to state clearly what should be done by us according to the opinion of the writer. For example,

(1) All the people should try their best to stand together.

In this sentence, the writer uses the modal auxiliary *should* to indicate that it is the duty of people to unite with each other to fight against possible disasters. In this case, the writer makes his/her own point of view sound like a kind of common sense, thus strengthening the persuasiveness of his/her opinion.

Moreover, modal clauses, such as *it's reasonable*... and *it's essential*... are also used to add objectivity to personal viewpoint. For example,

(2) It is essential for us to give supports to them to rebuild their home.

As for this expression, the modal clause *it's essential*... enables the writer to hide the subjectivity of his/her personal opinion successfully. With this clause, we will believe that it is not the writer but the common sense or morals that encourage us to help these people, who have suffered from the disasters.

Another device is the use of predicator constituents, such as *be ready/willing to*... and *be expected to*.... Undoubtedly, these expressions indicate certain kinds of inclinations of us, when we are facing certain situations. For example,

(3) When some people are in trouble, others are willing to help them.

Furthermore, some researchers, such as Qu Jiadan, have carried out valuable studies to broaden the range of the expressions of deontic modality. On the basis of his own research, he maintains that the open words (mainly including nouns, verbs, adjectives and adverbs) can also demonstrate certain kinds of modality (2005:107-108).

Consequently, in these 50 compositions, we perceive that despite those relatively typical ways of deontic modality that we have mentioned above, certain verbs like *want*, *deserve*... and adjectives like *undoubted*, *important*... are also applied to express deontic modality, thus conveying the writer's idea that what we should do or what we are supposed to do. For instance,

(4) This is an issue deserving deep concern.

(5) They all want to give help to the victims.

(6) Thus competition, honesty and cooperation are important to the development of our country.

In sentence (4) and sentence (6), what the writer tends to express is to warn us that something is so important that we should attach our deep concern/close attention to it, while through sentence (5), the writer expresses the intention/eagerness of people to help others.

All in all, despite various types of realizations of deontic modality, the writer voices the obligation or inclination pertaining to certain kinds of situations.

5.2.1.2 Different Values of Deontic Modality

According to Halliday, there are three basic values of modality, which are "attached to the modal judgment: high, median and low" (2000:358). He also attaches these three values to modal auxiliaries as in the following table (Table 5.2).

Table 5.2 Values of Modal Auxiliaries(Halliday 2000:76)

high	median	low
must, need, ought to, need, have/has/had to, mustn't, oughtn't to,	can't, mightn'twill, would, wouldn't, should, shouldn't, is/was to, won't (isn't/wasn't to)	can, may, could, might, (dare) needn't, doesn't + need/have to

According to this table provided by Halliday, this paper analyzes the modal auxiliaries in the compositions and presents more details about the frequency of different values of them. We can detect that these non-English majors prefer to use modality auxiliaries with median and low values.

Table 5.3 Frequencies of Modal Auxiliaries in the Compositions

statistics / values	high	median	low
number	28	93	56
percentage	15.82%	52.54%	31.64%

Generally speaking, modal auxiliaries of different values can convey different degrees of responsibility. In normal conditions, modal auxiliaries of high value indicate that the writer holds extremely great responsibility for what he says or what he is going to say, while those of low value reduce the responsibility that the writer needs to hold as much as possible. Undoubtedly, expressions of median value show that the writer only needs to hold a certain degree of responsibility (Wei Benli, 2005: 57). This paper selects several examples from 50 compositions to give a better understanding.

(7) The government *must* make some reforms. (high value)

(8) We *should* be united when facing disasters. (median value)

(9) Chinese people *can* help each other in the disasters. (low value)

In sentence (7), the word *must* makes us feel that the government has no choice but to make some reforms. With such a word of high value, the writer expresses a kind of extremely authoritative tone, thus leaving little room for our readers to carry out further negotiations. As for sentence (8), the writer chooses the word *should* with median value to voice his/her point of view. On the one hand, it indicates clearly and directly that we have an obligation to be united, or it is our duty to do so; On the other hand, it also leaves some space for others to make another kind of choice. When it comes to sentence (9), with a kind of consultative tone, the writer sounds more like hinting that Chinese people have the ability to help each other. In other words, they have no duty/obligation to do so.

5.2.1.3 Different Orientations of Deontic Modality

As we have discussed above, we know that besides the different values of deontic modality, there also exist different orientations in the system of modality, namely, subjective orientation and objective orientation, which can be divided into sub-types on the basis of implicitness and explicitness. Table 5.4 displays the frequency of the occurrence of different orientations in the compositions.

Table 5.4 Frequencies of Orientations in the Compositions

statistics / orientations	subjective		objective	
	explicit	implicit	explicit	implicit
number	67	121	6	14
percentage	32.22%	58.17%	2.88%	6.73%
total number	188		20	
total percentage	90.39%		9.61%	

Based upon the statistics shown in table 5.4, it is evident that the application of subjective sentences is much more than that of objective ones. In addition, the use of implicit subjective is also much more than that of the explicit one. In order to offer a clearer explanation about different orientations, some examples will be presented.

(10) We should give support to them. (explicit subjective)

(11) Chinese people should eliminate the jealousy in order to be united. (implicit subjective)

(12) Charity events should be organized with transparent mechanism. (implicit objective)

(13) It is essential for us to give support to them. (explicit objective)

Obviously, sentence (10) is of explicit subjective orientation, which means that it conveys the writer's opinion in a quite direct way, thus clearly demonstrating that this opinion purely results from the writer rather than some already well-known facts. On the contrary, as a kind of explicit objective orientation, sentence (13) enables us to conclude that whether the writer says or not, we should and we will give support to them, for it is our common sense or duty/obligation that lets us to do so. In this case, the writer successfully maximizes the objectivity as well as the persuasiveness of his/her opinion. As to sentences (11) and (12), with third-person pronoun Chinese people and the passive tense, the writer, to a certain extent, adds some objectivity to his/her viewpoint to make it easier for others to agree with and accept.

5.2.2 Interpersonal Meaning of Deontic Modality

5.2.2.1 Politeness and Respect

In a composition, the writer needs to show his/her proper politeness and respect toward others to guide them to begin and continue to read his/her article. It is well-known that as a country with a history of over 5000 years, China has a tradition of hierarchy, e. g. high power distance, which means that there exists inequality among different classes of people in the society.

According to the definition given by Hofstede (2001: 98), power distance is a type of dimension to measure cultural attitude toward inequality, or it can be thought as the extent to which a society will embrace and approve the unequally distributed power in certain kinds of organizations or institutions.

Normally, people from high power distance countries like China, maintain that both hierarchy and inequality can be accepted, namely power and social status are of critical importance. In this case, whether consciously or unconsciously, members of such kind of culture are always taught that people are not equal and everybody has his own right place (Sun Qiyao, 2012: 45-46).

Therefore, being Chinese, these sophomores are absolutely influenced by the hierarchical culture and believe that their own position in this society, to a certain extent, is lower than their teachers. Therefore, when they write composition or other articles that will be checked by teachers, they are likely to use auxiliaries of median and low values with a relatively consultative and modest tone. Those words would enable these students to show their proper respect and politeness to their teachers as well as other potential readers in a modest way.

5.2.2.2 Fulfillment of Self-protection

As Chinese, our sense of face is so deep-rooted that we will spare every effort to save our face. As for face, it refers to some kinds of emotional needs in social intercourse. Basically, face includes positive face and negative face. Positive face, which relates to self-esteem, refers to a feeling of being approved. This kind of approval results from the fulfillment of our needs, or the confirmation of our value. On the contrary, negative face has something to do with the desire for reasonable freedom and personal space, which should not be disturbed by others (Zheng Yuanhui, 2009: 93). Therefore, the writer should take both his/her face and the readers' face into consideration, for the purpose of protecting himself/herself and readers from losing face and getting hurt.

In order to satisfy this need, the writer chooses to use modality auxiliaries of median or even low value. On the one hand, those words could reduce the modal responsibility that the writer needs to hold as much as possible when he/she tries to speak out his/her personal opinion in the compositions; on the other hand, through using expressions of lower modal value, the writer voices his/her personal opinion with more euphemism, thus leaving much more space for the readers to choose to agree with the writer or not (Li Jie & Zhong Yongping, 2002: 13). In other words, it is a way for the writer to escape from undertaking some responsibility as well as a way of avoiding being forced to accept certain opinions for the sake of the readers.

In this case, if someone points out that what the writer says is wrong or unreasonable, the writer could, to a certain extent, save their face and avoid being hurt, for those words of median and low values indicate that even the writers themselves are not so sure about their own ideas. Namely, in their opinion, these ideas are just a kind of personal assumption about this issue. Moreover, as for the readers, considering the consultative of the writer, they are free to hold different opinions rather than being forced to agree with the writer, thus fulfilling their needs to protect their esteem.

5.2.2.3 Pursuit of Harmonious Relationships

As a kind of morals, *Li* (礼) and *He* (和) has been advocated and followed by our whole nation for over 5000 years. As we all know, these two kinds of morals that were proposed by Confucius, tell us how to develop and maintain a good relationship with others. To be more specific, they encourage people to pursuit identical views as well as allow other different views to exist at the same time. Under the impact of *Li* and *He*, these sophomores are apt to voice their own ideas without the attitude of extremely discriminating against different opinions of others. On the one hand, modal expressions of median or low value, together with implicit subjective expressions, enable the writer to convey his/her position properly and clearly. On the other hand, those expressions are so limited in the degree of authority and subjectivity that the use of them indicates that the writer admits and even permits that there are other kinds of opinions about this issue, thus avoiding hurting the feelings of other people that maintain different opinions and maintaining harmonious relationship with others.

5.2.2.4 Personal Opinion and Persuasion

Undoubtedly, the main purpose of writing this composition is to clearly take a position pertaining to whether Chinese people are united or not. In this case, it is reasonable for the writers to use more subjective expressions, which makes it clear that the opinion expressed in the composition comes from the writer himself/herself. As a result, the writer succeeds in conveying personal ideas.

Evidently, besides the purpose of expressing personal points of view, these compositions also try to convince others to accept the opinion of the writers. Therefore, any composition possesses the intention to persuade its potential readers. Given this potential purpose, the writer needs to consider his/her wording in the composition very carefully.

Compared with expressions of high value, those of median and low values, to a certain degree, will express a kind of relatively consultative tone of the writer, thus leaving enough space for potential discussions. As a result, it is much easier for the writer, who uses more expressions of median or low value, to transmit his own idea to his readers and even influence and change the attitude of readers successfully (Wei Benli, 2005:57).

Similarly, except the explicit subjective orientation, the other three kinds of expressions, to some extent, add some objectivity to the personal opinion of the writer. As a result, we will feel that it is much easier for us to accept and even agree with the viewpoint of the writer. To put it in another way, these expressions make it easier for the writer to persuade his/her readers.

5.3 Summary

This chapter has probed the deontic modality in the compositions written by non-English majors for the purpose of finding out certain kinds of interpersonal meaning expressed through it.

During the process of analyzing the compositions, we find that there are various ways of expressing deontic modality, such as modal auxiliaries, modal clauses and predicator constituents. Surprisingly, we still perceive that even certain verbs and adjectives can also be used to realize deontic modality. Given the fact that expressions of deontic modality possess systems of orientations and values, there is no doubt that modal expressions of different orientations and values will convey different kinds of interpersonal meaning of the writer. In this case, when we write a composition, we should pay close attention to our wording so that we will express ourselves more precisely and clearly, thus achieving certain types of interpersonal meaning that we tend to deliver.

As for the interpersonal meaning expressed in the compositions, it can be divided into five main kinds, namely, showing politeness and respect to the readers, fulfilling the need of self-protection of the writer as well as the readers, pursuing harmonious relationships with others, expressing personal opinion of the writer and persuading the readers.

In brief, this study of interpersonal meaning of deontic modality in the compositions written by non-English majors will help non-English majors realize the fact that deontic modality can be realized by various expressions, which can convey different kinds of interpersonal meaning. Consequentially, when these students write other compositions or expression themselves through other ways, they will become more careful with their selections of different expressions of deontic modality in order to succeed in expressing themselves more precisely.

Chapter 6 Interpersonal Meaning of Deontic Modality in Gender Language

6.1 Introduction

Thanks to the hard work of these linguists, the study on women's language is flourishing and now has attracted more linguists' attention. But the topic of the interpersonal meanings of deontic modality in female language is not paid more attention yet. Deontic modality is a new topic in the research field of modality system, and it is an important way to realize the interpersonal meaning.

This chapter analyzes the interpersonal meanings of deontic modality in female language. In recent years, a lot of American series TV plays focusing on American female's life come to people's daily life in China, here the author will choose some typical actor's lines as corpus to analyze the deontic modality in female language.

Modality system is one of the means to realize the interpersonal meanings. Thompson thinks that "What we have focused on has been the broad factors at work in the area of modality, particularly those which help in the analysis of spoken and written text." (Thompson, 2009:63). Female language research enlarges the field of language study. From a methodological point of view, female language research requires the multi-angle studies. It is a cumulative development of previous researches. Language is not just name, logo and communication systems, but also meeting point of power, which plays a role of link in the collaboration of human life. Language is not only a tool for expressing ideas through the exchange of concepts, but also a kind of behavior establishing interpersonal relationships (Hu Zhuanglin, 2000).

American TV Plays are not only the products of entertainment, but also play an important role for English learners to know the culture and the language better. Most of the researchers have studied TV Plays from such aspects as translation method, psycholinguistics or the literature analysis. Just in recent few years, some researchers treated the actor's lines in American TV Plays as the text to study the discourse analysis. Most of the studies aim at the understanding the interpersonal meaning. But none of the studies are about deontic modality. Thus, there is still a big research area to fill in. Therefore, the author is motivated to make a study on the interpersonal meaning of deontic modality in female language in American TV Plays.

6.2 General Review of the Study on Modality in Female Language

Geoff Thompson points out that "In functional approaches to grammar we essentially equate meaning with function" (2000:26), so the following discussion equates interpersonal function with interpersonal meanings. The interpersonal metafunction is concerned with the meaning of language when it is used to enable people to participate in communicative acts with other people, to take on roles and to express and understand feelings, attitude and judgments (Halliday & Matthiessen, 2004). Thompson gives a clear and elaborated definition on interpersonal meaning. He defines interpersonal meaning as the strand of meaning conveyed by language which is used to interact with other people to establish and maintain relations with them, to influence their attitudes to behavior, to express their viewpoints, and to elicit or change theirs (Thompson, 2000:28).

Besides Halliday and Thompson, many other linguists also committed to studying interpersonal meaning of language. Bex tries to explain the interpersonal meaning of two different ideas he received. He also judges that methods of address, forms of politeness, modality, words with different levels of cognitive certainty even certain features of the typographical layout can contribute to the relationships between the sender and the receiver that are encoded in those texts (Bex, 1996:108). In *Analyzing Causal Conversation* (Slade and Eggins, 1997:145), Slade and Eggins conclude that "the speaker makes meaning about such interpersonal dimensions as: the power and solidarity of their relationship; the extent of the intimacy; the level of their familiarity with each other; their attitudes and judgments" (Eggins, 1994:193). Appraisal Theory (Martin 2000:73), is an extension of the interpersonal meaning study in Systemic Functional Grammar and a further development of Systemic Functional Linguistics. It is employed in describing and explaining the way the language is used to adopt stances, to evaluate, to construct textual persons and to manage interpersonal positioning and relationships, that is to say, the responsibility that the speakers should take, is realized by the intervention components. "With evaluation, we are even more on the edge of grammar: much of evaluation is expressed by lexical choices and there are few grammatical structures that can be seen as having evolved with a primarily evaluative function. It is important to note that evaluation is a central part of the meaning of any text and that any analysis of the interpersonal meaning of a text must take it into account." (Thompson, 2009:65).

In the research field of the differences between gender and language, "female language" and "female status" as the basic theory of the research field, was put up with by Lakoff in 1973. He points out that the core of female language is reflected by this way: under the effects on many social psychologies, the changes of the female speech style are mainly reflected by euphemistic strategies, uncertain mood, etc, which are realized by modality.

According to the Appraisal Theory, the attitudes in the discourse contain *affect*, *judgment* and *appreciation*. In the viewpoint of judgment system, when we are judging something, we could judge a behavior in a classification of: moral or immoral, legal or illegal, acceptable or unacceptable, etc. In female's language, they always choose to use modality to realize their speech style, which results from aiming at gaining more social acceptance.

Besides, females are more inclining to use implicit judgment to express their ideas, which results in using more modality component to express their judgments, to achieve the goal of expressing ideas in an indirect way.

To sum up, under the special social cultural environment, females have been in a lower social status for a long time, which results in using modality components to express their thoughts in an indirectly way. Besides, employing the modality components makes female language own an outstanding characteristic of flouting politeness principle well, to make sure the occurrence of a better communication.

6.3 Mood, Modality and Key in Female Language

6.3.1 Interpersonal Meaning of Mood in Female Language

Interpersonal meaning of mood is realized by the lexical grammar tier and phonemic tier. Indicative mood in grammar categories is usually employed in exchanging information. In the indicative mood categories, the declarative mood is usually used to express a meaning of making a statement.

The declarative mood could express a meaning of persuading or suggesting others to agree with the speaker's ideas. Here is an example.

(1) Mother: Are you doing your homework, Maggie?

Maggie: No, I must get these chords right first, our group's playing in a concert on Saturday. This concert could change my life.

Mother: Oh, I think you had better finish your homework first; it won't cost your too much time.

The girl conveys the information "chords", "Their group's playing in a concert on Saturday", "The concert could change her life" to her mother, to get a goal of persuading her mother. And mother also conveys the information that Maggie should finish her homework first through declarative mood. Female is more sensible about language and good at using declarative mood to achieve the goal of communicating.

(2) Maggie: Can I go now, mum?

Mother: Don't you think it's too late, honey?

Interrogative mood expresses a meaning of questioning. The general interrogative sentence is a kind of questioning sentence about polarity, while WH- questions is questioning about the content. Maggie is asking permission for going out, "Can I go now" expresses a meaning of worrying about no permission of going out, and her mother should have answered "yes" or "no", but the mother chooses to use the interrogative sentence to express a meaning of not sure about whether Maggie will obey her or not. Besides, female are more likely to use the interrogative sentences which indicate that they are not willing to be thought so aggressive.

Imperative mood expresses a meaning of command, suggestion, threats and so on. The illocutionary meaning of them reflects the responsibility and the permission on the listener to make them take certain actions. Therefore, most of imperative sentences deliver the deontic modality. Meanwhile, female will choose to use indirect mood to express the meaning.

(3) Bring that here! (command)

(4) Could you bring that here? (Female will say in this way)

(5) Put the paragraph in your handwriting. (suggestion)

(6) You could include that paragraph in your handwriting if you like. (Female will say in this way)

(7) A: Excuse me, I want to get to LanTian Restaurant. (advice)

B: Take Bus 7.

(8) I think you could take a number 7 bus, but number 102 bus is faster. (Female will say in this way)

Besides, in order to avoid performing brusque or rash, female will choose to use a long sentence when female want to use imperative sentence to convey deontic modality.

(9) Tell the students to turn in these forms by Friday.

(10) Would it be all right with you if you had the students turn in these forms by Friday?

6.3.2 Interpersonal Meaning of Modality in Female Language

The author has already given a general introduction to modality. Here the framework the author may use will be summarized.

In the systemic functional grammar, modality is considered to be a major way to realize the interpersonal meanings. And it has different types and degrees. "People may signal a higher or lower degree of certainty about the validity of a proposition; or a higher or lower degree of pressure on the other person to carry out a command" (Thompson, 2000: 59). The values could be classified as high, median and low.

When the speaker chooses to employ modals to express their attitude or ideas, they should take the orientation of modality into account. According to Halliday, the orientation of modality is considered from subjective and objective way, and it could come to the scales of *explicitly* and *implicitly*. The modality expresses the personal attitude toward a proposition or proposal. Subjectivity is the basic characteristic of modality (Palmer, 1986: 16), objective orientation is not that direct as subjectivity. In some different context, the participants of the communication may want to conceal his ideas. He would adopt an indirect way to make it seem to be objective, such as *It is known by...* and *probably*. When the speaker wants to emphasize his own thoughts, she will take a subjective way. In this situation, she will employ the expression like *I think*, *I believe*, *will*, etc. However, the implicit orientation often expresses with the modal verbs or adverbs.

Explicit subjective orientation is an efficient method to make speakers' viewpoint to a certain proposition distinct. The speakers learn to state clearly that the viewpoints are their real thoughts or attitudes. For instance:

① I think you are right. (explicit subjective)

② In my opinion, she is a good teacher. (explicit subjective)

③ It seems that my grandpa doesn't like watching TV. (explicit subjective)

Implicit subjective orientation is to make the proposition not that obvious, thus the viewpoint is considered to be the fact itself but not from the speaker. Finite modal operators are the most representative way to realize the implicit subjective. Thompson believes that "modal operator exploits the finite slot and thus is firmly rooted in the interpersonal, subjective meaning of the clause" (Thompson, 2009: 61).

The mood adjunct is another component of modal adjuncts and it seems to be very indispensable in realizing the implicit objective orientation. Halliday thinks that all the modal adjuncts could demonstrate the objectivity of propositions in an implicit way.

Explicit objective orientation causes the participants in communication to have a feeling that thecontent they hear or read is not the speaker's own ideas but the facts are. Perkins argues that the view that nominal modal expressions represent the ultimate stage in the objectification of modality and play a very important role in conveying explicit objective orientation (Perkins, 1983: 137).

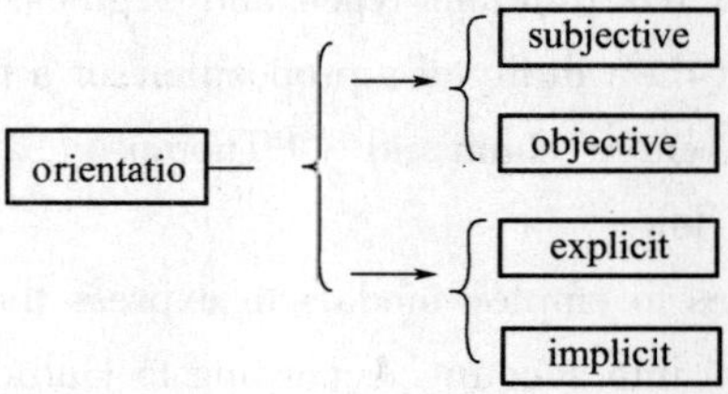

Fig. 6.1 System of Orientation in Modality

Table 6.1 System of Modality: Examples of "Type" and Orientations (Halliday, 2000: 358)

types of intermediacy		subjective explicit	subjective implicit	objective implicit	objective explicit
modalization	probability	I think/in my opinion Mary knows...	Mary will know...	Mary probably knows...	It's likely that Mary knows...
	usuality		Fred'll sit quite quiet	Fred usually sits quite quiet	It's usual for Fred to sit quite quiet
modulation	obligation	I want John to go	John should go	John's supposed to go	It's expected that John goes
	inclination		Jane'll help	Jane's keen to help	

Except mood and modality, key (also named tone), could reflect the interpersonal function as well. The difference is that the semantic feature is not expressed by lexical and grammar structure, but the tone of phonemic tier, which is also named contour. The basic unit of tone is "tone group"; one tone group contains one or several "foot"; one foot contains one or several "syllables".

Tone group is divided into single tone group and double tone group. Halliday (2000) divided the tone of single tone group into five kinds of simple key and two kinds of double key. Simple key contains: Tone 1 (the falling tone), Tone 2 (high rising tone), Tone 3 (low rising tone or flat tone), Tone 4 (falling intonation), Tone 5 (rising falling intonation). Double tone group contains: Tone 13 (the falling tone plus low rising tone), Tone 53 (rising falling intonation plus falling intonation). Symbol "//" means the boundary of Tone group. Symbol "/" means the boundary of tone foot. "T1, T2, T3, T4..." means types of tone group. "Capital letter" means the accent of tone group. Symbol "^" means transient intermittent.

The tone system of English is founded on the basis of opposition of rising tone and falling tone. The falling tone expresses the meaning of "sureness", while the rising tone "unsureness". Besides, the tone system also could be "neutral" (neither falling tone nor rising tone), and "combination" (both rising tone and falling tone).

Some samples of everyday expression will be analyzed // ^ That's very im/PORTANT /// What've/you/done //

A declarative sentence expresses the different ideas, protest or disproves of the speaker with T2, while the general interrogative sentence expresses a kind of unsureness of hearers about what they hear or see.

//2 he/can't be /RIGHT// //2 do you/take the /BIKE when you /go a/broad//

T3, a tone between rising tone and falling tone, expresses a semantic meaning of possibility, unimportance or unsureness. Sometimes a speaker finishes a clause, but the meaning he wants to express is not finished.

//3 he /could be /WRONG// //3 Lucy/likes to /TEACH him/while she's back//

T4 contains two semantic compositions. The speaker turns the semantic meaning to the opposite meaning when his speech is finished by half, which means "It seems or sounds the meaning he expresses is quite clear or full of possibility, but in fact it is quite complicated or not that possible." //4 ^ he /could be /WRONG//

T5 (rising falling intonation) also contains two semantic composition. The speaker turns the semantic meaning to the opposite meaning when his speech in finished by half, which means "It seems or sounds the meaning he expressed is quite doubting, which in fact is quite clear or believable." // 5 ^ he's /certainly/RIGHT //. // 5 ^ I/didn't /know he'd /ever/BEEN to / America //

T13 (the falling tone plus low rising tone) is double tone, which has two stress tones, but the second is much more important than the first one. If the last group is additional in the tone group, which the speaker doesn't want to make it outstanding at this time, the tone is adopted.

//13 Betty has/been to Austria/TWICE in the /last/YEAR or/so//

The new information the speakers want to provide, which contains "TWICE" and "YEAR", the latter is not that important as the former, so the speaker turns T1 to T3.

T53(rising falling intonation + falling intonation) is also double tone. Like T13, T53 has two stress tones too, the first of which is much more important than the second one.

//^Mary has/never/taken/Jim on /any of her/VITITS/though//

The semantic meaning that the speaker wants to express is "Maybe she likes Jim very much, maybe she has ever taken other children on her visits, but she's never taken Jim." The new information that the speaker wants to express contains both "Jim" and "VISITS", but the latter VITITS is her usual action, and the comparison among Jim and other children is much more important, so she turns T5 to T3.

6.3.3 Use of Politeness Principle in Female Language

According to Grice's Cooperative Principle, the participants ought to observe Cooperative Principle maxims when they communicate with each other. But in daily conversation, the participants often flout this principle, that is to say the cooperation principle cannot explain the following questions: why do people frequently flout this principle intentionally? Why do people often make hearers infer what is said instead of speaking frankly? Why are people often so indirect in conveying their thoughts or points of view? (He Ziran, 1997). Leech proposes that one of the most important reasons is politeness. It is for these reasons that Leech manifests that the Politeness Principle can be added to the Cooperation and proposes the Politeness Principle in order to rescue the Cooperative Principle from serious trouble.

In a communication, the speaker often shows his admiration and respect to the third party but not only the listener, who is the other participant in the communication. But the third party may or not stay at the situation. And the politeness principle concerns more other than self. This point is more obvious in female language.

In recent years, more and more linguists have paid more attention to the comparison study on the differences between female and male in the same cultural situation and share the same language. Their major findings show that most female could obey the Politeness Principle when they communicate with others, for avoiding the lame arguments and perverted logic and giving more respect to others. To employ modality to realize the interpersonal meanings is not the only aim to flout Politeness Principle, but there is the efficient and proper way. Why are female always so indirect to express their thoughts and ideas, it is relative to the gender characteristic, the special status in historic factors and so on. In the following section, the author will analyze the employment of deontic modality in realizing interpersonal meanings in female language aiming at flouting

Politeness Principle and the causes of it in different factors.

6.3.4 Interpersonal Meaning of Multi-Voice in Female Language

From the perspective of " multi-voice ", the modal intervention composition such as "maybe", "I think" have no connection with the proposition, but only indicates the meaning of the proposition referred by the speaker could be consulted or doubted by others who hold different ideas. It also indicates that the speaker gives enough respect to those people who hold different ideas.

The interpersonal meanings of multi-voice conform to the potential requirements of female in communications, thus, female are more intent to use modal intervention composition to convey the possibility of accommodating the anti-voice in the communication to avoid disputing, which benefits the speaker to express his own ideas and realize the aim of communication as well. For example:

(11) I brought some champagne, I thought we should have a toast. (Lynette)

Here Lynette suggests these ladies to have a toast to make Alice Young's soul be able to rest in peace, she adopts using I thought to make her advice have multi-voice feature, thus, to make other 3 female to accept her advice, and are not thought to be forced at the same time.

(12) When you read this morning's paper, you may come across an article about the unusual day I had last week. (Alice Yong)

Here *may* broadens the possibility of Alice's words, on the one hand, and it indicates the unsureness whether the audience will read the papers, and it also accommodates the possibility of not reading the paper.

6.4 A Discussion on Interpersonal Meaning of Deontic Modality in Female Language

In the previous parts, we have given a brief presentation of interpersonal meanings of the deontic modality. In this section, we will choose some samples of actor's lines in American TV series *Ugly Betty* to have an analysis of the occurrence of deontic modality in female language and ways of realization of interpersonal meanings in female language, and the reasons of realizing deontic modality in female language.

6.4.1 Methodology

We have chosen 50 samples from the actor's lines in *Ugly Betty* in Season One, the 19th episode and the 21st episode. Here the samples chosen are typical and clear. The theories mentioned above will be used to analyze the samples in this section. We will make an analysis of the data and statistics to see the ways of realization of deontic modality in female language.

Ugly Betty is an Emmy-winning American television comedy drama series. It premiered on September 28, 2006, on ABC in the United States and on City TV in Canada. The show tells us a story of a girl named Betty Suarez, who is not that glamorous but good-natured and hard-working.

Betty Suarez is a 22-year-old Mexican-American woman from Queens District, New York. She is sorely lacking in fashion sense. She is known to be courageous, good-hearted, and slightly naive. She is abruptly thrust into a different world when she lands a job at *Mode*, a trendy high fashion magazine based in Manhattan that is part of the publishing empire of the wealthy Bradford Meade. Bradford's son Daniel has just been installed as Editor-in-Chief of *Mode* following the death of Fey Sommers (Bradford's longtime mistress). Bradford hires the inexperienced Betty as his son's newest personal assistant to curb Daniel's habit of sleeping with his assistants. As time goes by, Betty and Daniel become friends and help each other in their professional and personal lives.

Life at *Mode* is quite difficult for both Betty and Daniel. Their most serious threat comes from creative director Wilhelmina Slater, a vindictive schemer who devises numerous plots to steal Daniel's job and seize the control of his family's company. In addition, Wilhelmina's loyal assistant Marc St. James and *Mode* receptionist Amanda Sommers continually mock and humiliate Betty for her lackluster physical appearance, awkward nature, and initial lack of taste in fashion. However, not everyone at *Mode* is against Betty; she gains loyal friends in Scottish seamstress Christina McKinney and accountant Henry Grubstick. She also receives strong support from her father Ignacio, elder sister Hilda, and nephew Justin. She also makes friends with Marc St. James and Amanda Sommers, the first being her neighbor in the last season, who also helped Justin with his coming out, and the latter even being her roommate for some time.

This Series is warmly welcomed by the viewers all around the world. The lines in it are funny and typical, and it will be of great help for our research about the interpersonal meaning of denotic modality in female language.

6.4.2 Analysis of Deontic Modality Orientation in Female Language

As we have already discussed above, when a speaker chooses to use modals to show their attitude or express their opinion, they should take the orientation of modality into account, which determines how explicitly the communicators want to take the responsibility.

Table 6.2 Distribution of Different Orientations in the 50 Piece Samples

	explicit subjective	implicit subjective	implicit objective	explicit objective
number	9	13	6	22
total number of samples	50	50	50	50
percent	18%	26%	12%	44%

From the table, we could clearly see that modality operators adopted in the examples with implicit subjective orientation (26%) and explicit objective orientation (44%) has taken a big percent. As we have mentioned above, in this section, we will classify subjective explicit and objective explicit as high value deontic modality, while subjective implicit and objective implicit as low value deontic modality. We could observe from the table that explicit subjective and explicit objective take a higher percentage in female language, which indicates that female are more inclining to take high value deontic modality orientation into consideration in communication.

No matter by which way to be realized, high value deontic modality has strong expressiveness in communication. Thus it conveys a function of efficient persuasion. The author thinks that the reason of adopting high value orientation deontic modality in female language resulted from many aspects, for instance, the character of female is more honest; female could adopt many other ways to make their expression in an indirect way to show euphemism.

6.4.2.1 Low Value Deontic Modality Conveys the Meaning of Obligation and Inclination

Implicit subjective is realized by some modal expressions generally, which makes the proposition not that obvious. Thompson thinks that "modal operator exploits the finite slot and thus is firmly rooted in the interpersonal, subjective meaning of the clause" (Thompson, 2009:61).

Table 6.3 The Frequency of Finite Modal Operator "should" "will" "would" in Samples in Implicit Subjectire

types of modals	finite modal operator	number	total number	frequency
modals of obligation	should	9	13	69.23%
modals of inclination	will/would	6	13	46.15%

The finite modal operators such as *should*, *will* and *would* could convey the meanings of obligation and inclination. In the expression of implicit subjective which possesses the low value deontic modality, the finite modal operator *should* takes a higher percentage in female language. *Should* as a deontic modality component, conveys an interpersonal meaning of obligation, and shows the speaker's attitude in a quite milder way. Some samples are as follows:

(13) Daniel: Betty, you worry too much.

Betty: Well, somebody should worry, and I take the role.

The modal adjunct *should* here indicates the speaker's viewpoint that Daniel, her boss, should have worried about the case. *Should* is mostly used to express the weak obligation which is employed to express that an action is merely suggested. So it shows a weak obligation. In this speech, Betty wants to express a meaning of "Daniel has an obligation to worry about the case but he doesn't". So she indicates a fact that "On this case, it should be paid more attention and worried about it" which makes the other participant in the communication and the third party in the communication focus on the fact itself and at the same time ignore Betty's own opinion. Let's look at another example:

(14) Betty: Where do they keep the menus?

Amanda: Uh, do I look like I eat?

Betty: Some of us do and have to work late. You would understand if you had something to do besides putting on lipstick.

Here, *would* is used to express the prediction as well as the tentative form of *will*, but *would* is weaker in force when the prediction is given. That shows the speaker adopts a milder way to express her thoughts. Here a fact that Betty wants to declare that "We work hard, sometimes until midnight, so it is quite normal to be tired and hungry. " And her own thoughts are "Amanda is so undisciplined, except putting on lipstick, she can't find anything else to do. So she cannot understand why we are so hungry and tired. " This efficient way to make the third party and the other participant in the communication pay more attention to the fact but not Betty's opinion. Although Betty is quite angry about the words which convey the meaning of disrespect to her, she also chooses to adopt a milder way to express her anger.

The finite modal operator *will*, as a modal of inclination, indicates that the speaker wants the other participants in communication to do something as she will. Let look at the following examples.

(15) Christina: Betty, will you stop saying that, please?

Betty: Why can' t you have any fun with it? You worked so hard for this.

Here the finite modal operator *will*, as a modal of inclination, indicates that the speaker wants the other participants in communication to do something as she will. Betty believes that Christina should have been happy about it for she has been working so hard to it", but Christina is the person involved in the case, she knows all the things that go on behind the scenes which Betty has no idea at all. So she is inclining to stop Betty. Christina is willing to express a meaning of "stop saying that (you do not know the things go behind the scenes)". *Will*, as a modal of inclination, is always employed to realize implicit subjective orientation.

(16) Willie: Bradford thinks his wife isn't really a monster. So let's show him what she's capable of. I want you to hit me as hard as you can.

Marc: Willie, isn't that a little extreme, even for you?

Willie: Don't pretend you've never wanted to do it. Now is your chance.

Marc: This isn't a trap?

Here "Don't pretend you've never wanted to do it. Now is your chance" is an implicit objective orientation conveying the truth that "Marc is eager to bit her, but he pretends to be not hardhearted enough to do so. Willie does not use the explicit subjective expression with deontic modality of possibility "I think you have wanted to do it for a long time", however, she chooses to adopt a negative form of imperative sentence to make the third party in the communication to believe that "Marc wants to beat me". This is not only her own opinion but a fact" which brings people to focus on the fact itself, not Willie's own thoughts.

(17) Daniel: Oh, you lost all your drafts!

Modal A: Betty will do it again, don' t worry.

As a modal of usuality, here *will* conveys the meaning of "Betty always solves the troubles those I make" or "For the most of the time, Betty will solve the troubles those I make". Compared with *would*, it is stronger in force in the prediction, which indicates the speaker chooses a strong way to express her thoughts.

As we've discussed above, deontic finite modal operators can be employed to realize implicit subjective orientation. From the data, we could observe a fact that *should* takes the most frequency in the modal of obligation and *will/would* takes the most frequency in the modal of inclination directly. If we only judged from this data from the table, it could be given the results that female prefer to adopt implicit subjective of intermediacy to realize the deontic modality.

6.4.2.2 Deontic Modality Conveys the Meaning of Necessity

All the dialogues in the following samples can express the deontic modality. They could be generally classified into three types of certain sources of cause: authoritative individuals of organizations, certain motivation (including the aspiration and demand of the speaker) and rules of laws.

The cause of authoritative individuals or organizations of deontic modality source could be described as: the speaker has the absolute right to judge the event or the other participant in the communication, and her judgment or suggestion could be always worthy of considering. The following example represents the deontic modality source of authoritative individuals or organizations.

(18) Hilda: So these two guys with money take you out to a fabulous dinner, everybody's having a great time, and you're feeling guilty, because?

Betty: I don't know.

Hilda: Betty, you deserve to have fun more than anybody I know. You spend every dime you make to live in the city, but you don't live in the city. Trust me, all your problems are gonna be there tomorrow, so will you please go have some fun? Just be careful, OK?

"You deserve to have fun" here conveys an interpersonal meaning of deontic modality, which expresses a meaning of "in my opinion, you are the one who should have fun without any doubt." Hilda is Betty's biological sister, who companies Betty from young to adult. They live in the same living condition, share the same growing experiences and they have the closest relationship. So Hilda has the absolute right to say "Betty deserves to have fun", which conveys the deontic modality meanings.

The cause of rules of laws of deontic modality source could be described as: The laws principles stipulate people to have to obey some rules, which represent a deontic modality of commanding.

(19) Hilda: My father's not here right now. What's this all about?

Lawyer: The message you left was passed on to me. I searched my files, and Mr. Suarez is not in the system.

Hilda: He has to be. His court date is in a month.

Everyone has his deadline of court date, which is determined by the laws. "he has to" here conveys a deontic modality meaning of "if he doesn't do this, he will break the law."

These two sources of deontic modality convey a meaning of necessity. The deontic modality meaning of necessity is always used by the speaker who wants to express his ideas in an explicit way and he absolutely holds the rights to express his ideas in public, in addition, it also indicates that he is so confident to undertake the responsibility about what he has said.

6.4.2.3 Deontic Modality Conveys the Meaning of *Possibility*

The causes of certain motivation of deontic modality source is the commonest one. Most of the deontic modality is caused by this source. In order to show the aspiration or the demand, the speaker will employ deontic modality to realize it. Let's have an analysis of the sample:

(20) Hilda: You're flipping out! He is threatening not to go to Mexico. He—he says, you know, we can't afford it, so he's just—he's just going to give up. You had to come home. You just got to help me talk sense into him.

Betty: Tell him I'm coming home, and I'm bringing the money for his ticket.

Hilda and Betty's father is going to give up and go back to Mexico. Hilda is so worried about it, and she is eager to keep their father in the USA, so she orders Betty to come home and talk some sense into him. So the source of the deontic modality here is "Hilda motivates her father to keep living in the USA, while there are two possibilities: one is her father keeps living in the USA, the other is being asked to go back to Mexico."

The source of deontic modality meaning of *possibility* indicates that the speaker wants to show the aspiration or the demand, but he has less authorities to make sure whether his proposition could be realized or not. This type of deontic modality is used in the highest frequency.

6.4.2.4 An Analysis of Deontic Modality Orientation in Female Language under Politeness Principle

We have already given a general summary to the characteristics of female language. The tact maxim and generosity maxim are aiming at benefiting and costing. The tact maxim requires speakers to minimize cost and maximize benefit to others, and the generosity maxim requires speakers to minimize benefit and maximize cost to the speaker himself. From the samples the author selected, the author will give a data analysis and generalized the results of deontic modality in female language. First let's look at the sample:

(21) Amanda (to Nick): Sorry to bother you. I thought you might be very hungry, or you won't eat my skittles.

Betty: It is likely that Nick is so tired after the all night long writing, you know Nick, always looking out for number one.

Nick eats Amanda's candy stealthily and is found by Amanda, and here Betty chooses to use *It's likely* to employ explicit objective to minimize Nick's costs, moreover, Betty here chooses to use "It is likely that Nick is so tired after the all night long writing" to convey an explicit subjective orientation to take the deontic modality, to make the third party in the communication and the participant in the communication believe the fact that Nick is so tired and hungry, or he won't steal eating Amada's candy, which results in the ignorance of Amanda's judgments on Nick and avoids the disputes in the communication in some way.

(22) Christina: Betty! I mean, look what it's done for you.

Betty: You know what, I think you should totally go back in there, people know your name, you're gonna be huge.

After being betrayed by her friend Christina, in order to encourage Christina, she chooses trying to express her real thoughts to Christina, and gives enough positive face to her. Here *I think* is *probability* modal, which conveys explicit subjective. As we have discussed above, females tend to adopt implicit subjective and explicit objective way to realize the interpersonal meaning more. Why does Betty here choose to employ explicit subjective way Betty and Christina are two best friends in the company. When Betty knows the fact that Christina has no choice but to betray her, she chooses to adopt *I think*, this deontic modality component, to take all the responsibility that she has commented on the affair. In this way, on the one hand, she uses the high value deontic modality to realize the interpersonal meaning of her comments in order to make Christian believe that Betty is willing to forgive her about what she has done to Betty. On the other hand, it helps to flout the generosity maxim, which gives enough positive face to her friend Christina. In this way, it could be able to make sure the smooth going of the communication.

In order to get the conclusion in which orientation is used more to flout tact and generosity maxim, the author will use a table to represent the adopting of different orientations to flout tact and generosity maxim.

Table 6.4 The Orientations in the Samples Which Flouts Tact and Generosity Maxim

type of intermediacy	explicit subjective	implicit subjective	implicit objective	explicit objective
number	4	0	1	3
Total number	9	13	6	22
percent	44.44%	0%	16.67%	13.64%

The data show that females are more inclining to employ explicit subjective to flout tact and generosity maxim. If we only observe this table, we could come to the conclusion that there are no implicit subjective employed in the occurrence of deontic modality in female language.

As we have talked about the orientation adopting circumstances to flout tact and generosity maxim, we will analyze the adopting circumstance to flout approbation maxim and modesty maxim.

The approbation maxim requires speakers to minimize dispraise and maximize praise of others. The modesty maxim requires speakers to minimize praise and maximize dispraise of him. Let's have a look at the following samples:

(23) Betty: Wait, Daniel, you saved somebody's life? You are a hero!

Daniel: OK, OK, it's over, I mean, I did my good deed for the year.

Betty: You know what? I have something else for Henry. You deserve this.

(24) Betty: I gave him a party.

Hilda: Are you crying?

Betty: I was so stupid to think he would like me, of course, he likes Amanda. I should know when he said I was beautiful, he meant on inside.

Hilda: You are...

Betty: You don't have to say that, I'm fine with who I am, but I am not beautiful.

Hilda: Man are stupid, they go for the obvious, trust me, I should know better. You are 24, it's OK to have a crash, act a little stupid, but you have to believe me, when I say this, you are beautiful.

(25) Betty: I am supposed to forgive you because you couldn't use your employee discount? Walter, go home.

Walter: I would, but we're in the middle of a game here.

(26) Claire: His wife's in prison. Wouldn't that make you just the tiniest bit depressed?

Willie: Of course it would.

Claire: Why are you really here, Wilhelmina? You're nothing but a selfish bitch. Oh, pardon my language.

The four samples above are chosen from *Ugly Betty*. We could directly observe that female like using some words full of praise to express their feelings, which indicates that the female characters in *Ugly Betty* try their best to maximize praise and minimize dispraise of the other participants in the communication when they have to flout the approbation maxim and modesty maxim. Here, *I was so stupid to think*, and *I am supposed to forgive you* are all explicit subjective, which indicate that the speakers are willing to undertake the responsibility about their words. What should be mentioned here for special purpose is the last sample. It is a dialogue between two women, who have tense relationship. Bradford is the ex-husband of Claire, who turns to Willie's husband now. And it is so obvious that the relationship between the two women is quite bad. Willie is making a challenge constantly, in order to anger Claire, which results in arousing the conflicting between the two participants in the communication. And finally Claire bursts into angers. Although she uses the direct expression *Oh, pardon my language*, it looks like she wants to obey the Politeness Principle, however, in fact, she has no sense of admitting the impolite way she communicates, but using the direct expression *Oh, pardon my language* to indicate that she would like to take the responsibility about what she has said. So *Oh, pardon my language* here is an expression with deontic modality.

The agreement maxim requires speakers to minimize disagreement and maximize agreement between speaker and the other participants in the communication. But when the speaker doesn't agree that much with the other participants in the communication, what will she do to flout agreement maxim? Let's have an analysis on the following samples:

(27) Alexis: Really? Daniel did that?

Betty: Look, I know the things between the two of you've been a little rough. And I know that you think he is totally screwed up. But he is really a very good person.

Alexis: Oh, yes, sometimes.

(28) Betty: Good morning, Amanda.

Amanda: Oh, hey, Betty. I was just thinking about you.

Betty: Really?

Amanda: Mm-mm.

Betty: Hmm, I think that's nice.

(29) Daniel: Can I get you girls some coffee?

Betty: Ahem, I'm sorry for the interruption, but you have a 5:00 p. m. circulation meeting.

(30) Amanda: I'm going nowhere at "mode" and now I'm apparently too old to be a wench. How long before I'm too old to be a receptionist? Sure, today I'm the eye candy, but tomorrow I'll be old candy—old, hard, wrinkly candy covered in lint.

Marc: Are you having a stroke?

Amanda: Maybe. I'm old enough.

(31) Henry: Betty, my grandparents had horses.

Betty: I never got near them because I am allergic, but I used to watch them out the window all the time. Let me do this for you.

The dialogues above all indicate that even if the females do not agree that much with the other participants in the communication, she will flout agreement maxim to give enough positive face to the other participants. No matter which maxim the female want to flout, she could employ the explicit subjective modality expressions to realize the deontic modality, which indicates that it seems female are more inclining to make subjectivity more explicitly when the deontic modality occurred.

6.4.3 Ways of Realization of Interpersonal Meanings of Deontic Modality in Female Language

6.4.3.1 Realization in the Ways of the Key

Except mood and modality, key could reflect the interpersonal function as well. In the expression with deontic modality, different tones indicate different interpersonal meanings. T1 in the declarative sentence conveys a meaning of affirmation. T2 in a declarative sentence expresses different ideas, protest or disproval of the speaker. T3, conveying a semantic meaning of possibility, unimportance or uncertain, is a tone between rising tone and falling tone. By using T4, the speaker turns the semantic meaning to the opposite meaning when his speech is finished by half, which means "It seems or sounds the meaning he expresses is quite clear or full of possibility, but in fact it is quite complicated or not that possible, while T5 contains two semantic compositions that the speaker turns the semantic meaning to the opposite meaning when his speech is finished by half, which means "it seems or sounds the meaning he expresses is quite doubting, which in fact is quite clear and believable. Now let's have a close look at the samples.

(32) Daniel: Whoopi? What did she do?

Betty: It's not out yet, but apparently, it's shocking. The Meades are next. He wants to destroy your family.

Daniel: A little late for that, huh?

//1^It's not out yet/but a/PPARENTLY// //1 it's shocking. //

This is a declarative sentence with deontic modality expressions. *Apparently* indicates the speakers' attitude and judgment about the thing they talk about. And the speaker has an accent tone on the deontic modality component modal adjunct *apparently* which conveys the meaning of undertaking the responsibility and certainty. In the dialogue, although Betty hasn't known what Whoopi has done, she knows that it is a shocking case, without any doubt. So in order to realize the interpersonal meanings of the deontic modality component *apparently*, she has a stress tone on it in the declarative sentence.

(33) Christina: Don't follow him around with a stun gun, love. So I'm supposed to sit around and watch a friend fall apart? He's not a friend. He's your boss.

Betty: He's both. I mean.

//1So ^I'm supposed to SIT around// //3 and WATCH a friend fall apart? //

Here the deontic modality component *be supposed to* doesn't have a stress tone on it. It is also a declarative sentence with T3, to express interpersonal meanings of distrust, shocking and anger. In this sentence, the two verbs *sit* and *watch* are stressed by the speaker. The real meaning that the speaker wants to express is: "I am not supposed to sit around and watch a friend fall apart."

(34) Christina: Betty, will you stop saying that. Please?

Betty: Why can't you have any fun with it? You worked so hard for this.

Christina: I don't know. I'm just... I'm—I'm Scottish. We're a humble people who like to drink. So what do you want?

//2^Betty WILL you STOP saying that please? //

It is general interrogative sentence with T2. Here the speaker gives an accent tone on the deontic modality component *will*, as a modal of inclination, to express a meaning of "not willing to listen to the content the speaker is talking about". The verb *stop* gives a deontic modality meaning.

Besides the five types of keys, different locations of accent could also realize the interpersonal meaning of deontic modality. If the accent is given on the modal operators, it mainly conveys the speaker's attitude, while if the accent is given on the notional verbs, it mainly conveys the interpersonal meanings of the degree that how deep the action could be accepted. Now let's look at the example:

(35) Betty: Daniel, if you get this while you're still at the restaurant, you may want to go out through the kitchen.

Christina: Betty!

Betty: I gotta go. Bye. We didn't speak. It was just a message. I'm not working. I'm here to have fun. Whoo-hoo!

//1You MAY want to // //1go out through the kitchen//

It is a simple declarative sentence with deontic modality expressions. Here *may*, modal of possibility is given an accent tone on it, which conveys the meaning of speaker's attitude toward the proposition.

(36) Combs: what exactly are you looking for?

Wihelmina: Insight. Fey kept that romance alive for years. She must have written something in those diaries.

//5She MUST have WRITTEN something//1 in those diaries//.

The author gives both *must* and *written* accent tone, where *must* has high value deontic modality meanings, and *written* is given a stress indicating that the speaker is quite sure about her inference. It also indicates that the speaker hopes to receive the positive response of the other participant in the communication very much.

(37) Aamanda: I don't like being played. You gave me hope that I could find some evidence to help my mother. There is no "love dungeon", and no diaries either, I'm guessing. Go find some other chump, because you just lost your best source.

Aamanda: // 1^You gave me hope/that // 3 I COULD find some evidence to help my mother // 3There is no "love dungeon" and no diaries either I'm guessing//

Could is stressed by the speaker, which indicates that she is so sure to find her mother, and using T3 indicates that actually no. And from *I am guessing*, we could infer the information that she still holds some faith to find her mother, but she is not willing to admit. "I'm guessing" here conveys the deontic modality in median value.

(38) Christina: Betty, if someone came to you and offered you help just to get closer to your dream, you...

Betty: No, I wouldn't. I have dreams, too, but I would never do something to hurt you like this.

Christina: I didn't do this to hurt you. Can we just—please, can we talk about it?

Betty: // 1No^ I wouldn't I have dreams too but // // 3 I WOULD NEVER do something to hurt you like this//

In the first two clauses, the speaker gives a positive response to the other participant in the communication, that is, "yes, you are right, I have dreams too." But the real meaning the speaker wants to express is "Although I have dreams, I will not betray my friend". So she adopts T3 to express the real meaning, and the deontic modal *would* and *never* are stressed to express the determination and the anger of the speaker.

(39) Willie: Claire, I'm simply a concerned observer. Just because your life has been put on hold, doesn't mean Bradford should have to be.

Claire: Oh, you poor, stupid woman, look at those toes, you're sleeping with him, aren't you? Well, I certainly hope you don't think it means anything.

//5 Well ^I CERTAINLY hope // // 1you don't THINK it means anything. //

Claire is so firm to declare her attitude that "I hope you should know you are not that important in Bradford's heart at all" or "I think you are not that important in Bradford's heart, so stop daydreaming." Here the accent is located on the deontic modal adjunct *certainly* and notional word *think* indicates the firm attitude towards the speaker.

T3 and T4 both have double semantic meanings, which are adopted to shift the meanings that the speakers want to express:

(40) Amanda: You mean the love dungeon?

Alexis: Do you know where it is?

Amanda: Sure, in never-never-land. It doesn't exist. It may be Fey's way of saying I'm hung over and I wanna go home.

Amanda: //4Sure^ in never-never land /It doesn't exist// //1 It may be Fey's way of saying I'm hung over and I wanna go home. //

When the speaker finishes a clause at "It doesn't exist", her meaning that she wants to express is not finished yet. T4 contains two semantic compositions. The speaker turns the semantic meaning to the opposite meaning when his speech is finished by half, which means "It seems or sounds the meaning he expresses is quite clear or full of possibility, but in fact it is quite complicated or not that possible." The real meaning she wants to express is that "The place you talked about does not exist at all; it is just a fake way which may be Fey's way of saying I'm hung over and I wanna go home." When the first two clauses are finished, the real meaning that the speaker wants to express is not finished at all. So the speaker chooses to adopt T4 to indicate that her real meaning will be expressed next.

(41) Whihelmina: Oh, you are still here? And it was wrong that *I thought* I was burning the midnight oil.

Bradford: What's that?

Wilhelmina: I forgot to include it with the earlier package. Mink if I... sit for a moment?

Whihelmina: //3Oh^ you are still here // and it was wrong /that// 3 I THOUGHT I was burning the midnight oil//

The speaker wants to express the meaning of "I thought I was alone, but you are here, I am not alone, so I am wrong". Here the accent tone is given on the deontic modality component *I thought*, which indicates that the speaker was so sure that she was alone, and burned the midnight oil. But when she finds she is wrong actually, she uses T3 to shift the real semantic meaning she wants to express.

(42) Angelica: Dentistry is not about fun. You always think you can bend all the rules because you are pretty and blonde, or maybe you are not.

Betty: Is she Okay?

Angelica: //1 Dentistry is not about fun //3 you always THINK you CAN bend all the rules because you are pretty and blonde or maybe you are not//

In the first clause, the speaker expounds a fact that dentistry is not about fun in T1, but use T3 to shift the meaning she wants to express. And deontic modal *can* and *think* are stressed.

Table 6.5 The Percentage of the Adoption of Different Tone in Deontic Modality Expression

types of tones	T1	T2	T3	T4	T5
number	76	4	59	3	32
clause number in total	104	104	104	104	104
percentage	73.07%	3.84%	56.73%	2.88%	30.77%

From the table above, we could observe that when the speaker speaks with deontic modality expression, T1 is mostly adopted to realize the interpersonal meanings. However, T3, a tone between rising tone and falling tone, expresses a semantic meaning of possibility, unimportance or unsureness. Sometimes a speaker finishes a clause, but the meaning he wants to express is not finished, so T5 ranks second, taking the percentage of 56. 73%. The speaker turns the semantic meaning to the opposite meaning when his speech is finished by half, which means "It seems or sounds the meaning he expressed is quite doubting, which in fact is quite clear or believable.", taking the percentage of 30. 77%. T2 and T4 are not employed that much in realizing interpersonal meanings of deontic modality in female language.

Besides, the location of the accent could also realize the interpersonal meanings of deontic modality.

Table 6.6 Realizations of Interpersonal Meanings of Deontic Modality by the Location of the Accent

the location of the accent	deontic modality component	notional verbs
number	96	64
total number of the clause	104	104
percentage	92.31%	61.54%

When the location of the accent is on the deontic modality component, it indicates that the speaker is quite sure about her speech. She is willing to undertake all the responsibility about what she has said. The notional verbs' accent location could also express this meaning of speaker's attitude, but it is weaker than the location on deontic modality. The speaker thinks that when the accent is on the deontic modality component, it indicates no matter how unbelievable the expressions are, the speaker is willing to take the full responsibility about the expressions; when the accent locates on the notional verbs, that expresses a meaning of "Although the speaker is willing to take the responsibility about what she has said, but actually, it is really unbelievable or unsure."

6.4.3.2 Ways of Realization of Deontic Modality in Multi-Voice

As we mentioned above, multi-voice is a kind of modal intervention component. Female adopt this way to convey the possibility of accommodating the anti-voice in a very high frequency.

(43) Betty: Daniel Meade's Office.

Betty: Oh, no, I'm sorry. He's not here right now.

Betty: He's um, in a breakfast meeting.

Betty: Oh, no, um. I'm sorry. He's all tied up.

Here the modal particle like *oh, no, um* have no connection with the proposition. If we take these words away, the real meaning that the speakers want to express could also be finished. In the communication, in order to flout the politeness principle, female always choose to adopt using modal particles to decrease the interruption. These modal particles could also realize the interpersonal meaning of deontic modality. It indicates that the speaker is not sure about what she has said, or maybe the content of her speech is not real, but in order to keep the communication going on, and give positive face to the other participant, she has to employ these modal intervention component. On the other hand, these modal intervention components could also help the speaker to realize the deontic modality interpersonal meaning. It is obvious that the speaker is not willing to take responsibility about what she has said, or at least, she is not sure about whether she wants to take the responsibility.

(44) Daniel: Look, I'm sure Alexis is handling everything just fine.

Betty: Oh, okay, so that's it? You're just gonna hand everything over to her?

So, that's it? is a modal intervention component. In other words, its interpersonal meaning is realized by the multi-voice. The speaker is out of anger here in the communication, but she wants to decrease the disputes in the communication. Daniel is her friend, but also her boss. She wants to give the positive face to her boss. Betty just wants to buffer the fierce conversation situation. She does not want to make the situation in such a tense way. If we take *Oh, okay, so that's it* these modal particles and phrases away, the meaning is also complete. That is "are you just gonna hand everything over to her?" So the speaker chooses to adopt multi-voice in using modal intervention components.

(45) Betty: He's both, I mean.

Christina: Uh, hey, don't cross that line.

As Betty's best friend, Christina thinks that Daniel is Betty's boss, so they shouldn't go so closed. She wants to remind Betty that she should treat Daniel as her boss. Her real meaning is just "don't cross that line between boss and friend", but in order to give the positive face to her friend

Betty, she has to use the modal particle as *uh*, *hey* to hint the sense of hesitation and worry. If she uses the imperative sentence to express the meaning, that is "Do not cross that line" as a command or order to her friend Betty, it will result in making the third party in the communication or the hearer ignore the fact that Betty and Daniel are in a relationship of boss and employee. They should keep a normal relationship, but pay more attention to Christina's attitude towards this case. Here she chooses to use two modal particles *uh*, *hey* to obey the politeness principle, and it is also used to realize the interpersonal meanings.

(46) Betty: Um, it's just that uh, if my lips are gonna be tingly, then, i-i-I want to be because of Henry.

Nurse: You are such a chick flick. I would totally pay $12 to see you.

Betty is so shy about her inner meaning, but she wants to express the meaning out frankly very much. Here she also wants to give a positive face to herself. "It's just that" is an expression conveying deontic modality which means "I think the thing I talk about is not worth paying much attention to." However, *um* here is a modal particle expressing a meaning of hesitation, which is an avoiding strategy. And the repetition of the word *I* also expressed the same meaning as *um*, the function here equals to the modal particle.

(47) Willie: Well, if I'm not, make sure they get their free hair products. Priorities, Marc.

Marc: Priorities. I still have so much to learn.

Here if we take the modal particle *well* and phrase *if I'm not* away, the meaning of Willie wants to express could also be finished. That is "to make sure they get their free hair products no matter what happens", but she also wants to indicate a possibility of uncertainty, which means "If I could come back on time, please give them their free hair products, and if I couldn't, give them too." So she uses the modal particle *well* to realize interpersonal meanings of uncertainty, worry and hesitation. *If I'm not* here conveys a deontic modality as "there exists a possibility that I will not be back", which helps to express the meaning of unsureness.

(48) Ben: Who is Daniel?

Betty: Oh, he's my-uh, you know what? We're not talking about him.

The speaker employs modal particle plus phrase to avoid talking about the topic she doesn't want to. Here *you know what* is an expression with deontic modality, having the same meaning with *I think*. But she chooses to realize the interpersonal meanings in multi-voice instead of *I think* directly, which indicates that modal particle and phrase are tenderer than modality component.

In the selected samples, the interpersonal meanings of deontic modality are realized by multi-voice taking up the following percentage.

Table 6.7 The Percentage of Interpersonal Meanings of Deontic Modality Realized by Multi-voice

ways of realization	multi-voice
numbers of multi-voice in deontic modality expressions	36
numbers of deontic modality expressions	97
percentage	37.11%

From the table, we could observe that the multi-voice employed by realizing the interpersonal meanings are taken in a relatively high percentage, which indicates that female are inclining to adopt this way to conceal the hesitation and the anxiety from her inner will. In fact, she is so unsure about whether she should express the real meanings she wants to express.

6.4.3.3 Ways of Realization of Deontic Modality of Possiblity in Interrogative Mood

As we have mentioned above, interrogative mood expresses a meaning of questioning. It could also realize the interpersonal meaning of deontic modality. This way of realization conveys the meaning of asking for agreement. Although it is the "wh-questioning sentence", but actually it expresses a meaning of positive, and indicates that the speaker would like to take the responsibility about the content of her question. Let's have a close look at the example.

(49) Willie: Don't you think it's time you move on with your life, our lives? You really care what a murderer thinks?"

Mr. Meade: She is not a murderer, and I will not leave her just because of one moment of insanity.

Here the interrogative sentence conveys the meaning of "I think it's time for you to move on with your life, our lives." "Don't you think" here also conveys a deontic modality even if it is in interrogative form. Willie would like to receive the positive response from Meade, whom she wants to marry to improve her status in the fashion field. Employing the interrogative form to convey the deontic modality indicates that the speaker is eager to receive the positive answer from the other participant in the communication. In addition, it also indicates that the speaker is not sure about whether she could receive the positive response or not. *Don't you think* here equals "I think", adopting an orientation of explicit subjective, which conveys a deontic modality of possibility. The speaker chooses to use such a direct way to express her meaning, which shows that she wants to suggest the other participant that she is willing to receive the positive answer to decrease the discrimination of the communication. It shares the stronger meaning than declarative sentence in mood, even if they both share the same meaning.

(50) Alexis: It would never work.

Constance: Of course it would, so why wouldn't you go to Brazil with me?

Constance here wants to express the meaning of "I think you should have wanted go to Brazil with me". *I think* and *should have done* carries the explicit subjective deontic modality. She is afraid of hearing negative voice from Alexis, so she adopts *should have done* to suggest that Alexis should go with her. But she is not certain about whether Alexis shares the same ideas with her. Using the form of interrogative sentence form, the participants of the communication may conceal her ideas. She would adopt an indirect way to make it seem to be objective. "Why wouldn't you go to Brazil with me" here could also convey the meaning of "It is obvious that it is wrong for you not going with me." or "It is known by all that you should go to Brazil with me, but you don't." In order to avoid being considered of making trouble out of nothing, and she chooses to adopt using interrogative sentence form to request polarity.

(51) Claire: His wife's in prison. Wouldn't that make you just the tiniest bit depressed?

Willie: Of course it would.

Claire: Why are you really here, Wilhelmina? You are nothing but a selfish bitch. Oh, pardon my language.

"Wouldn't that make you just the tiniest bit depressed?" is functioning as an expression of modality. "In my opinion, it should make you a little bit depressed." The proposition is "In my opinion, it should make you a little bit depressed, shouldn't it?" Not "In my opinion, it should make you a little bit depressed." By observing that we can see the clause is a metaphorical variant of "Maybe it will make you a little bit depressed." "*In my opinion*" conveys an explicit subjective orientation which is an efficient way to make speakers' own point of view to certain propositions clear. Claire makes her ideas to certain propositions clear that the fact that she is in the prison could make Willie have a sense of depressing. She inclines to make it clear that the viewpoints are their own attitudes or comments rather than some facts. The fact is that Willie is not feeling a little depressing at all. She treats Claire as her biggest enemy. She doesn't care about whether Claire is still in the prison or not. However, in Claire's opinion, although they are not friends, but not enemies neither, so she has an expectation of being cared about.

(52) Hilda: so these two guys with money take you out to a fabulous dinner, everybody's having a great time, and you are feeling guilty, because?

Betty: I don't know.

Hilda: Betty, you deserve to have fun more than anybody I know. You spend every dime you make to live in the city, but you don't live in the city, Trust me, all your problems are gonna be there tomorrow, so will you please go have some fun? Just be careful, OK?

Betty feels quite guilty in a fabulous dinner with two guys, which results from the worrying about Daniel. She is always thinking for others and ignoring her own life. Her sister persuades her to enjoy more time on herself. It is wrong to make her so tired for setting roots in the city. "Will you please go have some fun?" here *will* is a deontic modality, which represents the meaning of "You should go have some fun and you have rights to go have some fun" or the modals of obligation. *should* is mostly used to express the weak obligation which is employed to express that an action is merely suggestion. So it shows a weak obligation. It means that "you should have gone have some fun early, but you haven't yet".

(53) Christina: Betty, will you stop saying that, please?

Betty: Why can't you have any fun with it? You worked so hard for this.

Christina: I don't know. I'm just... I'm, I'm Scottish. We're a humble people who like to drink. So what do you want?

As we have discussed above, the finite modal operator *will* is a modal of inclination, which indicates that the speaker wants the other participants in communication to do something as she will. By saying "will you stop saying that, please?" Christina wished Betty to stop saying, in her opinion, Betty shouldn't say like that. So the clause conveys the meaning of "I think you should stop saying that" or "I think you shouldn't say that". The interrogative sentence "will you stop saying that, please" realizes the implicit subjective orientation, while "I think you should stop saying that" realizes the explicit subjective and *I think* here is a deontic modality component conveying a stronger deontic mood. The interrogative sentence to represent a weaker deontic mood to express the thoughts or ideas the speaker has. In order to analyze the percentage of interrogative mood sentences which realize the deontic modality, the author will give a table to show the adopting circumstances of the interrogative mood clauses.

Table 6.8 Percentage of Interpersonal Meaning of Deontic Modality Realized by Interrogative Mood

ways of realization	interrogative mood
numbers of interrogative sentence	8
numbers of deontic modality of possibility expression	83
percentage	9.64%

Compared with the ways of realization of multi-voice, interrogative mood takes less percentage, which indicates a fact that although interrogative mood could express their real meaning in an indirect way which seems more euphemistic, they will choose other methods, such as adopting multi-voice, putting different accent tone location, or using different keys to realize the deontic modality.

6.4.4 Motivation of Interpersonal Meaning of Deontic Modality in Female Language

Why are female inclining to adopt these methods the author has mentioned above to realize the interpersonal meanings of deontic modality? Are the reasons relative to the gender differences or the female speech characteristic? We will analyze the causes from different aspects.

6.4.4.1 Motivation of Realization in the Ways of the Key

Generally speaking, female all have a sharp sense on the using of the key. They pay much more attention to adopting different keys to realize the interpersonal meanings of their speech than male, and they also have the authoritative ways to pronounce words, in addition, they have more command to themselves on this aspect than male obviously.

In the expression with deontic modality, different tones indicate different interpersonal meanings. In this section, we have had a research on the adoption of different types of keys when female aim at realizing the interpersonal meanings of deontic modality in their expression through communication. Female inclined to be obedient, passive while speaking, and their voice is sharper than male, so when they determine to undertake the responsibility and certainty about what they have said, they will choose T1 (falling tone) to imply resoluteness and confidence.

Social nature of language use determines that language cannot depart from a matched environment, and cultural factors are related to the language use most closely among the factors in the social context. Context refers to the information the communicative sides need to be aware of before the conversation can proceed successfully. Hall (1976) indicates the high context and low context are actually the culture related with the communication. English is of low-context culture. There is not sufficient background information in the conversational context. Therefore, the speaking sides need clear, direct message in the communication. Different cultural backgrounds act a part in the language usage and speech act adoptions. The individualism and collectivism, the low context culture and high context culture, the Chinese traditional culture such as "the doctrine of the mean Confucian" and the concept of "equality" in America influence their females greatly in many aspects, especially the speech. All these factors may decide what strategies the speaker is likely to choose. Female's status has been in a low situation for a very long time due to many historical reasons. Since the feminist movement, their social status is improved gradually. They also have rights to fight for freedom, the work chance and being independent. This is a quite important reason for the formation of their speech characteristics.

6.4.4.2 Motivation of Realization in the Ways of the Use of Multi-Voice

Multi-voice is a kind of modal intervention component. Female adopt this way to convey the possibility of accommodating the anti-voice in a very high frequency. If we say multi-voices which are adopted to realize the deontic modality such as *I think*, *maybe*, and *It is obvious that* show the speaker's attitude in a direct way, then we can say the modal particles like *um*, *uh*, *oh* represent the speaker's attitude in an indirect way for certain. However, why are female inclining to use these modal particles?

Coleman (1990) presented the features of individualism and collectivism. In the individualist society, the personal interest comes before the collective interest. In the collectivist society, the relationship between the individuals is very important and everyone plays his role depending in the network. The Americans possess the concept of individualism. Individualists takes less consideration of others. But we could easily find that in a communication, the expression with deontic modality conveys the features of collectivism. Moreover, the face and courtesy consideration is significant in deontic modality. To some extent, the female will hide the opposite idea and show the agreement often when the deontic modality expression occurred.

These modal particles like *um*, *uh*, *oh*, convey both the deontic modality which realizes the interpersonal meaning of "I will take the responsibility about my expression, however, with a little hesitation and consideration about others."

6.5 Summary

All in all, due to the subordinate or lower social status, female have the habit to employ modal component to express their ideas in an indirect or euphemistic way which are determined by the specific social cultural environment, to accommodate different thoughts, that is to say respecting the different ideas to attach the possibility to be identified. Moreover, it indicates those females are trying to pursuit the equal rights and the identification in society through the employment of the modal component in female language to realize the interpersonal meanings.

Chapter 7 Interpersonal Meaning of Deontic Modality in Daily Communication

7.1 Introduction

According to the functional linguistics, interpersonal meaning can not only be embodied through the mood system and the modal system, but also can be expressed by means of addressing appellation, personal pronouns, and other specific terms such as verbs, nouns, adjectives and adverbs that can express the speaker's attitude (Zhu Yongsheng & Yan Shiqing, 2001: 33). However, Halliday just briefly deals with the interpersonal function of personal reference without detailed analysis in his works. Due to the fact that apart from the mood and modal system, personal system is a major means to express interpersonal meaning in discourse, so the author will mainly discuss different interpersonal meanings expressed by various personal pronouns. According to He Ziran (1997: 31), personal reference is the mutual call when the two parties are using speech language to convey information in a speech event. And different choices and uses of interpersonal reference in social communication can convey different referring information, hence expressing different interpersonal meanings.

Up to now, many researches on the interpersonal meaning of personal reference have dealt with the analysis of interpersonal meaning conveyed by the three kinds of person pronouns (*I/we, you and he/she/it/they*, etc.) in advertising, public interviews, public speeches as well as in the medicine directions. Besides, He Ziran and He Zhaoxiong (1997: 28-32; 2000: 62-66) have studied the basic use of personal reference in their works respectively; Chen Zhi'an and Peng Xuanwei (2003: 565-579) have done researches about the pragmatic meaning and concrete embodiment forms of the personal reference choice in a context from the perspective of vocabulary and grammar, which has further analyzed the use of personal reference in detail; Huang Guowen (1999: 47-49) has talked about the usage of personal reference from the style and discourse perspective, and Du Xiaohong (2003: 25-28) has explored the irregular choice and its application of personal reference in the literature works. All these studies have given us the discourse meaning of personal reference in a specific context, but no one has done a systematic research about the study on interpersonal meaning of personal reference combining deontic modality in discourse. Hence, the author will apply the basic use and pragmatic meanings of personal reference to explore various interpersonal meaning of personal reference used with different value deontic modalities in actual communication.

As is discussed previously, deontic modality of different values can convey different interpersonal meanings. The expression means of deontic modality are modal operators, modal adjuncts and metaphors of modality. In Halliday's point of view, each kind of modality has three degrees of values: high-value, median-value and low-value (2000:358).

Therefore, the author will discuss the interpersonal meaning conveyed by deontic modality of these three values respectively and to some extent enrich the previous studies. The value of deontic modality can reflect the authority identity of the speaker in real discourse. In general, the speaker with high social status is inclined to use high-value deontic modality, such as *must*, *certainly* and *surely*, to display his/her resoluteness, decisiveness and assertion while the speaker with low social status has the tendency to use median-value or low-value deontic modality, such as *perhaps*, *possible* and *may*, to show his/her tentativeness and politeness to the listeners by leaving enough space for them to make comments and come up with a resolution. (Martin, 1992; Zhang Delu, 1998)

7.2 Authority of High-value Deontic Modality

As the previous studies show that in grammar, high-value deontic modality is usually expressed by grammatical metaphor to express possibility and this kind of expression is explicitly subjective. Although responsibility stems from some kind of external authority such as rules or the law, typically and frequently the authority is the actual speaker, who gives permission to, or lays an obligation on the listener. Therefore, it can strongly indicate the speaker's subjectivity and absolute authority.

Besides, high-value deontic modality can demonstrate the strongest modality meaning, such as *must* and *shall*. Moreover, the strong expressiveness and absoluteness of high-value deontic modality and the authority of the speaker embody the subjectivity. And in the speech act, directives (where we try to get others to do things) and commissives (where we commit ourselves to do things) (Searle, 1983:166) are the two major speech acts with high-value deontic modality to express obligation and permission, which can be seen in:

(1) You must be here at seven.

(2) John shall have the book tomorrow.

Here, in sentence (1), *must* reveals that it is the listener's obligation to be here at seven. Also, it shows the speaker's firm attitude. And in sentence (2), the speaker commits himself to ensuring that the event takes place by guaranteeing to arrange that John will receive the book. Apart from the promises conveyed by commissives, Palmer (2007:72) believes that they also can be seen as threats and the only difference between promises and threats seems to be what the speaker undertakes to do or whether it is welcome to the addressee.

7.3 Euphemism of Median-value Deontic Modality

Median-value deontic modality is between the high-value and the low-value, so the modality meaning conveyed by median-value deontic modality is neither like the absolute subjectivity of high-value deontic modality nor like the explicit objectivity of low-value deontic modality. In general, the speaker uses median-value deontic modality to make his/her speech euphemistic, subtle, polite and easy to perceive in discourse. Without strong obligation modality meaning, it usually appears in the descriptions of the medicine to express the possibility and usuality such as *should*, *will* and *supposed*, which can effectively provide the necessary information for the patients as well as get the producers free from much responsibility. That can be seen from the following sentence:

(3) The solution should be prepared immediately prior to use, but can be stored at 4℃ or up to one week.

Here the producer uses modal metaphor *should to* weaken his/her responsibility in a subtle way.

7.4 Consultative Tone of Low-value Deontic Modality

Expressions in low-value deontic modality are usually explicitly objective, so the speaker often uses low-value deontic modality, such as *may*, *might*, to express his/her uncertainty in a consultative tone.

Besides, Lyons (1997:793-823) asserts that modality is concerned with our opinions and attitudes, and it isn't merely limited to modal verbs, other expressions such as *frankly*, *fortunately*, *possibly* and *wisely*, express modal meanings as well. In addition, they play an important role in the comprehension of discourse modality and interpersonal meaning. All these words are linked with the inclination and attitude of the speaker and they have more or less displayed the interpersonal meaning of taking the responsibility. Moreover, since it conveys the objectivity of deontic modality and expresses in a consultative tone, it has contributed to the effectiveness of communication. Also it is used to make a quite positive suggestion, as in:

(4) You might have told me the truth.

Here the speaker advises the listener positively that he/she might tell the truth when he/she had known it.

Furthermore, low-value deontic modality is often concerned with identity, social status and personal power. Therefore, it is usually used out of the speaker's politeness in a consultative tone in order to exactly transmit information and is often used in questions as a more tentative, more polite form for asking permission (Palmer, 2007:80):

(5) Might I come in at the moment, Chairman?

Here the speaker uses the low-value modal metaphor *might* to show his/her politeness in a consultative tone.

7.5 Interpersonal Meaning of Deontic Modality in Terms of Personal System

As deontic modality expresses the speaker's attitude towards a proposition as a whole, it involves degrees and scales of the speaker's commitment to his/her obligation, or in order to request other people's obligations, or to express their own wishes. Besides, the personal reference, which includes three kinds, if used properly, can make the communication sincere in attitude and mild in tone.

Generally speaking, the singular first personal pronoun *I* can give the listeners or readers a sense of subjectivity, egocentricity or authority as well as responsibility, while the plural first personal pronoun *we* is usually used to express the speaker's politeness, modesty, care, persuasion as well as self-protection from taking too much responsibility. Therefore, the singular first personal pronoun *I* is seldom used in actual discourse except for the condition that the speaker wants to show his/her authority or take certain responsibility for what he/she has said or done. And the plural first personal pronoun *we* is often used in reports (we-inclusive-of-addressee), works (inclusive authorial we), newspapers or magazines (we-editorial) as well as in the interview or in public speech. Besides, through analyzing the president campaign speeches given by Lincoln,

Obama and McCain, we can find that the former two speakers prefer using the plural first personal pronoun *we* to using the singular first personal pronoun *I* in their speeches, on the contrary, McCain uses more *I* than *we*, which gives the listeners an impression that he is presenting a lot of his personal opinion without considering the listeners' feeling. So in discourse, especially in public speech, it is very helpful for the speaker to choose appropriate personal reference to embody his/her identity, position and fit for the speech situation and the plural first personal pronoun *we* usually comes into the consideration of the speakers, because it can help them shorten the psychological distance between the speaker and the public, leave the public a feeling that the speaker is presenting the resolution or thoughts of an intelligent group or a team rather than his/her personal ideas and then win the trust of the public. Whereas the singular first personal pronoun *I* often puts the speaker in an authority or leader's position, so the public speaker may as well use it little. This is the pragmatic strategy to make the public speech as well as the communication successful.

The second personal pronoun *you* can sometimes be used to refer to anyone without considering the context in order to leave a distance between the speaker and the listener and hence to show the speaker's objectivity, but this kind of usage mainly applies to oral expressions and in written works. Authors prefer using the third personal pronoun *one*. Besides, the second personal pronoun "you" can be used as a vocative to indicate that the listener has been chosen as the communicate object. Therefore, by making use of the strong interact function of the second personal pronoun "you", it is often used in advertising to get the potential consumers into the interaction with the advertisers by shortening the psychological and communication distance between them and leaving the consumers in an equal, intimate and harmonious discourse situation, and then persuade the potential customers into buying the products.

And the third personal pronouns are usually used in the condition that the two sides are not talking face-to-face, such as on the telephone, one is introducing him/herself to the other, or in the situation that this listener is not on site. Besides, the third personal pronouns, such as *one*, *each person* and *everyone*, are often used when the speaker is announcing certain rules or regulations to show their objectivity and credibility through making use of the distance created by the third personal pronouns and to protect him/herself from taking unnecessary responsibility as well as to persuade the listener to act as what has been suggested willingly. Moreover, the third personal pronouns can sometimes be used to express irony, especially when the speaker uses a third personal pronoun which is higher than the targeted listener's actual identity to refer to the listener. Also it can sometimes be used to express the speaker's care for the listener, in particular, when the speaker tries to comfort the listener. For instance, when mother tries to comfort her daughter she may use *my dear girl* or *my darling* instead of other nouns to refer to her daughter to show her care. Last but not least, the anaphora and anaphora of the third personal pronouns are among the major forms which play a vital role in discourse cohesion and coherence. Therefore, the application of the third personal pronouns can help listeners or readers better understand the interpersonal relationship and meaning in discourse.

When it comes to the interpersonal meaning of deontic modality in terms of personal reference, here we mainly discuss six different interpersonal meanings embodied when deontic modality and personal reference work together.

7.5.1 Politeness and Modesty

Generally speaking, the plural first personal pronoun *we* and the third personal pronouns are often used in works, reports or announcements to express the authors' or speakers' politeness and modesty. And the second personal pronouns are usually used in advertisement to show the advertisers' politeness to the potential consumers and to embody the advertising concept of regarding the consumers as the center. Furthermore, sometimes the second personal pronoun *you* is called polite reference, for it can create an equal, intimate and harmonious communication situation and present vividness, immediacy and camaraderie. Let's have a look at the following examples:

(6) This proposal is really fantastic in general, but could we possibly make it more feasible in action?

In this sentence, the speaker uses the low-value modal operator *could* to request the listener's obligation for making his/her proposal practical and feasible in action. In addition, the speaker applies the plural first personal pronoun *we* instead of the second personal pronoun *you* to give his/her order in a polite and subtle way, making the listener feel comparatively more comfortable than using direct vocative *you* to blame the unfeasibility of this proposal in public. The speaker tries to leave listeners the feeling that they are equal and that they are together and show his/her politeness in a consultative tone, in the hope of saving the listener's face and simultaneously persuading the listener into shouldering the obligation that he/she requests.

(7) I am afraid that the proposal you put forward just now is not feasible.

In this sentence, the speaker uses the metaphor of modality to show his/her attitude on purpose. Although the speaker uses the second personal pronoun *you* in the clause to directly refer to the listener, his/her application of the expression *I am afraid* shows that he/she wants to cooperate with the listener in spite of the fact that it is his/her subjective conjecture with high deontic modality meaning. It can help maintain the relationship of each other without offending the listener. Thus the speaker realizes his/her communication goals. One is to transmit the information exactly and show his/her attitude or judgment. The other is to influence the listener's behavior and get the listener to do what is expected by the speaker.

(8) Each person has to clean up after him/herself.

In this sentence, the speaker uses high-value deontic modality *has to* to strongly impose the obligation upon the listener, but the distance and objectivity expressed by the third personal pronoun *each person* and *him/herself* in the above sentence can make the potential blame of the speaker less direct and at the same time save the listeners' face. Therefore, sometimes the speaker will resort to the third personal pronoun plus high-value responsibility to express his/her strong requests or wishes in the actual discourse, hoping to show his/her politeness and to persuade the listeners effectively.

Besides, reporters or authors often use the plural first personal pronoun *we* instead of the singular form *I* in their reports or academic works to show their modesty, that is, they do not owe their achievements totally to their own efforts, but this is not always true. As some researchers have put forward, sometimes reporters and authors need to use the singular first personal pronoun *I* to take responsibility for his/her own findings or statement bravely.

7.5.2 Self-protection and Persuasion

During the process of the real communication, apart from the fact that the speaker wants to express his/her attitude or idea, he/she also wants to influence the listeners' behaviors. By using appropriate deontic modality and proper personal pronoun, here especially the third personal pronouns, the speaker can achieve this goal easily. It can leave sufficient room for the listener to make a choice and at the same time it can protect the speaker him/herself from being regarded as tyrannical or rude. Let's look at the following sentences:

(9) It is required that everyone here should obey this rule.

In the above sentence, the median-value modality operator *should* is used to show the speaker's subjective opinion or advice and indicate that it is the listener's obligation to obey the rules here. Besides, the application of the metaphor of modality *it is required* and the objectivity as well as the distance created by the third personal pronoun *it* and *everyone* makes the speaker's statement uneasy to deny, thus realizing the purpose of protecting him/herself from being thought of arbitrary when introducing rules or laws to the public and persuading them to carry out their obligation.

(10) One cannot lose what one never had.

In the above sentence, the negative high-value deontic modality operator *cannot* is used to express strong modality meaning. But the objectivity carried by the third personal pronoun *one* lowers the speaker's subjective status. Thus, the speaker achieves the goal of protecting his/her own subjectivity, making his/her speech easily accepted by the listener and successfully persuading the listener into complying with the advice. In addition, in oral English the speaker can use the second personal pronoun *you* to replace the third personal pronoun *one* to realize his/her friendly communication purpose, because you can get the listener to come into the talk easily and strengthen the interaction between the speaker and the listener. And Li Zhanzi (2000) holds the similar idea about the interpersonal meaning of the second personal pronoun in *Interpersonal Meaning in Discourse*.

Additionally, in some discourses, when the speaker wants to shorten the distance between him/her and the listener, he/she will try to use a proper noun to refer to him/herself from the perspective of the listener, hoping to persuade them into making a promise or saying "Yes" to his/her coming request. This kind of usage often appears in children's words when they want to persuade their parents into buying something for them.

7.5.3 Care and Irony

In discourse, the speakers can use the plural first personal pronoun *we* to refer to listeners to show his/her care for them. This kind of usage is usually applied in the communication between the superior and the inferior, such as that between the teachers and students or between the doctors and the patients. For example:

(11) Now then, let's have a look at that project, shall we?

In this sentence, the teacher uses the median-value deontic modality *shall* to initiate a request in an euphemistic way. Besides, the application of the plural first personal pronoun "we" instead of the second personal pronoun "you" refers to students creating an intimate relationship between the teacher and the students and simultaneously gives the students a feeling of equality. Thus through combining appropriate deontic responsibility modality and proper personal reference the teacher has effectively expressed his/her care for the students.

Besides, because the third personal pronouns are not the direct participator in the discourse in reference, so as an outsider, it must enlarge the distance between the speaker and the listener. When the speaker uses *it* to replace the second personal pronoun in discourse, *it* conveys the feeling of being estranged. But this kind of usage can be applied to create irony or humor, especially when the speaker applies a proper noun higher than the target listener's actual identity.

Let's look at this sentence:

(12) Would his highness like some coffee?

This is what words that a busy woman in the kitchen said to a lazy man sitting in the hall. Here we can see the irony. The woman uses the third personal pronoun *his highness* which obviously puts the lazy man in a higher status than it is instead of the direct addressing—the second personal pronoun *you* to show her anger with the lazy man. Moreover, the application of the median-value deontic modality operator *would* expresses the woman's humor in a question and euphemistic way.

7.6 Summary

Based on Halliday's systematic functional grammar theory and the previous studies on the interpersonal meaning of deontic modality and personal reference, the author has discussed how deontic modality and personal reference work together in discourse and the main interpersonal meanings expressed by them.

In the process of real discourse, in order to express different interpersonal meanings and communication purposes, such as effectively establishing his/her subjectivity or authority, showing his/her courtesy and expressing his/her attitude, the speaker should be careful in the selection of different value deontic modalities and also be cautious in his/her choice of proper personal reference, since different value deontic modalities and various personal reference convey different interpersonal meanings. As is analyzed in the previous chapters, high-value deontic modality usually shows the speaker's authority; median-value deontic modality often expresses the speaker's courtesy in an euphemistic tone and low-value deontic modality frequently indicates the speaker's attitude in a consultative tone. In addition, when deontic modality and personal reference work together in the real discourse, there are mainly six kinds of interpersonal meanings conveyed by them, and they are politeness and modesty, self-protection and persuasion as well as care and irony.

The study on interpersonal meaning of deontic modality in terms of personal reference in discourse can help the authors or speakers better realize the goal of communication. And at the same time, it can also make the readers or listeners better understand the interpersonal relationship and different interpersonal meanings expressed in the real communication.

Chapter 8 Interpersonal Meaning of Deontic Modality in Business English

8.1 Introduction

With the rapid development of economy in the worldwide, there are more and more communications between different countries, especially business negotiations. Language, as a tool for human communication, plays an important role in the process of business communication, thus the effective use of language in business communications is considered as a lifeline for the success of business. Thus, business negotiation as one of the most important business communications got more and more attention. By analyzing the language use in business negotiations, the author finds that the deontic modality metaphors have been used widely in *business negotiation English.* So how the negotiators use deontic modality metaphor to express their ideas appropriately and strategically deserves our attention. In addition, it is important for negotiators to grasp the various interpersonal meanings that deontic modality metaphors express. Thus, our aim is to find out what interpersonal meanings are expressed by deontic modality metaphors. In order to find out the answer, the author sets out to analyze deontic modality metaphor in business negotiation English.

Halliday proposes that "there are three metafunctions of language labeled as ideational, interpersonal and textual" (2000:132). Interpersonal meaning is to use language "to interact with other people, to establish and maintain relations with them, to influence their behavior, to express our own viewpoint on things in the world, and to elicit or change theirs" (Thompson, 2000:28). According to Halliday, modality can be used in a metaphorical way to express interpersonal meaning, that is, interpersonal grammatical metaphor including metaphor of mood and metaphor of modality. Modality metaphor has been used widely in various discourses and has been studied by many researchers. Deontic modality as an important type of modality has been studied as well, but the deontic modality metaphor bearing a lot of interpersonal meanings hasn't got the deserved attention. Therefore, it is our aim to study the interpersonal meanings that the deontic modality metaphors express in business negotiation English from a systemic functional perspective so as to understand business negotiation discourses comprehensively and use the deontic modality metaphors properly.

Theoretically speaking, the study of the interpersonal meanings of deontic modality metaphors in discourses may enrich Systemic Functional Grammar theories. In other way, the study proposes a new perspective for studying the language use in business negotiations and many other discourses. Also, it attracts negotiators' attention on some special language use, and helps them understand the negotiation discourse better. What's more, it gives negotiators a hand to enhance their language competence, and then they can employ appropriate language forms to express their attitudes, make judgments, and win the negotiation. Finally, studying the interpersonal meanings also helps negotiators establish a certain relationship with each other.

8.2 Studies on Business Negotiation

Business negotiation is a common way of commercial exchanges, and has been studied from different perspectives for a long time. Because it involves many aspects, such as cultural factors, language features, negotiate skills and principles in the process, so the studies involve many domains.

Donald W. Hendon, Rebecca Angeles Hendon, and Paul Herbig (1996) do their research from the perspective of cultural factors. They have revealed the different cultures in the business negotiations. Zou Yong (2008) points out that it is important to use some skills and strategies for negotiators to reach an agreement in international business negotiations. He gives some bargaining skills and strategies for negotiators to win the negotiation.

In recent years, especially after China's entry into WTO, there are increasing business negotiations for Chinese companies. More and more researchers realized the importance of business negotiations; what's more, the use of language sometimes determines the success. Zeng Wenxiong (2002) points out that it is crucial for negotiators to use different language forms cooperatively and harmoniously rather than use them respectively. Wang Lei (2004) studies the language features of negotiation English register, which helped many negotiators win their negotiations.

Although the work by researchers has contributed a lot, few researchers pay their attention to the interpersonal meanings of deontic modality metaphors in business negotiation English. Thus it is necessary for us to explore the deontic modality in business negotiation English discourse and its interpersonal meaning. The author expects to find out some implications for English business negotiations through the analysis.

8.2.1 Data Analyses

Relevant systemic functional grammars will be used to analyze the data collected from the corpus. The three research questions will be dealt with through the analysis. Then the author will present a detailed description of the results from the data. After analyzing the occurrence of deontic modality metaphors in business negotiation conversations, the author concludes various interpersonal meanings that deontic modality metaphors employ in the business negotiations English discourses. Finally, the author tries to find out the reasons that the negotiators choose this kind of language.

8.2.2 Research Questions

In order to achieve the goal of the study, the author attempts to deal with the following questions:

(1) Are there many deontic modality metaphors being used in business negotiation English conversation?

(2) What are the interpersonal meanings that deontic modality metaphors realize in business negotiation English?

(3) What are the reasons of using deontic modality metaphors?

8.2.3 Research Methods

For this study, the author selects 30 business negotiation dialogues randomly as corpus. Some of them are from the internet, and some are selected from the textbook: *Business Negotiation English*. Among them, conversations 1-27 come from the internet, and conversations 28-30 are from the book. All the conversations are the real business activities for negotiating business. So the reliability and factuality of the data are guaranteed. In this book, both qualitative and quantitative methods are adopted to analyze the statistics and describe the results.

8.2.4 Data Collection

Firstly, the author picks up some sentences to illustrate what deontic modality metaphor is. Secondly, the author collects 30 pieces of price negotiation conversations as materials to analyze the use of deontic modality metaphor. In order to find out whether the deontic modality metaphor is used widely in business negotiation, the author counts the number of deontic modality metaphor in each conversation. Finally, the author makes a table to illustrate the use of deontic modality metaphor in business negotiation English.

8.2.5 Discussion

At the negotiation table, the negotiators get the result of the negotiation instead of the thing they deserved. In order to achieve the success in the negotiation, the two parties not only grasp enough negotiation skills, but they should also pay attention to language use. To some extent, using language strategically and appropriately will help negotiators a lot in the negotiation, and even determine the result of the negotiation. Here, the author aims to explore the interpersonal meanings of deontic modality metaphors expressed in business negotiation discourses, so in this part, the author wants to find out the realization of deontic modality in business negotiation discourse.

8.2.5.1 Realization of Deontic Modality Metaphors in Business Negotiation English

After carefully reading the selected conversations, the author finds out that deontic modality metaphors can be realized through two ways, they are: projecting clause, and nominalization. Based on the theories in the third chapter, we know that some of the subjective projections such as *I think*, *I believe*, *I am afraid* can express explicit subjective orientation, and some projections like *everyone knows*, *it's needless for me to point out* are expressed in objective orientation, and all of these projecting clauses are modality metaphor which we have proved in the previous chapter. But what is deontic modality metaphor? Whether all modality metaphors are deontic modality metaphors or not? We can define deontic modality metaphor from the perspective of grammar, that is, the metaphorical pattern of deontic modality sentence. Thus, deontic modality metaphor should have two characters: firstly, it must be a modality metaphor; secondly, it must be deontic modality sentence. To be specific, it is a sentence with a projecting clause. However, it doesn't mean all the modality metaphors are deontic modality metaphor. The author picks out some of the sentences and lists them in the following:

Explicit subjective orientations:

(1) I'm sorry to say we have to close business at that price.

(2) I think the price is a little bit higher.

(3) I'm afraid I can't agree with you there.

(4) I hope you'll be able to meet our requirements.

(5) I'm glad we've come to an agreement on price.

(6) I agree that yours are of better quality.

(7) I can assure you that our price is practical and reasonable.

(8) I suggest you make an appropriate reduction.

(9) I admit your pens are of good quality.

(10) I've told you that we were already in a tight corner and there wasn't any room for us to move.

(11) I thought it might be a good idea for us to start with the points we have in common.

(12) I believe it would be difficult for us to make any sales at these prices.

(13) I don't know if those prices will work for us.

(14) There is one thing I wish to have your attention.

(15) I'm confident in saying that we are the most suitable for your needs.

(16) I'm sure you'll have a ready market at your end.

(17) We promise you can have our full cooperation.

(18) We are sorry to say that we can bring our price down a still lower level.

(19) We believe it will be appropriate to organize some major events to support the promotional activities.

(20) We think the facilities of BBTP's Exhibition Center should be good enough for this event.

All of the sentences are modality metaphors, and are all explicit subjective orientations. Among 20 sentences, 18 sentences are deontic modality metaphors, and only sentence (4), and (10) are not deontic modality metaphors, but they are modality metaphors expressing the speaker's hope and wish. For deontic modality metaphors above, 41% of them are expressed in high value, and 59% of them are expressed in low and middle value comparatively. Deontic modality metaphor sentences express the degree of the speaker openly accepts the responsibility for what he/she said. In the business negotiation table, the negotiators must pay more attention to these clauses that contain the first person "I" and "we", because in the business negotiation, the negotiators express their attitudes in a strategic way, sometimes clearly, sometimes fuzzily, and sometimes euphemistically. These clauses in a direct way always contain some special interpersonal meanings, and we will analyze them in detail.

Explicit objective orientations:

(21) It is difficult for us to push the sale of your digital cameras nowadays.

(22) It would be impossible for us to push any sales at such a price.

(23) Everyone in the trade knows that US's bristles are of superior quality to those from other countries.

(24) It is unnecessary for me to point out that supply exceeds demand at present and that this situation is apt to continue for a long time yet.

(25) It's a pity we can't put the business through.

(26) It's well known that your company has great experience in this field.

This kind of pattern also shouldn't be ignored, because they express explicit objective orientation, and all of them are expressed in low value. Among 6 sentences, three of them are deontic modality metaphors. They are sentence (23), (25), and(26). They are all metaphorical realization of modality, and they are all concerned with modal responsibility, so they are deontic modality metaphors. The speaker uses this kind of expression to prove the objectivity of his point, so as to convince the opponents to accept it. In business negotiation conversations, the negotiators would like to use this kind of expression to disguise the responsibilities, and to protect themselves.

In addition, nominalization can also express objective orientation. We have mentioned that nominalization is one type of modality metaphor. Here nominalization expresses deontic modality meaning we can fall it into the category of deontic modality metaphor. Because this kind of pattern is used less than the two former patterns, the author only finds several examples from the materials and lists them.

(27) It is the best that we can give.

(28) There is one more thing I wish to have your attention.

(29) There is possibility that we can discuss this later.

All of the three sentences are deontic modality metaphors in business negotiation conversations. The speakers use nominalizations also to objectify their opinions. Except explicit objective expression, nominalization is also a sentence pattern which can help the speaker disguise the responsibility and can be used in persuasive discourse, although the number of them is limited.

Negotiators sometimes like to employ this kind of pattern, and sometimes prefer that kind of expression. However, no matter what kind of expression, there is one goal for them to arrive at, that is, to express their attitudes politely and strategically so as to achieve a win-win result.

8.2.5.2 The Occurrence of Deontic Modality Metaphor in Business Negotiation Discourses

Firstly, the author counts how many sentences each conversation has, and among of them, how many are said by the seller and how many are said by the buyer. Secondly, the author counts the number of modality metaphors in each conversation. Finally, the author counts the number of deontic modality metaphors in each conversation. At the same time, the author counts the number of explicit subjective expression and explicit objective expression respectively.

Table 8.1 The Use of Deontic Modality Metaphor in 30 Pieces Business Negotiation Conversations

NO.	NTS	NS	NB	MM		DMM		ESO		EOO	
				NS	NB	NS	NB	NS	NB	NS	NB
1	9	4	5	0	3	0	3	0	2	0	1
2	39	18	21	0	1	0	1	0	1	0	0
3	30	18	12	0	2	0	2	0	2	0	0
4	16	8	8	0	0	0	0	0	0	0	0
5	19	11	8	2	0	1	0	1	0	0	0
6	10	5	5	3	2	2	2	1	1	1	1
7	59	29	30	10	9	8	8	7	4	1	4
8	23	11	12	3	4	3	3	3	2	0	1
9	15	9	6	4	3	4	3	4	3	0	0
10	11	4	7	4	3	3	3	3	2	0	1
11	16	8	8	0	0	0	0	0	0	0	0
12	27	14	13	1	3	1	2	1	1	0	1
13	9	5	4	1	1	1	1	1	1	0	0
14	24	12	12	2	3	2	3	1	2	1	1
15	23	10	13	1	3	1	1	1	0	0	1
16	11	5	6	0	2	0	2	0	1	0	1
17	17	8	10	1	1	0	1	0	2	0	0
18	35	19	16	0	2	0	2	1	3	0	0
19	24	12	12	1	3	1	3	1	1	0	1
20	16	8	8	1	2	1	1	1	0	0	0
21	19	8	11	1	1	1	0	2	0	1	0
22	21	8	13	2	1	2	0	1	0	0	0
23	18	11	7	1	0	1	0	1	1	1	0
24	28	13	15	1	1	1	1	0	0	0	2
25	17	9	8	1	2	0	2	2	4	1	1
26	53	29	24	3	6	2	4	0	0	1	1
27	18	7	11	2	1	1	1	4	3	1	2
28	18	9	9	6	4	4	4	1	3	1	0
29	9	6	3	2	3	2	3	5	3	1	1
30	26	16	10	1	5	6	4	3	6	4	0
total	660	333	326	60	71	48	60	42	24	11	20

NTS represents the total number of sentences in a conversation; NS represents the number of sentences said by the seller; NB represents the number of sentences said by the buyer; MM represents the number of modality metaphor; DMM represents the number of deontic modality metaphor; ESO represents explicit subjective orientation; EOO represents explicit objective orientation and nominalization.

The statistics above shows that modality metaphors are extensively used in business negotiation discourses by the negotiators. What's more, we can see that there are 119 modality metaphor sentences in total, among which, 102 sentences are deontic modality metaphors. So 85.7% of the modality metaphors are deontic modality metaphors, either subjective orientation or objective orientation. It also proves that deontic modality metaphors have been widely used in business negotiation conversations.

From the statistics, we can see that the number of the sellers using deontic modality metaphor is more than that of the buyers using deontic modality metaphors. On the one hand, it proves that the sellers have realized the importance of deontic modality metaphor in business negotiation discourses and can use them fluently to help them realize their intention. On the other hand, due to the different positions of the sellers and the buyers in this kind of conversation, there are differences in their use of deontic modality metaphors. In business negotiation conversation, the main task of the sellers is to persuade, thus how to use language strategically is of great significance.

Another statistics we should notice is the number of subjective orientation and the number of objective orientation. We can see clearly that subjective orientation is used more than objective orientation. That is to say, explicit subjective orientation is used more than explicit objective orientation. The high value explicit subjective orientation mainly expresses that the extent of the speaker openly accepts the obligation or responsibilities for what he/she says is high. In business negotiation conversation, the sellers use explicit subjective orientation with the purpose to persuade the buyer in a tentative way. Explicit subjective orientation can express politely and kindly, so the listeners are willing to accept. Instead, the explicit objective orientation shows the two parties are estranged from each other. The buyers in business negotiation discourses always express his attitude towards the price, and the use of explicit subjective orientation can express his attitude directly and firmly. However, explicit objective is important as well in certain conditions.

8.2.5.3 Interpersonal Meaning Analysis of Deontic Modality Metaphor in Business Negotiation English

After analyzing the statistics of the occurrence of deontic modality metaphors in the business negotiation conversations, we can conclude that deontic modality metaphors have been used widely in business negotiation conversations by both the sellers and the buyers. Then in order to answer research question 2, the author will try to analyze the interpersonal meaning of deontic modality metaphors in real business negotiation environment. The author selects conversation 14, 26, and 30 as cases to study the use of deontic modality metaphor in detail. According to the process of negotiation, negotiation conversation usually can be divided into three stages: the beginning stage, the bargaining stage and the decision stage. The author will illustrate the interpersonal meanings of deontic modality metaphors in the different stages respectively.

1. The Beginning Stage

The beginning stage is the preparatory stage of a negotiation. In this stage, negotiators aim to establish a friendly relationship with each other or to acquire certain information of the market, product or potential partner. So there is no conflict in this stage.

At this stage, the sellers will introduce their products to the buyers. They usually emphasize the advantages of their produces and arouse the buyers' interests. Then they persuade their opponents to buy the products. In this phrase, as the sellers' main task is persuading, so they will choose a tender voice, and they must speak in a polite way. In addition, they show their sincerity to their guests so that the negotiation can develop smoothly. A good beginning influences the later bargaining even the decision of the buyers. At this time, deontic modality metaphor plays an important role in the conversation. Let's look at some examples in detail.

Conversation 1:

Mr. Wang, director of a Chinese building materials manufacturing, is negotiating with Mr. Andrews, general manager of a British company. The project under discussion involves both the purchase of equipment and technology transfer for the manufacture of high-quality wooden plastic sheeting.

A: Hello, Mr. Wang. It's a great pleasure to see you again so soon.

W: Pleased to see you again, too, Mr. Andrews. I'm glad we could start a more detailed discussion of the project now.

A: We really appreciate your cooperation and personal visit to here to discuss the project with us.

W: I believe a face-to-face talk will make it easier for us to exchange views and thus quicken the process of our negotiations.

A: I can't agree with you more.

W: Mr. Andrews, since the technical people have almost finished their discussions, we'll deal with the commercial part today. I believe you have studied the proposal we sent you on March 1.

A: Yes. Thank you very much for sending us the proposal. We hope we can reach an agreement. But I think there are still some points that need to be discussed.

The underlined sentences are all deontic modality metaphors, among which, three deontic modality metaphors are used by Mr. Wang, the seller, and only one said by Mr. Andrews, the buyer. Besides, all of them are explicit subjective expressions. We know that explicit subjective expressions show the highest degree of the speaker's acceptation of the responsibility for what he/she said. By this kind of expression, the speaker shows his utmost sincerity to cooperate with the buyers, and it will be helpful for the success of business.

For instance, at the beginning, the seller uses *I'm glad* to begin his conversation, it is a polite expression showing that he wants to cooperate with his opponent Mr. Andrews. Then the sentence "I believe a face-to-face talk will make it easier for us to exchange views and thus quicken the process of our negotiations" has the same meaning with the sentence "It will be easier for us to exchange views by a face-to-face talk." However, the speaker uses the former explicit subjective orientation to express this meaning: what is the intention of the speaker? That is to answer, what kind of interpersonal meaning the original sentence expresses. We know that Mr. Wang is the seller in this negotiation, and he wants to sell his equipments and transfer technology to Mr. Andrews. In order to persuade Mr. Andrews to do business with him, he must speak in a tentative, polite, and kind way to express his sincerity in this deal. The clause *I believe* expresses the seller's positive attitude towards this business, and shortens the distance between the two parties. However Mr. Andrews uses just one deontic modality metaphor to show his willingness to continue the negotiation. The projecting clause "I think" in the sentence "I think there are still some points that need to be discussed" also expresses the speaker's positive attitude towards this deal. If the speaker said "there are still some points that need to be discussed", the opponent may feel they are forced to do something, then they may be unwilling to cooperate. But this expression transfers the speaker's intention correctly.

In this conversation, we can find that the underlined sentences are expressed in high value. High value modal expression usually shows the speaker's affirmativeness about what he said. In this stage, the sellers use this kind of expression to attract the buyers' interests on their products. In addition, high value expressions shorten the distance between the two parties.

In this conversation, the seller, Mr. Wang, employs more deontic modality metaphors than the buyer, Mr. Andrew, and all the deontic modality metaphors are subjective orientation. That is because Mr. Wang is influenced by China's cultural value. Firstly, ever since the ancient times, Chinese people consider "politeness" as the basic principle to regulate people's action. When Chinese people communicate with others, they would like to express themselves in a polite way, with sincerity. So in the communication, Chinese people would like to express their minds in the explicit subjective orientation. Secondly, Chinese people are influenced by collective culture value. According to Hofstede (2001), members of collective culture emphasize on the cooperation and group harmony. In the business negotiation conversation, in order to maintain a close relationship between each other, we find that Chinese people use more deontic modality metaphors to express their politeness and to shorten the distance between the two parties. Thirdly, Chinese people focus more on social position, because hierarchy system has deeply influenced Chinese people. In China, in the social environment, people have their own positions. People are supposed to pay attention to their own positions when they communicate with others in the social actions. In this business conversation, Mr. Wang is the seller, and Mr. Andrew is the buyer. In the social position, Mr. Andrew has a higher position than Mr. Wang in China, because there is one saying in China "customer is the God". So in order to win the negotiation, Mr. Wang, the seller must use language properly and strategically. So he uses a lot of deontic modality metaphors.

2. The Bargaining Stage

After the initial stage of the negotiation, there comes the bargaining stage. The bargaining stage is the core stage of a negotiation, because to some extent, it decides whether a deal is possible or not. In this stage, a series of substantial items that a deal needs should be negotiated in detail. However, the main subject of the negotiation is the price. In most of the time, the two parties negotiate around the price. The buyer tries to buy the products in a low price; however, the sellers want to sell in a high price. Compared with other stages, this stage is complex. Thus, in this situation, how to use language strategically to achieve the final success is of great significance for the negotiators.

Conversation 2:

(Representatives of Blossom's Department Store of the U. S. and of China's Textiles Imp-Exp Corporation are in the course of discussing the publicity and promotion of Chinese goods in the United States. A = Textiles; B = Blossom's)

B: It would be our expectation that during the six-week period, between three and four million people would visit the Blossom's stores.

A: That's very interesting. On our part we will supply you with all the goods and supporting materials you need for displaying purposes.

B: We expect to purchase merchandise direct from China. However, since Blossom's is a store rather than an importer, we need understanding of the corporations in China that we cannot purchase in the same quantity as an importer.

A: That's perfectly understood. We believe it will be appropriate to organize some major events to support the promotional activities, to which VIPs and guests can be invited.

B: It is our expectation that key political, social and well-known American and international celebrities will attend these events, thereby generating significant publicity and creating greater interest in China.

A: As far as the participation by the Chinese side is concerned, what would you like us to do to help?

B: It is important that our buyers, merchandise managers, fashion coordinators and vice presidents receive all possible cooperation.

A: That's for sure. We promise you can have our full cooperation.

B: It is most important that delivery dates be adhered to both for samples and final shipments. If there is any delay, we should be notified directly.

We can find that there are six deontic modality metaphors being used in this conversation. Among them, four deontic modality metaphors are from B, the buyer, and two sentences are from A, the seller. This implies B tries his best to do business with A.

After observing the deontic modality metaphors in this conversation, we find that all the deontic modality metaphors from B are in explicit objective orientation, but all expressions expressed by A are explicit subjective orientation. The four deontic modality metaphors by B in this conversation can be classified into two sentence patterns "it is our expectation that..." and "it is important that...". The first pattern can be paraphrased as "we expect that...." However, the later expression shows a stronger expectation. If the speaker uses this expression, the hearer will feel pressure on him. In this situation, B just wants to express the expectation, not requirements. So an explicit objective expression expresses the speaker's opinion properly. The other sentence pattern "it is important that..." emphasizes the importance of the cooperation. The speaker uses this expression to arouse the hearer's attention. If the sentence "it is important that delivery dates be adhered to both for samples and final shipments" was transferred into "delivery dates should be adhered to both for samples and final shipments", the two sentences have the same literal meaning, but they have different interpersonal meaning. Through adding the projecting clause, the speaker realizes the emphasis intention. Let's look at the two sentences by A. In this conversation, A wants to promote his products in America, so A has the lower position in this conversation, and he is trying his best to persuade B to do business with him. So his tone should be gentle and polite. For this reason, he employs two high-degree modal expressions, "we believe" and "we promise". By using these two high-degree expressions, the speaker wants to shorten the distance with the hearer and show the determination of cooperating with him.

Taking cultural background into account, the two people come from different cultural backgrounds. A is a Chinese and B is an American. A is deeply influenced by Chinese culture, so he would like to express himself in the explicit subjective orientation, the reason of which we have analyzed in the first stage. For the American B, we can find that he is influenced by American's culture. American people would like to express themselves in an explicit objective orientation. That is because, American is an individualistic culture. People from this culture might only emphasize on self and control. So people from this culture are different from collective members. So they don't give enough attention to polite expressions as Chinese do and they just claim the fact. Another cultural factor is that American society is a low power distance one. They consider everyone has the equal right and position. In their mind, the position of the seller and the buyer is the same, so most of them will not use different tones and expressions when they are in different positions.

3. The Decision Stage

After the discussion of the first two stages, the negotiation comes to the decision stage. Through the bargaining stage, some agreements have been made. In this stage, the two parties will make straightforward statements toward the agreement and make their decisions. At this time, negotiators try to make clear the detailed items such as price, quality and terms of delivery and so on. These matters may relate the two parties' benefits, so language use is also important in this situation. In addition, their decisions determine the result of the business activity. Thus in this stage, to study the interpersonal meaning of deontic modality metaphors is of great significance.

Conversation 3:

A: Your price for bristles is much too high. It's almost 25% higher than that of last year.

B: I'm a little surprised to hear you say that. You know very well that the market for bristles has gone up a great deal in recent months.

A: To be frank with you, your price is higher than some of the quotations we have received from other sources.

B: When we compare prices, we must first of all take quality into consideration, mustn't we? Everyone in the trade knows that China's bristles are of superior quality to those from other countries. I can assure you that our price is practical and reasonable.

A: I'm sorry to say that your price is not acceptable. It's a pity we can't put the business through.

In this conversation, there are four deontic modality metaphors, two explicit subjective orientations and two explicit objective orientations. The projecting clause *everyone in the trade knows* seems a subjective orientation, but actually, it expresses the objective meaning. "Everyone in the trade knows" means it is a fact, nobody can deny "China's bristles are of superior quality to those from other countries". By using this projecting clause, the speaker's opinion was objectified and authorified, and then it will be easy for the buyer to believe what he said. After this, the seller at once gives a firm tone by using *I can assure you*, by which, the seller hopes that the buyer accepts the price and agrees to do business with him. But the two deontic modality metaphors by the buyers end the negotiation. *I'm sorry* and *It's a pity* indicates the failure of the negotiation. *I'm sorry* expresses the fact that the buyer can't do business with the seller in this price euphemistically. *It's a pity* is an explicit objective expression, and it means it's not his responsibility for not putting the business through. Thus the speaker disguises the responsibility.

To sum up, the deontic modality metaphors in the business negotiation can employ the following interpersonal meanings:

(1) to show politeness and sincerity

Politeness always plays an important role in the whole process of negotiating. Showing politeness is a basic principle human beings are supposed to observe in communication. Thus, in the process of negotiation, negotiators use polite expressions as many as possible, especially in the beginning stage. For instance: ① I'm glad we could start a more detailed discussion of the project now. ② I'm afraid I can't agree with you there. ③ I think it's always more convenient to discuss things face to face. All of the projecting clauses can be removed without changing the original meanings of the sentences; however, the speakers just use these projecting clauses aiming to express his ideas politely. With them, there will be a friendly atmosphere.

Sincerity is another important attitude that negotiators wish to express in the beginning stage. In order to avoid the opponents' doubts about the speaker's sincerity, the speaker would like to employ deontic modality metaphors to express their sincerity of cooperation. ① I hope we can come to an agreement this time. ② We expect we can reach an agreement. ③ I'm confident in saying that we are the most suitable for your needs. All of these sentences show the speaker's positive attitude towards this business cooperation.

(2) to shorten distance

Negotiators would like to use deontic modality metaphors strategically to shorten the distance with the opponents, especially in the beginning stage of a negotiation. This kind of expressions is shown as follows: ① We promise you can have our full cooperation. A high scale deontic modal expression *promise* in the projecting clause shortens the distance between the two parties. ② I admit the present market is very unfavorable to us. The projecting clause *I admit* indicates the speaker is standing on the position of the opponent to think about this deal, and this will shorten the distance between them.

(3) to show confidence of his own products

In order to win the business, the sellers should show all the advantages of their products. What's more, they must be confident of their own products by themselves, sometimes this must be shown in language use. Deontic modality metaphors can be used to realize this function strategically. Let's look at some examples: ① I believe we'll win the project. This expression seems to express the speaker's ambition; however, it is the speaker's tactic. He wants to make the opponent be sure of the products quality. ② I can assure you that our price is practical and reasonable. A high scale modal expression "I can assure" shows the speaker's confidence of the products, and he wants to attract the buyer's interests on his products by using this expression.

(4) to objectify the speaker's opinion

We know that explicit objective orientations are used to disguise subjective opinions, such as: ① It's needless for me to point out that supply exceeds demand at present and the situation is likely to continue for a long time to come. ② It's a pity we can't put the business through. ③ It's well known that your company has great experience in this field. Negotiators disguise the real responsibility source through the use of explicit objective orientation. However, sometimes a subjective expression can express objective meaning, such as: ① You are well informed that some countries are selling their goods at lower prices in large quantities. ② You know very well that the market for bristles has gone up a great deal in recent months. ③ You can't be ignorant of the fact that India has come into the market with a lower price. Three subjective expressions realize objective meanings. *You are well informed*, *You can't be ignorant of the fact*, and *You know very well* are three high scales modal expression which indicate that it is a fact instead of the speaker's own opinion. This kind of expression is a kind of negotiation strategies as well.

(5) to affirm the offer

In the last stage, the negotiation comes to an end, so it is the last time for the buyer and the seller to deal with the price problem. No doubt, the buyer wants the seller to give a further reduction, while the seller wants to insist on the high price. At this time, the seller wants to win the negotiation, and the selection of language is a kind of tactic. Sometimes, the seller uses this kind of expression *it's about the best that we can do* implies that the seller has given the least reduction. If the buyer wants a further reduction, the negotiation will fail. This deontic modality metaphor realizes the speaker's intended meaning euphemistically.

(6) to avoid direct denial

The use of deontic modality metaphors can not only avoid refusing the other party flatly, but it can also explore what attitudes the other party is holding. For example: ① I'm sorry to say we have to close business at that price. ② May I suggest that we go half-way to meet each other and close the deal? ③ I'm afraid that 10% is beyond my negotiating limit. Instead of saying "No, we can't agree with you", negotiators use this kind of expression to save other's face; besides, it will not destroy the relationship between the parties. Thus, it not only reduces the intense atmosphere, but it is also helpful for the two parties' further cooperation.

8.2.5.4 Motivations of the Use of Deontic Modality Metaphors

Through the analysis above, we find a lot of deontic modality metaphors are used in business negotiations, and they can realize various interpersonal meanings. In this part, the author aims to answer the third research question. Then the author analyzes the reasons that deontic modality metaphors can exist in this kind of discourse. The author explores the reason from these three perspectives: business principles, language characteristics of deontic modality metaphor, and social and psychological factors.

1. Business Negotiation Characteristics

Business negotiation is a phenomenon of human communication which contains various interpersonal meanings. According to Halliday, one of the three metafunctions of language is to realize interpersonal meaning; however, the characteristics and principles of business negotiation will influence the expression of the interpersonal meanings, so that the characters and principles of business negotiation influence the language use.

Three principles are supposed to be observed by negotiators. The first is the equality principle. Without equal status, the negotiation cannot go further. Equality and mutual benefit is the very basic principle in modern negotiation. So both parties must be in the equal status. In this situation, negotiators should focus on their language use, neither too powerful nor too weak. The second is the sincere cooperative principle. Business negotiation is a special human communication which closely relates to two parties' economy interests. Negotiators should show their sincerity to each other so that results will be achieved in the success of the negotiation. The third is the flexible and fluid principle. It means that some flexibilities are needed to keep negotiation develop smoothly. Thus different strategies and tactics should be adopted to deal with different negotiation opponents. In this situation, deontic modality metaphor should be taken into consideration. Through tactic language, negotiators could assess to what is the least concession in other party's mind.

2. Social and Psychological Factors

Firstly, according to Leech, in order to establish and maintain successful and harmonious social relationship, people should obey politeness principle. According to Brown and Levinson, politeness is universal to all cultures, because all people have the need to be appreciated and protected. Thus in the communication, we should obey politeness principle, and maximize the politeness through appropriate language use. In order to maintain the friendly relationship with each other in the communication, negotiators must use some strategies, especially positive politeness strategies. These strategies mainly show in the language they use. Business negotiation is a communication, through which, a clear purpose is to gain benefit from each other. So a good communication atmosphere is important, thus positive strategies are of great significance to negotiators. Deontic modality metaphor can be regarded as the positive politeness strategies used in the conversations.

Secondly, because of cultural differences, negotiators from different countries have different opinions towards language use, not to mention deontic modality metaphor. For Chinese, "politeness" is the basic principle in communicating with others, thus Chinese negotiators would like to use explicit subjective deontic modality metaphors to show their politeness. For Japanese, "strictness" is their national spirit, so they would like to use serious language, especially when it relates to responsibility, thus they employ more objective deontic modality metaphors.

Thirdly, people in different social positions use different languages. In the business negotiation, the buyer's social position is higher than the seller's, so the seller is supposed to use polite language to communicate with the buyer. However, different countries have different opinions towards this kind of cultural value. For example, since the ancient time, China is influenced by hierarchy system, and people have their own position in the society. So in the business negotiation, they distinguish each other's social position, and they choose different languages according to their different roles in the social action.

Although deontic modality metaphors are used widely, different people have different orientations, and what kind of interpersonal meaning it can realize depends on the context. Thus, in order to maintain certain relationship, we must pay attention to deontic modality metaphors.

8.2.6 Results

After analysis and discussion, the author finds the answers to the research questions. First, the author finds that deontic modality metaphors have been used widely in business negotiation discourses. By analyzing the statistics, the author finds that both the sellers and the buyers are adept in using deontic modality metaphors. By contrast, we find that explicit subjective expression is used a little more than explicit objective expression.

Second, the author finds that deontic modality metaphor can help the negotiators realize various interpersonal meanings in the actual discourses. Deontic modality metaphors are always used to show the speaker's politeness, sincerity and affirmativeness, to shorten the distance between the two parties, to show confidence of his own products, to objectify the speaker's opinion, to affirm the offer, to avoid direct denial. Showing politeness and sincerity is important in the process of the negotiation, especially in the beginning stage of the negotiation. At this stage, negotiators mainly use explicit subjective deontic modality metaphors, especially the sellers use a lot of this kind of expressions. They use deontic modality metaphors in order to have a happy start, hoping that the following stage will be developed smoothly. Negotiators would like to use deontic modality metaphors to shorten the distance between the two parties. By using explicit subjective expression, the speaker can produce more utterances tentatively, which will shorten the distance between the speaker and the listener. Then it will be beneficial for the negotiators to cooperate with each other. It is important for the sellers to show their confidence of his products. By using some explicit subjective orientations, such as *I believe*, *I can assure*, and the sellers show their confidence of the products, and this will be helpful for them to persuade the buyers to buy the products. Sometimes negotiators use explicit objective expressions to objectify their opinions, because this kind of expression can disguise the real responsibility source and they can escape from taking responsibility for their opinions. In addition, the objective orientations make the proposition look like a set fact, not the speaker's opinion, and it is easy for the listener to accept. In the last stage of the negotiation, negotiators would like to use deontic modality metaphors to affirm the offer. By using deontic modality metaphors, the seller implies his least reduction. In order to have a further cooperation, the two parties will refuse euphemistically by using deontic modality metaphors. Some polite expressions such as *I'm sorry* will be used to avoid refusing directly. It will be helpful for the two parties' further cooperation.

Third, the author analyzes the reasons from three perspectives. Firstly, the author accesses it from the perspective of business principles to illustrate the possibility of the existence of deontic modality metaphors. Secondly, the author illustrates the functions that deontic modality metaphors have in the real discourse to prove the value of deontic modality metaphors in the business negotiation conversations. Thirdly, the author from the perspective of social and psychological aspect analyzes the language use.

8.3 Summary

To sum up: the findings the author gets: firstly, as the author expects, deontic modality metaphors have been used widely in business negotiation discourses. Both the sellers and the buyers would like to use deontic modality metaphors to realize their intended interpersonal meanings. Secondly, deontic modality metaphors can help the speakers realize various interpersonal meanings. The author selects three negotiation conversations as cases to analyze the interpersonal meanings that deontic modality metaphors employ in the three stages of the negotiation. In the beginning stage, negotiators mainly use explicit subjective deontic modality metaphors to show their politeness, and sincerity. When the bargaining stage comes, negotiators use explicit subjective orientations to shorten the distance between the two parties, and use explicit objective expressions to objectify their opinions aiming to disguise the real responsibility resource. In the decision stage, negotiators use fewer deontic modality metaphors than the two former stages. The sellers would like to use deontic modality metaphors to affirm the least reduction and to end the conversation politely in order to avoid refusing. Thirdly, the author analyzes the reasons from three perspectives. In the first place, the principles of business negotiation provide the possibility of the existence of deontic modality metaphors. In the second reason, deontic modality metaphors have many interpersonal functions and these functions can help negotiators achieve the goal of communication. In the third place, the social and psychological are taken into account to analyze the motivation of using this kind of expression.

Chapter 9 Interpersonal Meaning of Deontic Modality in Cross-cultural Study

9.1 Introduction

In Halliday's functional linguistics, a language has three functions: ideographic, interpersonal and textual functions (Halliday, 1985). Because modal expressions and modal terms are various in different cultures, the interpersonal meaning of modality in different cultures is different from each other.

Previous investigators study the modality from grammar-level to discourse-level, and their understanding and research on the subject is deepening. Lyons (1997: 793) thinks that there are two types of modality—epistemic modality and deontic modality. Epistemic modality is about knowledge and belief while deontic modality is about possibility and necessity of morally responsible main body's behavior. This is dichotomy from the perspective of logic. Previous researches mainly concern the interpersonal meaning of epistemic modality, orientations of modal expressions, the interpersonal meaning of modality in different contexts or situations and the modality part in the cross-cultural construction of inter-personal meaning in transition, while no one has done a systematic research about cross-cultural studies on interpersonal meaning of modality.

This chapter mainly concerns cross-cultural studies on inter-personal meaning of modality by comparing the differences of the interpersonal meaning of modality in Chinese and English, in order to fill in the gap for the research of the interpersonal meaning of modality to some degree and provide inspiration for later work. In this chapter, we will try to explore the differences of the interpersonal meaning of modality in terms of modal terms and ways to express modality by making use of examples mainly from the achievements of the predecessors. Besides, we also try to dig out the deep cultural reasons of the differences.

9.2 Differences Caused by Modal Terms

In English and Chinese, people use modal terms to express a certain meaning. Because of cultural differences, people make use of modal terms in various ways and the interpersonal meaning they express is different thereupon. In the following parts, we will explore this in three aspects: value, word meaning and some special situations.

9.2.1 Different Value of Modal Terms Expressing Dissimilar Meanings

Halliday (2000) described the value of modality: Low: *can*, *may*, *needn't*, *doesn't/didn't need*; Median: *will*, *shall*, *won't*, *shan't*; High: *must*, *need*, *ought to*, *mustn't*, *can't*, *oughtn't to*. Let's take two advertisements as examples. The first one is in Chinese about a floor's maintenance note:

(1)不允许用碱水/肥皂水擦洗(to use alkaline /soap scrub is not allowed.)

千万不可用汽油擦拭(Do not clean it with gasoline.)

若遇漏水于地面,必须及时擦干净,不能直接太阳暴晒或用电炉烘烤,以免干燥过快,地板破裂。(In case of leakage on the ground, it must be cleaned in time. No direct sun exposure or baking furnace. If one side dries too fast, it will break.)

铺装完后的油漆地板应尽量减少太阳直晒,以免油漆经紫外线的照射过多,提前干裂和老化。(After painting, the floor pavement should not be exposed to sunshine, so as to prevent the paint against drying and aging.)

漆好的地板如不长期入住,切忌用塑料布或报纸盖上,时间一长漆膜会发黏,失去光泽,同时切忌高温物体直接接触地板。(If you do not move into the house a long time after the painting, do not cover it with plastic sheeting or newspaper because if it is covered by them for a long time, the floor will be sticky. And at the same time, you should prevent the floor from direct contact with hot objects.) (Li Zhanzi, 2002: 120)

In this 300-hundred-word advertisement, there are seven strong denotic modalities, four consequences mentioned with *in order to avoid* and four consequences without using *in order to avoid*, which makes people feel that they are not buying floors but a bomb.

Then let's look at the following advertisement in English:

(2) scratch resistant

chemically resistant;

pressure resistant;

abrasion resistant;

resistant to caster mounted chair;

easy to care (Li Zhanzi,2002:121).

We can see in the second advertisement, there are five modalities expressing ability and a weakened demotic modality. Through a simple comparison, we can see that it is very common to make use of demotic modality (high) in Chinese advertisements; especially in the form of *Product Using Notes*. We can understand this situation in two ways. The first one is that the manufacturers are responsible for their customers and let them know all the notes exactly, which is positive. The other one is that the customers feel it is too complex to use and maintain the floor, and then they give up buying it, which is negative. And if we use weakened deontic modalities, better effects will appear. While the potential bad result is that customers maybe violate the notes because it is not that detailed.

Besides, there is another comparison from English and Chinese public service advertisements (PSA for short). The first ones are in Chinese:

(3)请不要食用鱼翅(Do not eat shark's fin.)

(4)奥运来了,文明交流方便快捷,别忘了说普通话(Olympics comes and it is convenient to have a friendly exchange, so do not forget to speak Mandarin.)(Zhang Fan,2009:28)

And there is also one in English:

(5) When a child's only future is surviving day to day, we can help provide the love and care. Where children live in fear, we will help to protect them. And when they are sick, we will help to nurse them better...(Zhang Fan,2009:28)

In this comparison above, it seems that there are more modalities (high), such as "不要", "别", "不许", "禁止" and "勿", etc. in Chinese PSAs than in English PSAs. Those modalities transfer the information to the audience that they should not do something rather than they are supposed to do something. The gruff tone used carries absolute authority over the audience, which will set a barrier between the advertiser and the audience. Compared with Chinese PSAs, the English ones use more expressions of inclination with more modalities (low) advertiser. Those expressions indicate that what I said is what I expect you to do rather than force you to do.

And there exist cultural reasons for the differences in the two comparisons above. Chinese people put much emphasis on collectivism, and generally the government or an organization may have absolute authority over the individuals, so when the government or an organization makes an announcement, they tend to listen to it. Here this authority is shown through those modal terms with high value. On the contrary, people in the western world put more emphasis on individualism, and under normal circumstances the opinions of individuals will influence the decision the government or an organization will make. As a result, when the government or an organization there announces something, they will try to persuade the general public or use a more tender way.

9.2.2 The Differences in the Meaning of Modal Terms

Many English learners think that modality in both English and Chinese is represented by a group of modal verbs and is fairly easy to learn. But whenever they meet with modality, they cannot work out its accurate meaning, but rely on the equivalent modal words in their mother tongue. In fact, the seemingly similar modal words are quite different from language to language. So modality deserves a contrastive study between English and Chinese. Through an analysis of the meaning of modal words of English and Chinese in the following context, this section verifies that modality is not as simple as what the English learners think.

The main form to express modality is finite modal operator. Based on the study of R. W. Zandvoort (1975) and Chen Gaochun (1989), we can include the comparison of infinite modal operator in English and Chinese like this:

Table 9.1 Comparison of Infinite Modal Operator in English and Chinese (Liu Yanqin, 2008)

type		English	Chinese
modality	possibility	must, can, could, may, might, ought to, should	能、会、应该、应当、该、能够、可能……
	usuality	will, would, must	
modulation	responsibility	must, need, have to, should, ought to, can, could, may	应该、应当、该、必须、得、能、准许、可、可以、允许、务必......
	tendency	might, will, would, must	甘心、宁可、急于、愿意、愿、肯、懒得、只要、会、自愿、情愿、要......

In English and Chinese, a finite modal operator can express different types of modal meanings, which is a common phenomenon with many languages. And the finite modal operator of languages from different pedigree has the same characteristics. Besides, it is clear in the form above that the meaning in English and Chinese finite modal operator is almost in correspondence.

However, we do not pay too much attention to the similarity in our work but to the differences of it in these two languages.

There is not a finite modal operator in Chinese that expresses usuality, but in English there exists specialized finite modal operator having this function. For example, "She will sit there for hours, waiting for her son to come home." In this sentence, *will* expresses usuality. In Chinese, in order to express usuality, people use modal adjuncts like"往往"、"经常"、"常常". For example, "她常常在那里坐几个小时,等她的儿子归来."(She will sit there for hours, waiting for her son to come home.)(Liu Yanqin, 2008)

9.2.3 Discrepancies in Special Situations

It is shown in many resources that many researchers probe the English translation of Chinese titles when they write a pasper. And many researchers have focused on the translation of the Chinese words like "窥探"、"浅析" and "试论", which seems like a question concerning the usage of words, but it arouses many researchers' thinking of the interpersonal meaning. Some people think this is a form of polite words that derives from traditional Chinese feudal ethics and people use them to show their caution; others hold the idea that Chinese people value harmony and show their respect to readers. However, this language phenomenon does not keep with the habit of westerners, so that they think it is a hollow language with procrastination due to a lack of appropriate means in their language. Through the discussion above, we can see the differences of expressing a certain interpersonal meaning between Chinese and other languages. Based on the differences, now people often delete the translation of these polite words from Chinese to other languages.

Besides, Chinese people and westerners make use of different modalities to describe religion and the Gods because they hold different attitudes towards them. Let's look at the following example:

(6)这都是天地神佛不忍我叫这些小人们糟蹋,所以才叫我知道了。

(7)I think Heaven and Earth and the Lord Buddha must have taken pity on me in letting me know about this marriage. They didn't want me to be destroyed by a pack of scandal two mongering servants. (Translated by Hawks)(Zheng Yuanhui, 2005)

In the translation above, Hawks used a modal metaphor *I think* and a *must* (high), which is not in accordance with the original Chinese. Based on this, we assume that Hawks had his own consideration, or he did not understand the interpersonal meaning of the Chinese passage.

According to Bakhtin's Dialogue Theory, the text is a result of consultation between communicators and multiple voices of a language environment (Li Zhanzi, 2002:114). In order to discuss the translation above, we should take readers into consideration. The differences of interpersonal meaning between the original text and the English translation are caused by readers' different attitudes to religion and the Gods. The attitude of Chinese people to the Gods is practical while that of westerners is holy. From the perspective of the interpersonal meaning, Wang Xifeng gets wronged so that she thinks that the Gods should call the shots for her, which is hard to understand for westerners. And the interpersonal meaning in the English translation is that she guesses the Gods may have known everything, which is an adjustment from the original text. The adjustment does not affect the interpersonal meaning of the whole passage, but becomes closer to English readers' taste.

9.3 Different Interpersonal Meaning Caused by Ways of Expressing Modality

There exist many ways to express modality, such as modal metaphor, orientations and mood. The ways to express modality vary from culture to culture, which is reflected in languages expressing different interpersonal meanings. In the following part, we will study it in three aspects.

9.3.1 Disparity of Interpersonal Meaning in Terms of Modal Metaphor

When a speaker expresses the possibility of what he says by making use of an independent main clause to constitute a sentence with a main clause and a subordinate clause, this independent main clause is a modal metaphor. For example, "I think it is going to rain." We can test it with a tag question like this: "I think it is going to rain, isn't it?" But not "I think it is going to rain to rain, don't I" So this sentence is a variant of "It is probably going to rain (isn't it)," but not a corresponding first person sentence.

Similarly, we can also regard *I am certain*, *It is likely*, *You cannot seriously doubt that...* and *Everything admits that...* as modal metaphors because they all express the meaning of *I believe*.

The differences of Chinese and English modal metaphor are in the following form:

Table 9.2 Differences of Chinese and English Modal Metaphor(Li Liu,2005)

comparison project	English modal metaphor	Chinese modal metaphor
subjective modal metaphors with tag questions	The subject and qualifier of tag questions are in accordance with those of the main sentence in form	The subject and qualifier of tag questions are not in accordance with those of the main sentence in form
expressing forms of objective modal metaphors	Mainly start with form subject "it"	Absolute sentences can be used
the level of modalities	declarative sentence、modal metaphor、interrogative sentence	modal particle and modal adverb
negative transfer	transferred	not transferred

Apart from the differences existing between different languages, people from different cultures have their own tendency to use modalities even in the same language. Compared with native speakers, language learners use modal metaphors not with some interpersonal purposes but for other reasons. For example, Chinese students often start a sentence with *I think*, not to show that they are not sure about what they say but as a way only to start the sentence and gain time for them to organize the whole sentence. This phenomenon has something to do with culture. Chinese tend to be modest and they do not want to show themselves very directly, so that they use *I think* more frequently than native speakers.

9.3.2 Disparity in Orientations of Modality

The basic distinction that determines how each type of modality will be realized is the orientation. According to Halliday (2001), the speakers may express their opinion in the way that makes it clear whether it is their subjective point of view or it is objectively a quality of all event itself. There is some intermediate ground of expression between the highlighting subjectivity and creating objectivity. Besides, there is another variant in the modal expression, implicitness and explicitness. Implicitness is usually realized when the modality is expressed in the same clause as the main proposition, while explicitness is used when it is expressed in a projecting clause (Halliday, 2000:355).

Zhao Nan (2004) made a comparison of modal orientations used in English and Chinese news report in her paper for the master's degree. And she made a conclusion that English is more explicit in objective orientation and implicit in objective orientation. Consequently, objectivity is emphasized and subjectivity is concealed to some degree, which makes news reports more objective and believable to readers. However, Chinese is more explicit in subjective orientation and implicit in objective orientation. In this way, the objectivity in news reporting is minified and subjectivity is magnified to certain extent, which might make news reporting seem a bit subjective to readers.

This outcome has deep-seated cultural reasons. On the one hand, Chinese reporters may care less that readers will consider their reports as subjective and maybe they think their subjective opinions are just right. On the contrary, their English counterparts present their views in a more implicit way, which makes those opinions not too subjective and more credible to the readers. On the other hand, in China, *People's Daily* and *PH Corpus* are the most important and authoritative newspapers and they dominate in journalism, so maybe Chinese people get used to receiving the information from them and think it is true even though they hold different opinions. They tend to listen to the government or what other authorities have announced. However, *New York Times* and *Washington Post* seem to persuade readers. Although they also try to lead the readers to their mode of thinking, it seems that the method they take is concealed designedly.

9.3.3 Discrepancy in Mood

First, mood and modality are often mingled together, and in many studies, the two concepts are usually viewed as one unity and are not separated. Li Zhanzi (2002:81) has concluded that mood is the result of grammaticalization of modality. That's to say, in the basic kinds of mood, we may use different means to realize modality, including the speaker's attitudes, emotions and intentions, etc.

Then let's look at the differences of mood systems in English and Chinese. Obviously, we cannot deny that the entry conditions for the mood systems are more or less similar in these two languages: mood is the expression of basic speech functions, coated with the speaker's attitudes. But we notice that the options in the two mood systems are very different, owing to the different standards of classifying mood. In Chinese, each set of the rich meanings of mood may be grouped under a general title, that is, one kind of mood. While in English, mood is classified only in light of speech functions it is supposed to perform. In English, the choices for mood are basically four ones: the declarative, the interrogative, the imperative and the exclamative. The comparison is finally focused on the realization of mood, which can be reflected at the different levels of language system.

The reason for this is maybe English is a language of hypotaxis, which means people use it in certain kinds of language forms, just like four choices for mood while Chinese is one of parataxis, which means not with the help of languages forms but logical links between the meanings of words or sentences.

9.4 Summary

This chapter is based on many predecessors' research, aiming at a study on the differences of interpersonal meaning of modality in different cultures.

In order to study those differences, first we know many aspects of modality through the basic research made by Halliday, Li Zhanzi and many other researchers. Then we probe the differences from the perspective of modal terms and ways to express modality. The aspect of modal terms mainly involves the differences in value and word meaning, and the aspect of modality expressing mainly covers the differences in modal metaphor, orientations and mood. The differences of interpersonal meaning caused by modality in English and Chinese are not accidental phenomena but have their deep-seated cultural roots.

Chapter 10 A Contrastive Study of Interpersonal Meaning of Deontic Modality in Chinese and English Advertisements

10.1 Significance of the Study

Modality shows the speaker's or writer's attitude to a certain proposition, the subjectivity or objectivity toward an utterance (Palmer, 2007:117). Meanwhile, modality plays a significant role in daily communications. Therefore, many researches in modality have been done by logicians, philosophers and linguistics. From linguistic aspect, certain linguistics of Traditional Grammar, Semantics, Transformational-Generative Grammar, Pragmatics, and Systemic Functional Grammar have shown their own interests. However, what had taken the dominant position in those analyses is the research of modality auxiliary while other expressions were neglected. Functional grammar broadens the researching scope of modality and takes many other modal expressions into consideration. Halliday (2000) provides an explanation of the types of modality, system of orientations and values which attach to the modal judgment. With the more participation of linguistics into the research in modality, attention has been shifted to the study of modality in discourse analysis. Thompson argues that "what we have focused on has been the broad factors at work in the area of modality, particularly those which help in the analysis of spoken and written texts" (Thompson, 2000: 63). Moreover, he provides an example in *Introduction Functional Grammar* to present how modality works in novels and short stories. Actually, the study of modality has already begun in the field of literature, semantics, stylistics, and discourse analysis. In *Language and Control*, Fowler (1979) indicates that Critical Discourse Analysis should particularly pay attention to transitivity, modality and transformation (Li Zhanzi, 2002:10).

However, a great number of modality researches are limited to modality auxiliaries. The contrastive study of it in English and Chinese is ignored. Moreover, lots of researchers have analyzed epistemic modality in various texts. Few of them have researched deontic modality in detail, not to mention its contrastive study in different languages.

As a type of discourses, advertising is the medium for realizing the interaction between the advertiser and the potential consumers. As a tool, it plays an indispensable role for modern institutions and corporations. Advertising, as an acknowledged genre and a cultural, social and language phenomenon, has aroused the interest of worldwide linguists. Most researchers have studied advertising from such aspects as translation, stylistics, lexicology, pragmatics and psycholinguistics. Few of them have paid attention to the negotiation and interaction between the readers and the advertiser. Just in last few years, certain researchers have studied advertising texts from the respective of contrastive discourse analysis. The vast majority of the studies are based on interpersonal meaning. However, none of them have related deontic modality to the study of advertising texts. Therefore, there is still untouched research space. Due to these factors, the author is motivated to the Chinese and English advertising texts and makes a contrastive analysis of interpersonal meaning of deontic modality in them.

This part aims at finding out how deontic modality is realized in English and Chinese advertising texts respectively. Through the contrastive analysis we could find the differences and similarities between the applications of deontic modality in those two kinds of texts. What's more meaningful is to explore the causal factors for those differences.

The authors believe that a contrastive analysis of deontic modality in advertising texts of two languages is likely to achieve a kind of domain extension from the previous studies both on advertising discourses and on interpersonal meaning, which in turn may broaden the relevant theoretic studies through application in specific field, namely, advertising texts analysis. Besides, it will be able to deepen our understanding of the interpersonal meaning of deontic modality of languages. More significantly, it is of much significance since there are so many cultural differences between China and western countries. For the practical purpose, through the detailed and thorough discussion, the findings of the study can be considered reliable in providing insights into the further studies of deontic modality.

10.2 Research Questions

The present research, from the perspective of interpersonal meaning, attempts to make a contrastive discourse analysis of deontic modality in Chinese and English advertising texts. In the research, following questions should be concerned:

(1) How deontic modality is realized in advertising texts in both Chinese and English?

(2) What are the differences in realizing deontic modality between Chinese and English

advertising texts?

(3) What are the causal factors for the differences?

10.3 Different Ways of Realization of Deontic Modality in Chinese and English Advertising Texts

In the section above, studies on modality, deontic modality and interpersonal meaning are presented. Through the discussion, we come to understand modality system deeply. Moreover, some detail analyses of deontic modality make us know what deontic modality is and how does it realize interpersonal meaning in discourses. All of those provide the further research with the theoretical framework and make it more justified. In this chapter, a contrastive study of deontic modality in English and Chinese advertising texts will be presented in detail from the perspective of interpersonal meaning mainly including the analysis of the frequency of deontic modality occurrence, modality orientation and modality value. Through the contrastive analysis, certain differences and similarities between Chinese and English advertising texts will be discovered.

10.3.1 Data Collection and Methodology

The advertising texts in two languages are in written form. The titles and slogans of the text are not included. The author chooses 25 examples respectively from the public press, magazines and the Internet. Besides, the author will make efforts to select international and domestic famous brands.

10.3.2 Analysis of Deontic Modal Expressions in Selected Samples

10.3.2.1 Different Frequencies of Deontic Modality Occurrence

We had made clear that deontic modality implies that the speaker "intervene in the speech event by laying obligations or diving permission" (Downing & Locke, 1992:382). It can be realized by modal adjuncts, modal verbs, modal auxiliaries or even certain types of sentences in advertising discourses and then in turn realizes according interpersonal meaning to persuade or influence the potential customers. Then in this part, we will discuss how deontic modality is realized in advertising texts in both Chinese and English. First of all, an overview of the distribution of deontic expressions in both Chinese and English samples should be given.

Based on the analysis of our selected samples, a summary of frequencies of those deontic modality expressions is presented in the following table.

Table 10.1 Frequencies of Those Deontic Modal Expressions

samples / number	Chinese samples	English samples
with modal expressions	15	8
total number	25	25
percent	60%	32%

As shown in table 10.1, it is found that both Chinese and English advertising texts involve deontic modal expressions. 15 pieces of Chinese samples apply those expressions which covers 60% while 8 of the English samples in which deontic modal expressions are employed amounting to 32%. We could get the great difference between these two frequencies. But it is not enough. In order to analyze the differences systematically, we will do more detailed analysis about it from the aspect of modality orientation and modality value.

10.3.2.2 Different Modality Values

Modality has different degrees and scales. Thompson points out that applying modality, speakers can assess the probability (how likely it is to be true) of the proposition or the degree of allowed to/ supposed to/ determined to (Thompson, 2000:59). In Halliday's view, modal verbs, modal adjectives modal operators and expansions of the predicator all have three scales of value which are "attached to the modal judgment": high, median and low. His illustration is shown in the following two tables with the first one being the values of modal adverbs, modal adjectives and some expansions of the predicator and the second one being the values of the English modal verbs.

Table 10.2 Values of Modality (Halliday, 2000:358)

	probability	usuality	obligation	inclination
high	certain	always	required	determined
median	probable	usually	supposed	keen
low	possible	sometimes	allowed	willing

Table 10.3 Modal Auxiliaries Attached to Certain Value in English (Halliday 76)

low	median	high
can, may, could, might, (dare) needn't, doesn't + need to/ have to	will, would, should, is/ was to won't, wouldn't, shouldn't, (isn't/ wasn't to)	must, ought to, need, has/ had to, mustn't, oughtn't to, can't, couldn't, (mayn't, mightn't, hasn't/ hadn't to)

As it is a contrastive study, we also should have an idea of divisions of Chinese modal verbs. In China, according to Halliday's modality types and values for their interpersonal functions, Ma Qingzhu (1992) combines the semantic and grammatical characteristics of Chinese modal verbs and summarizes them as follows:

Table 10.4 Value of Chinese Modal Verbs (Ma Qingzhu, 1992:49-50)

	low	median	high
positive	可能,会,可,可以,能,能够,好,得以,容易,来得及	乐意,愿,愿意,情愿,想,想要,要,希望,企图,好意思,了的,高兴,乐于,肯,敢于,勇于,甘于,苦于,懒得,忍心,值得,配,便于,有助于,易于,善于,适于,易于	得,应,该,应该,应当,必须,须得,必得,要,务必,务须,须要,犯得着
negative	可能不,不会,不必,无须,不须,不能够,免不了,难免,不免,不(容)易,来不及	不乐意,不愿,不愿意,不情愿,不想,不要希望,不好意思,不肯,不敢,不忍心,不值得,不配,不便于,无助于,难于,不善于,不适于,不宜(于)	不可能,不可,不可以,不能,不得,不该,犯不着

Our study is based on Halliday's and Ma Qingzhu's classifications and focused on those ones which can realize deontic modality.

According to table 10.3 and table 10.4, through analyzing the deontic modal auxiliaries in both sample texts, we could list the next two tables.

Table 10.5 Value of Deontic Modal Auxiliaries that Occur in English Samples

value	low	median	high
total Number	1	4	1
percentage	14.28%	50%	14.28%

Table 10.6 Value of Deontic Modal Auxiliaries that Occur in Chinese Samples

value	low	median	high
total number	1	2	7
percentage	6.66%	13.33%	46.66%

From table 10.5, we detected that 14.28% (only 1) of the deontic modal auxiliaries commits to both low value and high value, while 4 modal verbs are with median value which accounts for 50%. And the number of Chinese modal auxiliaries 15 in total number committing to high value adds up to 7 (46.66%) while median value to 2 (13.33%) and low value to 1(6.66%). The figure indicating the distribution of Chinese and English deontic modal operators in advertising texts is distinct, especially, the occurrence frequency of deontic modal auxiliaries with high value. With 30% percent margin, the occurrence in Chinese is much higher than that in English. Most of the deontic auxiliaries adopted in Chinese samples are with high value (46.66%) while in English samples that with median value (42.85%) take the dominant role.

As for the choice of modality auxiliaries or whether a modality auxiliary can be applied, different advertisers with different culture backgrounds may have different preferences. The result shows us that English advertisers prefer to apply modal verbs with lower value to avoid committing advertiser themselves to the certainty or the truthfulness of the statements. In this way the accuracy of the advertisement can be enhanced. Just as a researcher said: "a non-absolute statement can reflect the present state more exactly than an absolute one." (Yang Shu, 2007) As far as the customers are concerned, they feel that they come to understand the quality and effectiveness of the products objectively and become more trustful to the goods.

By examining the samples, one can find that both Chinese and English texts commonly apply the low value modal operators like "能" and *can*. These words can offer the potential customers a possibility of obtaining certain benefit of the product. Low value modal operator means the lowest degree of pressure. It leaves the decision to the readers and enables them to take purchasing actions.

The figure also uncovers that the percentage of deontic modal verbs with median value in

English is much higher than that in Chinese by a 36.67% margin. Generally, *will*, *should*, "想(要)""将" can indicate what will happen. They also provide information about the statements of future occurrence which are based on the speaker's beliefs, predications or intentions, rather than one's knowledge of the "fact". Moreover, *will* could indicate an obvious promising attitude. Some samples both in Chinese and English are as follows:

(21) 想要身体好,请喝健力宝。

(22) 北京要加油,我要喝红牛。

(23) This super charged perfector helps skin feel stronger, balanced and more refined. In just 5 days, you'll see radiant results. Over time, your skin will look healthier and be more resistant to the sighs of premature aging.

(24) Your skin should glow, not shine! If you have oily skin, our popular Daily Oil Control will help keep your skin balanced so it looks radiant instead of oily. Helps keep impurities from clogging pores, makeup from streaking, and skin from shining, all day long. A great addition to the 3-Step System. Gentle and oil-free. 1.7oz.

In the above examples, "想(要)" are applied to express a mental process. The potential consumers have a desire to keep their bodies healthy. The word *will* gives information about what the customer's skin will be like after applying the advertised products. *Should* is used to indicate what the customer's skin will benefit after applying the products.

In contrast to English samples, there is more percentage of modal verbs with high value used in the Chinese examples. The Chinese samples have expressions like "应""勿""别" and "一定", while English examples only have one high value deontic verb "bet". Some samples will be shown in the following:

(25) 你常感到肌肤干燥不适吗? 你是否用了多种滋润护肤产品,可肌肤仍不够润泽,甚至出现细纹干纹? 那你一定要关注羽西给你的超凡科技!

(26) 防御日晒是一个复杂的"细胞工程",首先应从保护细胞内部的 DNA 开始。最新的兰蔻柔皙深护防晒乳 SPF50 + + + 可为肌肤提供 DNA 保护、UV 保护和污染保护,完美保护伞让你不再为防晒苦恼。

(27) 今夏,Clinique 倩碧皮肤学专家为你的双唇精心调制了 8 款水润的"夏日特饮",赶快来畅饮! 你的双唇,一定会上瘾。

(28) 趁早下"斑",请勿"痘"留。

(29) 酸酸甜甜宝宝才爱喝。记住买蓝瓶的! 别买错了呀!

In these examples, the high value deontic modal operators are used to indicate the advertisers' confidence in the products and in turn to convince the potential consumers. In this way, they make the readers have positive impressions of the effects that can be brought by applying their products.

Therefore, the potential customers' desire will be aroused.

Except for above three value modal verbs, samples in both languages use imperative sentences to convey deontic modality, such as:

(30) 喝汇源果汁,走健康之路。

(31) 保护嗓子,请用金嗓子喉宝。

(32) Come; join us in the magic of the Pacific and the pageantry of its people.

(33) Ask for more.

Advertisers cannot override the consumers and cannot fundamentally affect their purchase intentions. Therefore, as a matter of fact, the imperative sentences in advertisements all imply certain obligations of different degrees such as *You are allowed to. . . / You are supposed to . . . / You are determined to . . . .* Applying imperative sentences, the advertiser attempts to appeal the potential consumers to experience the benefit that can be brought by the products. Sometimes, the imperative sentences in Chinese imply a harsh tone and cold attitude which could build a barrier between the advertiser and the customers. Therefore, advertisers apply mitigators such as "请" in our samples to make the advertisements polite and less offensive.

10.3.2.3 Modality Orientations

Modality orientations distinctively determine how every type of modality is realized. From Halliday's point of view, speakers could express their own opinions clearly no matter what their subjective viewpoints or objective events are. Halliday (2000:355) points out that "The term 'implicit' is used when the modality is expressed in the same clause as the main position, while 'explicit' is used when it is expressed in a separate clause." Besides those intermediate grounds of expression between the highlighting subjectivity and creating objectivity, explicitness and implicitness are other variants of the modality orientations.

Explicit subjective orientation is an effective way to make speakers' own point of view to certain propositions clear. The speakers inclined to make it clear that the viewpoints are their own attitudes or comments rather than some facts. As the most representative modal expression to show explicit subjective orientation, projecting clause can also be applied in explicit objective orientations. For instance:

(34) In my opinion, it is wrong. (explicit subjective)

(35) It is likely he likes this kind of movie. (explicit objective)

If we study them from the ideational metafunction aspect, they belong to different processes in transitivity. The first example which presents subjective orientation is the mental process which gives prominence to the subjectivity of the viewpoint, while the later one which indicates objective orientation belongs to relation process. According to Perkins, lexical verbs also are the realizations of explicit subjective orientation (Perkins, 1983:96).

Implicit subjective orientation is to make the proposition less obvious, so that the viewpoint is just as if the fact itself rather than from the speaker. It is realized by some modal expressions, among which the finite modal operator is the most typical one. Thompson also believes that "modal operator exploits the finite slot and thus is firmly rooted in the interpersonal, subjective meaning of the clause" (Thompson 61). Moreover, from Hoye's point of view, comment adjuncts which are the typical of modal expressions are fundamentally subjective (Hoye, 1997:176).

In implicit objective orientation, the mood adjunct which is the other part of modal adjuncts appears to be very important. Halliday argues that all the modal adjuncts indicate the objectivity of propositions in an implicit manner. Same as mood adjuncts, the passive verbs predicators are also closer to the objective end of the scale from subjective orientation to the objective one. Therefore, they also function in showing implicit objective modal orientation. An example is provided:

(36) You are supposed to be doing your homework.

In this sentence, we can perceive that the pressure seems not to come from the speaker, but other sources.

Explicit objective orientation enables readers to feel that what they are reading is not the speaker's own idea but something objectively accepted. Perkins holds the view that nominal modal expressions represent the ultimate stage in the objectification of modality and play very important role in conveying explicit objective orientation (Perkins, 1983:137). In addition, as we have discussed above, the projecting clauses which belong to the attributive relational process and verbal process also indicates explicit objective orientation.

①The distribution of different orientations in both kinds of samples

Through the analysis of the selected samples, we find that most of the examples adopt those modality operators with implicit subjective orientation. The distribution of different orientations can be perceived from the following table:

Table 10.7 Distribution of Different Orientations in both Kinds of Samples

	explicit subjective	implicit subjective	implicit objective	explicit objective
English samples		6		
Chinese samples	1	11		

Combining Table10.1 and Table 10.7, we should get that, in English samples, there are 6 examples with implicit subjective modality expressions which account for 75%. And the number of

Chinese modal auxiliaries 15 in total number committing to implicit subjective modality adds up to 9 (73.33%) while explicit subjective modality to 1 (6.66%). According to the outcome of the comparison, with one implicit subjective modality, it seems that Chinese advertisements incline to make subjectivity more explicitly than English ones.

②Comparison of the finite modal operators in Chinese and English

As we all know, finite modal operators can be applied to realize implicit subjective orientation. The frequency of this expression in both Chinese and English samples is as follows:

Table 10.8 Finite Modal Operators in English and Chinese Samples

	language	number	frequency
Finite modal operator	Chinese	9	81.82%
	English	5	83.33%

It can be perceived from the table that the expression in English advertisement samples reaches 5 in number and 62.5% in frequency of occurrence, while it adds up to 9% and 60% in Chinese. The data displays that finite modal operators appear a little more frequently in English samples than in Chinese ones. If merely judged from this table, it can be apprehended that English advertisements prefer to make subjective orientation more implicitly.

Not all auxiliaries have access to being applied in the samples. In the selected samples, positive finite modal operators markedly overrun the negative ones. It is clearly presented by the proportions they each take which are demonstrated by the next table.

Table 10.9 Positive Finite Modal Operators in English and Chinese Samples

	positive finite modal operator	frequency
English samples	4	80%
Chinese samples	6	66.66

Table 10.10 Negative Finite Modal Operators in English and Chinese Samples

	negative finite modal operator	frequency
English samples	1	20%
Chinese samples	3	33.34%

Those samples adopt positive deontic finite modal operators such as: *will*, *can*, *should*, "能", "一定要", and "应". For example,

(37) Your skin should glow, not shine! If you have oily skin, our popular Daily

(38) 水润肌肤,谁不想拥有? 强生婴儿润肤油,能在微湿肌肤表面形成锁水保护膜,有效防止水分流失,让你的肌肤拥有如婴儿般的水润娇嫩。

Negative deontic finite modal operators as "won't" "别" "请不要" "勿" are employed in samples. For instance:

(39) The all-in X that won't limit your creativity ability

(40) 球是拍的一部分,拍是手的一部分,鱼翅是鳍的一部分。请不要食用鱼翅——没有买卖,就没有杀害!

Besides the finite modal operator, in selected samples, English ones also adopt comment adjunct which is another device that is taken to be committed to the implicit subjective orientation. Only one example (16.67%) can be provided.

(41) Is your microwave cooking fast? You bet!

Bet here means *certainly*, *surely* or *of course*. While in Chinese samples "请" is employed two times (18.18%) to convey implicit subjective deontic modality.

(42) 保护嗓子,请用金嗓子喉宝。

(43) 胃炎,胃溃疡,请用斯达舒。

Through the above analysis, the conclusion we could get is that English seems to be inclined to make subjective orientation a bit more implicitly than Chinese.

10.4 Summary of the Similarities and the Differences

The analysis above displays that both Chinese and English advertisement samples adopt deontic modality expressions. Chinese samples are richer in deontic modal occurrence than English ones. In the distribution of different modal expressions in advertisement texts, the similarity may lie in the dominant position of modal operators in both Chinese and English samples. The second important position is for imperative sentences and scarcity of comment adjuncts.

Through analysis, we find that despite the approximation of the proportion of modal auxiliaries with low value, the figure illustrates that the frequency of modal auxiliaries with median and high value is greatly different. The occurrence frequency of modal auxiliaries attaching to high value (46.66%) is much higher than that of median value (13.33%) in Chinese, while it is on the contrary in English (median value 50%; high value 14.28%). It indicates that English advertisers incline to apply modal verbs with lower value to avoid committing advertiser themselves to the certainty or the truthfulness of the advertisements.

In terms of modality orientations, the analysis displays that both Chinese and English incline to adopt those implicit subjective oriented deontic modal auxiliaries. Moreover, most of samples in both languages employ finite modal operators to realize implicit subjective orientation (Chinese 81.82%; English 83.33%). Among those finite operators, 80% in English are positive finite modal operators and 20% are negative ones. While in Chinese 66.66% of them are positive finite modal operators and 33.34% are negative ones. Besides the finite modal operators, comment adjunct which is another device that is taken to be committed to the implicit subjective orientation is employed in the samples. In English only one example (16.67) can be provided, while in Chinese two examples (18.18%) are available. In addition, one sample in Chinese applies explicit subjective oriented deontic modality which does not occur in English. All in all, through the contrastive analysis, those data show that English inclined to make subjective orientation a bit more implicitly than Chinese.

10.5 Different Cultural Value System in Deontic Modality in Chinese and English Advertisements

Although the function and the purpose of advertisement are globally the same, in different cultural backgrounds, the ways of expression are distinct. Advertisements in both Chinese and English attempt to clearly convey the information about the products to potential consumers by applying concise, catchy and pleasant language and persuade them to buy the products. However, the ways of using the techniques and strategies of the languages by advertisers are different because language has something to do with certain national cultures

To some degree, advertisements symbolize the national cultures and represent the cultural traditions. People's world views, values, traditions, religious, marketing concepts, advertising policy-making, and ideas about advertising effects etc. are all manifested in advertisements. Every nation forms its own philosophical system during the long process of development and takes the relationships between people and nature as the center of the ideology. The philosophical concepts in Chinese culture and western culture are very different. And the differences are embodied in the choice of words in the English and Chinese advertisements. We only discuss the different cultural value systems including collectivism & individualism, large power distance & small power distance.

10.5.1 Different Cultural Value Systems

A value, formally, is taken as an ending belief meaning the end-state of existence or a specific mode of conduct that is socially or personally preferred to another. According to Rokeach, a value is "a learned organization of rules for making choice and for resolving conflicts" (1973:161). Albert points out that a value system "represents what is expected or hoped for, required or forbidden (1968:32). It is not report of real conduct but is the system of criteria by which conduct is judged and sanctions applied." Therefore, those "rules" tell us what is good, right, useful, and wrong, how to live our lives, and what to strive for.

Everyone has a unique set of individual values, but there are also values called cultural values prone to pervade a culture. Cultural values are derived from the philosophical concepts and transmitted by various sources such as media, school, family, church and so on. The most important is that cultural values guide communication and perception. The awareness and understanding of cultural values enable us to appreciate other people's behaviors and understand our own actions. We will analyze cultural values reflected in advertisements in the following aspects.

10.5.1.1 Collectivism and Individualism

Our analysis will be based on the Hofstede's value dimensions (power distance, individualism, masculinity, uncertainty avoidance, long-term orientation). So firstly, something about these dimensions should be presented. By doing 30 years' quantitative researches, Hofstede develops a comprehensive model of culture. After collecting data from an extensive IBM database for which 116,000 questionnaire were used in 72 countries and in 20 languages, he developed the model. Therefore, the model has been widely applied in categorizing, comparing, contrasting and ordering different cultures and societies.

In his famous "Hofstede Dimensions", Hofstede theorized and explained the difference between collectivism and individualism. As Hofstede defines, collectivism-individualism is the relationship between the collectivity and individual. In individual cultures, people are more *I*-oriented and tend to express their own opinions. Moreover, self-sufficiency, self-actualization and individual accomplishments are what one must strive for and personal decisions are more highly valued than group ones. Individualism culture is low-context culture, because there is more explicit verbal communication in it.

In contrast, collectivistic cultures are more *we*-conscious. People's identity in this culture is based on the social system to which he belongs. Losing or having "face" is the expression adopted by those people who belong to this kind of culture. The group's views, needs and goals are more highly valued than individual ones. Social norms of the group are highly valued over individual pleasure and shared beliefs in group are more important than unique individual ones. According to Hofstede (2001:114), the members in individualism culture are more of:

① a self-orientation

② an emphasis on self and control

③ the pursuit of individual goals that may or may not be consistent with ingroup goals

④ a willingness to confront members of the ingroup to which a person belongs

⑤ a culture where people derive pride from their self being

While those members of collective culture are more of:

① the subordination of personal interest to the goals of the group

② emphasis on sharing, co-operation and group harmony

③ a concern for group welfare

China and western countries differ in this dimension. The western countries are considered to be countries with an individualistic culture. However in China, the interdependent relationship within a collectivity is more important, therefore, it is taken as a country with a collectivistic culture.

10.5.1.2 High Power Distance and Low Power Distance

As Hofstede defined (1980:98), power distance is a dimension to measure cultural attitude about inequality. He also pointed out that power means the capacity which can guide or determine other's behaviour. Moreover, the power distance refers to the extent to which a society can permit and accept unequal distributed power in certain organizations or institutions.

People in high power distance countries such as China, Singapore and Japan believe that hierarchy and inequality is accepted and status, power and authority are important. Members in this culture both consciously or unconsciously are taught that people are unequal and everyone has a right place.

On the contrary, in low power distance culture countries like New Zealand, Austria, Norway and especially America, inequality is minimized. People in these cultures hold the view that a hierarchy is an inequality and they should have access to power. People in power consider their subordinates to be the same kind of people as they are. Leaders and other people in power always attempt to be less powerful than they really are. In the west, egalitarian is advocated as the social convention and the difference between people, groups, and ranks are identified but not emphasized. Every one strives for justice and power equalization.

10.5.1.3 Comparison of These Two Value Dimensions in Deontic Modality in Chinese and English Advertisement

Hofstede (1980) proposed five dimensions of culture, two of which are power distance and individualism-collectivism. It is acknowledged that Hofstede takes them as two distinct dimensions with separate scores for each. Hofstede believes that individualism can be computed for countries while power distance can be computed for not only countries but also organizations. Whereas, he also realizes that these two dimensions are substantially the same and inclined to be correlated. The collectivist countries are more likely be the ones with high power distance, and the individualist countries tent to be the ones with low power distance.

In China, we regard dealing with relationship as the most important principle almost permeating all aspects of the people' life and is the most significant characteristic in the collectivist societies. Obviously, in China, relationship must be predominantly valued. Actually, everyone was placed in a complex and orderly society of hierarchical relationships since he was born. According to Hofstede, collectivistic culture is more likely to be with high power distance. Therefore, the power distance in China is relatively high. The people in China try to build up a harmonious relationship that is based on the fulfillment of the responsibilities and obligations distributed to every member of the society according to his social position.

Hence, in Chinese advertisements, more high value deontic modal auxiliaries are employed. As for the advertised products, advertisers know more than potential consumers and have more authority. By applying high value deontic modal auxiliaries, advertisers express their confidence in the products and make the readers believe the products' properties and qualities.

On the contrary, the English-speaking countries are characterized by individualistic culture (qtd. in Wang Xiaochao & Yang Xi'nan, 2006: 107). In the west, only one principle regulates the interpersonal relationship—individualism. Accordingly, the power distance is low in those countries. People in these countries usually focus on individuals and the relationship between people will never be influenced by power, authority or different status.

All of those are reflected in the English advertisements. Unlike Chinese advertisements, English ones are more likely to apply lower value deontic modal auxiliaries. It is to avoid committing advertiser themselves to the certainty or the truthfulness of the statements. In this way the accuracy of the advertisement can be enhanced. Moreover, as individual's rights are more valued, the English advertisements usually just introduce the properties and advantages of the products to the readers and leave the decision to the potential consumers themselves. Let's refer to example (24): Your skin should glow, not shine! If you have oily skin, our popular Daily Oil Control will help keep your skin balanced so it looks radiant instead of oily.

In this sample, median value deontic modal operator *should* makes the consumers believe the following kind of skin is their dream. And *will* shows a strong probability and indicates a predication. It seemed that what the advertiser states *will* exactly happen in future and the statement he makes is based on his predications or beliefs rather than on his knowledge of "fact". Therefore, using the auxiliary will shows a confidence in the high quality of the product and make the tone cordial and sincere. Moreover, it further makes the potential consumer believe the advertised products will bring those benefits. At the same time, the psychological distance between the reader and the advertisers is shortened and makes a solid foundation for the following purchasing behavior.

In addition, the difference in applying modal orientation also can reflect this kind of cultural difference between Chinese and English speaking countries. As analyzed above, being distinct from Chinese samples, English ones appear to be more implicit in subjectivity orientations without using explicit subjective orientation.

All of these can be attributed to manifest the western countries' emphasis on individualism and the high power distance in China. In the next part, causes of those differences will be discussed.

10.5.2 Motivations of the Differences between Two Cultural Values

The comparison of deontic modality in Chinese and English advertisements from the aspect of cultural values has been made. In order to get a deeper understanding of it, it is necessary for us to analyze what causes the differences between Chinese and western countries' cultural values especially the American one.

10.5.2.1 Historical Factors

As the cultural value system is developed as time goes by, history is reasonably one of the determinant factors.

Chinese culture has developed from agriculture which generations of Chinese lived on and worked for about 5000 years. The collectivism can be explained by the agrarian lifestyle. Although China's reform and opening up in 1978 brought a fantastic change of cultural values, the deep rooted cultural values still exist and influence people's life. Moreover, China has been a central power governed nation. This kind of sovereign makes the country as a collective one and everyone is a part of the mechanism. The sovereign also leads to a hierarchy of power distribution among various groups and classes. Whereas, the history of western countries, especially that of America, cannot be separated from immigration. Therefore, people there are featured by pursuit of freedom, hard work, practicality, improvement, responsibility, equality and individuality. In their opinions, the meaning of lives lies in people's self-fulfillment by hard working. And they believe that the dignity of individual right cannot be deprived. All of these shaped Americans' national personality of individual achievements and independence. The notion of individuality and independence there is so strong that "some Americans believe that there is something wrong with someone who fails to demonstrate individualism" (Samovar 2000:63).

10.5.2.2 Religious Factors

As we all know, religion plays a significant role in every aspect of our life and has a great influence in the formation of one nation's culture value system.

In fact, not so many Chinese people believe in any religion so much as American people do. But the influence of Confucianism on Chinese cannot be ignored. It plays a dominant role in the formation of Chinese social ideology. Confucianism focuses on unity and social harmony instead of individualism and aggressiveness and considers the relationship between human beings as the basis of society which involves such things as the protection of dignity, face, honor, prestige and reputation. Li doctrine ascribed five key relationships known as "五伦" that is "父子有亲,君臣有义,夫妇有别,长幼有序,朋友有信" (relationship between parent and child, ruler and subject, husband and wife, elder sibling and junior sibling, elder friend and junior friend). With parents loving, children reverential; rulers being benevolent, subjects loyal; husbands good, wives obedient; elder siblings gentle, younger sibling respectful; friend faithful, the relationships are inherently hierarchical (Huang Junjie, 2002: 98). Generally, Confucianism cultivates and advocates the consciousness of group, the concept of harmonious interpersonal relationship and the hierarchy of power system.

As we all know, most of the western countries believe in Christianity which advocates everyone is born equally. Additionally, the concept that Christianity discovered the individual could be partially related to individualism which has been discussed in detail in the last section.

10.6 Summary

Adopting Chinese and English advertisements as samples, we have conducted a contrastive study of those samples for finding out how deontic modality is realized to fulfill the function of advertisements. The major findings of present study can be summarized as follows:

Firstly, in the selected samples in both languages, modal auxiliaries and imperative sentences are applied to realize deontic modality. As for the similarities and differences, we analyze them from three aspects including: deontic modality occurrence, deontic modality value and modality orientation. After the contrastive analysis, we can see that Chinese examples adopt more deontic modal expressions than English does. The similarity is that the dominant position of the distribution of different modal expressions is taken by modal operators in both Chinese and English samples.

The second important position is for imperative sentences and scarcity of comment adjuncts.

In terms of the value of the deontic modal auxiliaries occurring in both kinds of samples, the analysis reveals that despite the approximation of the proportion of modal auxiliaries with low value, the frequency of those with median and high value is greatly distinct. Generally, English advertisers incline to apply modal verbs with lower value, while in Chinese ones modal auxiliaries with high value take a larger proportion.

As for modality orientations, the contrastive analysis displays that both Chinese and English examples tend to apply implicit subjective oriented deontic modal auxiliaries. And finite modal operators take the dominant position to realize the orientation. Among those finite operators, in Chinese 66.66% of them are positive finite modal operators and 33.34% are negative ones; while 80% in English are positive finite modal operators and 20% are negative ones. Additionally, one example in Chinese employs explicit subjective oriented deontic modality that is not occurring in English samples. All of those analysis show that English advertisements incline to make subjective orientation a little more implicit than Chinese does.

Secondly, the analysis of different cultural value systems embodied in deontic modality in Chinese and English advertisements provides certain explanations for the divergences discussed above. Through contrastive analysis, we discover that two cultural factors contribute to the differences. The western countries are considered to be countries with an individualistic culture while China is taken as a country with a collectivistic culture. It leads to the relatively high power distance in China and low power distance in western countries.

Thirdly, the explorations of causal factors of the differences between Chinese and western countries' cultural values help us further understand the cross-cultural disparities of deontic modality. The study is from two aspects: historical factors and religious factors. It is found that the collectivism in China can be explained by the agrarian lifestyle adopted in the past. Immigration in the history of western countries, especially in America, made people there are featured by pursuit of freedom, hard work, practicality, improvement, responsibility, equality and individuality. Moreover, Confucianism plays a dominant role in the formation of Chinese social ideology. Confucianism cultivates and advocates the consciousness of group, the concept of harmonious interpersonal relationship and the hierarchy of power system, while Christianity believed by most of the western countries makes the concept individualism rooted in the mind of people there.

Chapter 11 Contrastive Study of Deontic Study in Western and Chinese Political Speeches

11.1 Research Background

The present study attempts to make a contrastive analysis of deontic modality in Chinese and American leaders' speeches at Climate Summit in 2009. As the issue of global warming becomes increasingly serious, people attach unprecedented concern to climate summit. On behalf of developing countries and developed countries, the attitude of China and U. S. has drawn the attention of the whole world. Thus, the contrastive analysis of deontic modality is based on the sample speeches of the leaders of the two countries. Generally speaking, politicians do not deliver speeches as individuals, but as representatives of political parties, governments, or nations in political speech. In those circumstances, they are limited as political actors as to proper speech context and way of delivering. Political speech is characterized as a hybrid genre of epideictic address, a genre that combines the goal of reaching persuasion with the offer of verbal means that is used to establish consensus regarding norms and values in society. Any political speech prepares for a larger, more extensive communicative process, and it can be characterized as strategic move in a principle communicative plan.

On climate summit, leaders of different countries are supposed to manifest their efforts and clarify their substantive commitments. Occasions like these no doubt provide a wider platform for the study of deontic modality. However, as leaders of different countries, they are endowed with two different identities: a positive advocator before the mass media as well as a bargainer for the interests of his country. Therefore, the observation of deontic modality becomes more challenging. Nevertheless, their attitudes, stances and ideologies all manipulate deontic modality to achieve the desired construction of interpersonal meaning. And vice versa, by observing interpersonal meaning of deontic modality, we can also find the attitudes, stances and ideologies of the leaders of the two countries.

The study of modality has been broadened to a great degree since it has been discussed under the framework of interpersonal meaning in recent years. The focus is shifted from modal auxiliary words to modal meanings at discourse level, and the corpus is not merely limited to English. Nuyts (2001) analyzes epistemic modality of Dutch and German in the framework of cognitive-pragmatics. Papafragou (2003) constructs his own frame: semantic-pragmatic by referring relevant theory. He discusses the four modal verbs: *can*, *may*, *must*, *should*, with a probe into the comprehension of pragmatic system by grammatical operation. Facchinetti (2003) elaborates modal meanings of modern English which include the semantic and pragmatic features of main modal verbs, newly emerged modal expressions, stylistic variants of modality and sociolinguistics.

Domestic researchers further make researches on English modality on the basis of foreign results. Meanwhile, they apply those theories in the studies of Chinese and foreign language teaching. Liang Xiaobo (2001) conducts a detailed research on the emergence and evolvement of modality from the perspective of cognition. Others like Peng Xuanwei (2000) compare mood and modality of Chinese with those of English. Li Zhanzi (2002) studies the realization of interpersonal meaning in academic discourses and autobiographies by widening Halliday's conceptual framework. In 2005, she makes a survey of the discussions by Martin and Lemke on appraisal types and constructs the continuum from mood, modality to appraisal, and she emphasizes the significance of the angle of continuum in semantics and discourse analysis.

Retrospecting the results by foreign and domestic researchers about modality, the author finds that though they have broadened the scope of modality to a considerable agree, the branches remain yet to be perfected. In other words, we need to continue the research modality from more subtle perspectives. "Deontic modality" proposed by Thompson (2000:60), which is the very essence of modality, is a worthy problem to study in such a complicated modern world since it shows the extent to which the speaker openly accepts responsibility for the subjective assessments being expressed. It has important implications in a number of different corpus analyses. Thompson exemplifies that "in an academic paper, a writer has to judge very carefully the extent to which s/he advances a claim as certain or as still open to doubt; while in giving advice a speaker has to judge very carefully to the extent to which s/he appears to putting pressure on the other people" (Thompson, 2000:60). It might also serve as a common technique for them to disguise the source of responsibility to a greater or less extent, or amplify it to influence people according to different discourses or ideologies. In recent years, deontic modality has been mentioned in some works and journals but with few going further. Li Zhanzi (2002) implicates that there are cultural differences in the embodiment of deontic modality by analyzing some household product instructions. Li Jie (2005) points out that deontic modality is a fascinating problem to explore because writers and speakers may resort to various methods of masking their viewpoint in an apparently objective way, for a number of reasons. Zhang Man studies the configuration of modal commitment and responsibility in abstracts, analyzing modal commitment and responsibility realized by modal elements in the corpus statistically. Others mainly discuss deontic modality together with the term of *hedges*, which often appears in news English. However, people place too much stress on the aspect of disguising the source of responsibility, neglecting the fact that deontic modality is a cline which needs to be studied more completely. Besides, the text to which deontic modality is applied is not just limited to one genre.

As a parameter of the value of modality, the study of deontic modality shouldn't have suffered such stagnation. Hu Zhuanglin (2000:7) holds that the development of any discipline is a process of innovating, debating and incorporating of different theories and school. Inspired by Li Zhanzi whose work is devoted to interpersonal meaning of epistemic modality in autobiographical discourse, the study of deontic modality bears more similarities to deontic modality. And its flexibility enables it to adapt into more practical discourses. This paper aims to make contrastive analysis of deontic modality in Chinese and American political speeches by integrating Halliday's Systemic Approach and Martin's Appraisal Theory. Different values and ideologies will also be explored to make the analysis more complete.

11.2 Research Questions

With the purpose demonstrated above, in this thesis, the author attempts to explore the following questions:

①What are the salient linguistic characteristics for expressing deontic modality in Chinese and American political speeches on climate change?

②In what way is interpersonal meaning of deontic modality in Chinese political speeches similar to or different from that of English political speeches?

③What kind of values and ideologies are encoded in the two cultures through their application of deontic modality?

11.3 Data Collection

After explaining research significance and research questions, we will give an introduction to samples obtained in this book. In the following part, the validity of the samples will be discussed.

This part takes the speeches by Chinese President Hu Jintao, Prime Minister Wen Jiabao and U. S. President Obama as samples. All the four sample transcripts are obtained on the theme of climate change based on the United Nations Framework Convention on Climate Change (UNFCCC). The samples are collected for comparative analysis in which Chinese and English speeches each occupy half. The Chinese transcripts are downloaded from official website of Foreign Ministry of China. The English transcripts are downloaded from the official website of White House. The selected four speeches are all delivered in 2009. Therefore, they are the latest ones. In addition, it is in 2009 when Obama takes the office American attitude towards climate change tends to be positive than previous U. S. presidents. The arrangement here is to ensure the comparability between speech samples from different cultures, in other words, speech samples to be compared should be subject to similar situation, that is, similar discourse participants, similar places, similar genre, similar field and mode. The following table will demonstrate the transcripts collected in detail.

Table 11.1 Speeches by Chinese and American Leaders Collected for Comparative Analysis

speech / theme	Chinese speeches	American speeches
political speech on climate change	胡锦涛在联合国气候变化峰会开幕式上的讲话(C1)	Remarks by President Obama at United Nations Secretary General Ban Ki-moon's Climate Change Summit (A1)
	温家宝在哥本哈根气候变化会议领导人会议上的讲话(C2)	Remarks by President Obama at the Morning Plenary Session of the United Nations Climate Change Conference (A2)

(C1 = Chinese speech transcript released in September 22, 2009; C2 = Chinese speech transcript released in December 18, 2009; A1 = American speech transcript released in September 22, 2009; A2 = American speech transcript released in December 18, 2009)

11.3.1 Contrastive Analysis on Deontic Modality at Halliday's Systemic Functional Level

In this section, a contrastive analysis of deontic modality in Chinese and American political speeches will be carried out based on the analytical framework in detail. Through such a detailed analysis, we aim to exploit the similarities and differences of the realization of deontic modality in the two types of speech transcripts at Halliday's grammatical level. Furthermore, to dig out the values and ideologies behind the linguistic manipulation remains our concern.

11.3.1.1 Deontic Modality Embodied by Mood

1. Mood Structures: Syntactical Presentation for Deontic Modality

The following analysis is a contrast of the specific mood structures applied in Chinese and American political speeches. Firstly, we need to identify the specific speech roles carried out by the speaker/writer before coming to explore the specific mood structures employed in political speech.

Speech roles are originally discussed in tenor of commercial advertising texts—a kind of tenor in which the advertiser/writer informs the potential consumer/readers of the characteristics of the product or service advertised and tries to persuade the potential consumers/readers to buy the product or service (Halliday, 2000:69). While in the tenor of political speech we are concerned, instead of giving information of products or services and demanding actions of buying products or services, the speakers provide the information of climate change and demand actions of doing something for that situation. In this perspective, the speech roles of this political tenor resemble the functions in commercial ads. In the following subsection, we will explore how the leaders interact with the listeners by the choices of mood structures in Chinese and American transcripts.

A. Information Giving

According to the theoretical framework we discussed in the last chapter, the most typical realization of the speech role of giving information is by use of declarative mood structure.

(A) Declarative

In political speech, especially for leaders who have double roles—an inexplicit politician and a confident one, declaratives are the most commonly used mood structure for them to give the appropriate information and thus realize their interpersonal meaning of deontic modality. Declaratives in abundance can be found in our transcripts. For example,

(1) Most importantly, the House of Representatives passed an energy and climate bill in June that would finally make clean energy the profitable kind of energy for American business and dramatically reduce greenhouse gas emissions.

(2) That's why we've taken bold action at home—by making historic investments in renewable energy; by...

(3)中国已经制定和实施了《应对气候变化国家方案》,明确提出2005年到2010年降低单位国内生产总值能耗和主要污染排放……

(4)发展中国家应该根据本国国情,在发达国家资金和技术转让支持下,努力适应气候变化,尽可能减缓温室气体排放。

Such kinds of declaratives are in abundance in the sample transcripts. Relevant information about the climate situation and their endeavor is conveyed by those declarative clauses. Example (1) and example (3) tell that the bills have been passed by the two countries to express their concern about the issue. Example (2) and example (4) further specify measures that will be taken according to the situation of their countries. Through such declarative clauses, the audience is informed of the speaker's basic attitude about the issue by the information they provide.

(B) Imperative

Along with declarative mood structure, some of imperatives in our transcripts, especially in Chinese transcripts, aim to give information rather than demand someone to take action. Surprisingly, we find few such cases in American transcripts on that situation. Examples in Chinese transcripts are given below:

(5) 加强节能、提高能效工作……大力发展可再生能源和核能……

大力增加森林碳汇……大力发展绿色经济……(C1)

(6) 深入推进循环经济试点,大力推广节能环保汽车,实施节能产品工……(C2)

All those clauses have imperative functions. They are often used for requesting actions; however, their functions go beyond that on this situation. Examples (5) and (6) are actually giving information about measures that Chinese governmentovertly commits to taking. Palmernotes that imperative closely associated with deontic modals—deontic modality of a high degree (80). In this perspective, Chinese political speeches seem not to be in line with its traditional national character—a kind of culture has long been characterized as indirect and implicit. Similarly, we can find another case in Chinese classical literature:

(7)三人焚香再拜而说誓曰:"念刘备、关羽、张飞,虽然异姓,既结为兄弟,则同心协力,就困扶危,上报国家,下安黎庶,不求同年同月生,但愿同年同月死,皇天后土,实鉴此心,背义忘恩,天人共戮(qtd. in Hu Zhuanglin, 1985:190)。

The example above abstracts from *Three Heroes Swear Brotherhood in the Peach Garden*. Bearing the same ambition of reglorifying Han Dynasty, the three brothers commit themselves to the promise that they would never betray. Chinese culture gives priory to morality and justice. When it comes to responsibility, the utterances tend to be direct, coherent and avoiding obscurity which can be seen in example (7). In this perspective, deontic modality in Chinese political speeches enjoys representability of a high degree through this mood structure. Therefore, it possesses more powerful functions to appeal to others.

B. Action Demanding

With the theme of climate change in mind, the ultimate goal of political speech is to persuade the other countries to take emission action including the speaker himself. This kind of action demanding is often achieved by imperatives or declaratives.

(A) Imperative

According to systemic functional grammar, imperative mood structure is the typical way to demand actions from the listeners. And we found such clauses which are used to demand actions in both Chinese and American sample transcripts:

(8) So let us begin (A1).

(9)应该建立政府主导、企业参与、市场运作的良性互动机制,让发展中国家用得上气候友好技术(C1)。

(10)必须始终牢牢把握以下几点……

The imperatives above are employed to urge the audience to take emission action. They all present an explicitly subjective attitude, whereas Chinese deontic modality conveys tougher interpersonal meanings than that of American. Moreover, although imperative is the most direct way to help political speakers to achieve the ultimate goal, it is found that imperative clauses are seldom used in American speech samples. The reason of it may be illustrated as the following aspects: Firstly, the ideology of the two countries differs. In American public discourse, the relationship between the speaker and the audience is symmetrical solidarity because Americans have been long influenced by Enlightment philosophy: "liberty, egalitarian and fraternity" (Ron Scollon, 2000: 114). From speeches with political leaders, they try to eliminate any suggestions of hierarchy in any interpersonal or social relationships. There is a reinforced emphasis on "avoiding elaboration and extravagance, on popular appeal and commonness, and on promoting close, egalitarian social relationship" (Ron Scollon, 2000: 115). Political speakers are expected to be considered as one of us in their public communication. Chinese people are influenced by concept of hierarchical Confucian relationships. They are quite conscious in any interaction who is older and who is young, who has a higher level of education, who has a lower level, or who is a teacher and who is a student. The use of imperative enhances the sense of dominance as a passionate political speaker as well as an advocator. By those imperatives, deontic modality of a high scale is fully realized. Secondly, speakers' willingness to assume responsibility of gas emission differs. In other words, interpersonal meaning of deontic modality conveys the degree to which they would make substantive commitment publicly. By analyzing interpersonal meaning of deontic modality, it is not difficult to observe their real stance encoded in speech.

(B) Declarative

Declarative clauses are also used to realize the speech function of demandingaction. And its effect of appeal bears more interpersonal meaning. Here are some examples in point:

(11) Unease is no excuse for inaction (A1).

(12) In 2002, I announce our first step... (A1)

（13）应对这一挑战，需要国际社会同舟共济、齐心协力（C1）。

（14）世界期待着我们就事关人类生存和发展的气候变化问题做出选择（C1）。

The declaratives above function as imperatives to demand actions from the audience, meanwhile, they soften the speakers' tone and make the audience feel less pushed to take action. Example (11) and (13) convey the fact that the journey ahead of us is hard. The application of deontic modality, and be it implicit or explicit, creates an inviting tone to appeal countries and people that are concerned to support and participate. In example (12), American leader is showing his endeavor by declaring an official announcement for steps. Example (14) the word "期待" (look forward) is asking for positive choices of the countries and people who are concerned. Those declaratives convey deontic modality with lower intensity compared with that of imperatives.

(C) Exclamative

A small number of Chinese exclamative clauses is employed in our Chinese transcripts. While in American sample transcripts, exclamatives are even more scarcely distributed. Some of exclamatives in Chinese transcripts are placed at the beginning or in the middle to retain the audience's attention. Others appear in the end of the speech to show strong emotional response to something. Examples below are found in Chinese sample transcripts:

（15）各位同事！

（16）中国愿同各国携手努力，共同为子孙后代创造更加美好的未来！

The examples above highlight Chinese leader's deontic modality toward the mission. Example (15) can be seen as an elliptical exclamative clause which appears in the body of the transcripts for several times. It is used to retain the audience's attention and give people a sense of mission. Clauses like Example (16) are placed at the end of the transcripts. They are employed to evoke the audience to make their effort to ameliorate the deteriorated conditions of climate.

C. "Dialogue" in Political Speech

Political speech is an art. A successful speech on this occasion lies in whether it can impress the audience with their art, which could be different in culture. In our samples, the Chinese leader tends to impress the audience with the seriousness by conveying deontic modality of a high scale. He uses bunches of imperative mood and declarative mood to express strong emotional response, hence creating a monologic sense. As for their American counterparts who are influenced by western rhetoric art, the core of American leaders' oral rhetoric is the control of its audiences' beliefs for political purpose, during that process languages are used to engage audiences in an exchange of symbols to accomplish political goals. They tend to create an atmosphere of dialogue between the audience and themselves to achieve a back and forth communications. Even in this serious style, we can still find such examples:

(17) ... for if we fail to meet it—boldly, swiftly, and together—we risk consigning future generations to an irreversible catastrophe.

(18) Yes, the developed nations that caused much of the damage to our climate over the last century still have a responsibility to lead...

(19) That's why we've renewed our leadership within international climate change negotiations. That's why...

(20) What we are seeking, after all, is not... We seek...

By those clauses, the American political speaker projects a corresponding role to the audience which may expect them to participate. They tend to weaken the scale of their deontic modality to represent multiple interpersonal meaning: a confident and vague politician. For example (17), the speaker asserts a catastrophe instead of compelling the people to implement certain policy. To meet that catastrophe or to live at ease depends on your choice. Example (18) and (19) unveil the assessment of the American leader by making an assumed interlocutor. Similarly devious method can be seen in example (20), during the process of which deontic modality of a low scale is expressed.

So far, we have discussed two speech roles realized by mood structures in the Chinese political speech and the American political speech. What we are going to do next is to present a distribution of the mood structures including declarative, imperative, interrogative and exclamative in Chinese and American political speech on the climate change. The distribution is illustrated by the table below:

Table 11.2 Distribution of Mood Structures in Chinese and American Leaders' Speeches

political speech / mood structures	Chinese speeches		American speeches	
	occurrence	percentage	occurrence	percentage
declaratives	96	86.4%	139	99.3%
imperatives	11	10.0%	1	0.7%
exclamatives	4	3.6%	0	0%
interrogatives	0	0%	0	0%
total	111	100%	140	100%

Table 11.2 illustrates that Chinese leader's speeches share a similarity with their American counterparts in terms of the use of declarative mood structures. In political speech on such an occasion, the majority of sentences are declaratives, taking up 86.4% in Chinese political speeches and 99.3% in American political speeches respectively. By contrast, no interrogatives occur in the two countries' speech samples as this kind of mood structure involves indecisive elements of deontic modality which seems to be not in line with political speech associated with obligation. In Chinese speeches, imperatives enjoy the second highest frequency, with 11 imperatives employed, covering 10.0%. While in American speeches, imperatives only take up 0.7%. As the typical mood structure embodied deontic modality, imperatives are favored by Chinese leaders on political occasion because they help the speaker express their deontic modality to a higher degree by avoiding obscurity. And for the similar purpose, exclamatives are used in Chinese speeches, covering 3.6%, whereas no such structures are employed by their American counterparts.

2. Subject Alternatives as to Manipulate Deontic Modality

Halliday's mood system mainly consists of two parts: subject and finite element. The subject is the proposition/proposal to be addressed, which often appears as noun. The subject carries a heavy semantic load concerning with the proposition/proposal as it is the benchmark of affirming or denying a proposition/proposal. Besides, it is an element which is responsible for availability of the proposition/proposal. In this perspective, when a speaker chooses an element as subject, he/she endows it with certain deontic modality (Miao Xingwei, 2004: 6). Look at example (14) again, there is a skillful arrangement for the subject of this sentence. "世界" is quite an abstract word which cannot have the feeling of humans. Here, the Chinese leader is actually conveying his expectation, during the process of which the subject weakens his own deontic modality.

The concern of subject also deals with the actor and goal that we often discuss in passive structures. Jesperson (1933) makes a comprehensive generalization about the use of passive structure. He holds that it is mainly used in the following five circumstances: ① The actor is not known or not easy to point out. ②The actor is obvious according to the context. ③ The actor could not be pointed out for special reasons. ④ More concern is attached upon the subject (the goal) in the passive voice than the subject (the actor) in the active voice. ⑤For the purpose of syntactical cohesion. In those five circumstances, we focus on the third and fourth point because they involve the speaker's attitude and intention of different degrees, hence possessing certain interpersonal meaning. Let's look at the following examples:

(21) On shrinking islands, families are already being forced to flee their homes as climate refugees.

In the example above, we can find that the American leader attempts to present a fact, and make his utterance more objective. By making "families" as subject, he attaches more concern upon humans. Consequently, the audiences feel the necessity to do something for climate change by their own deontic sense rather than through the speaker's advocacy. This passive structure possesses implicitly objective feature which estranges the speaker from his/her assessment. Hence, it helps the speaker detach from his deontic modality. While in Chinese sample transcripts, such passive structures are rarely found.

In this section, we attempt to find out linguistic characteristics of deontic modality in Chinese and American political speeches in terms of mood structures. We firstly brief the functions of the speech roles in political speech, i. e. giving information and demanding actions, and then we analyze how deontic modality is realized in terms of those two roles. Leaders of the two countries bear resemblance in the use of declarative mood and interrogative mood. Both the Chinese and American speech transcripts employ declarative mood in abundance to address the issue of climate change, with no occurrence of interrogative mood. As to the differences between the two kinds of speeches, firstly, Chinese leaders are more inclined to use imperatives and exclamatives to clarify his stance. In this way, deontic modality reaches a high degree, thus possessing more power to appeal and evoke people's awareness. Secondly, the American leader uses "dialogue" and passive structures in his speeches, which rarely appear in Chinese speech transcripts.

Those differences are partly from ideological influences. The origin of the Chinese pattern of thought should be traced back to Confucianism, which was more concerned about politics, morals and rules in the realistic society. Correspondingly, they have been used to putting themselves into the whole society and proposing responsibility and devotion to the whole society. On such political occasion, the deontic sense impels the Chinese leader to be formal and determined, clearing his deontic modality with interpersonal meaning beyond Chinese stereotype of being indirect. By contrast, American values advocate free and individual choice. They diversify their speeches with "dialogue" and passive patterns. Rather than demanding by imperatives, by the approach of reasoning, weakened deontic modality enables them to let the audience weigh the issue by themselves. However, its potential disadvantage is that whether the American leader has addressed the seriousness of the issue to a profound degree and whether the audience could hear their substantive commitment towards the issue. In addition, Chinese language belongs to a high-context culture in which people might understand the discourse according to the context. Hence in many cases the subjects are omitted, which contributes to the larger number of imperatives.

11.3.4.2 Deontic Modality and Main Elements of Modality

In Thompson's framework (2000), deontic modality is conceptualized on the basis of the types, values and orientation of modality combined. Considering that the values of modality are often embodied by modal operators, we will make a contrast of modality in Chinese and American sample speeches mainly in terms of modal operators and orientations, aiming to find out how the deontic modality helps realize interpersonal meaning in transcripts of the two countries in this aspect.

1. Modal Operators as Tools to Adjust Deontic Modality

Modal operators are important aspects among various resources of expressing deontic modality to realize interpersonal meaning. Halliday identifies different modal operators with different values based on the degree the speaker overtly accept his/her subjective assessment. The more certain a modal expression is, the more heightened its deontic modality conveys. According to the theoretical framework we discuss in section 3, Halliday attributes three values to modal operators: low, median and high. What follows next is an analysis of how each value in deontic modality realizes the desired interpersonal meaning.

A. Low Value Modal Operators

The use of low value modal operator signifies a low degree of certainty about the validity of a proposition/proposal, thus a weakened deontic modality will take on. In our American sample transcripts, low value modal operator "can" is the most frequently employed by American leaders, which can be seen in the following examples:

(22) No nation, however large or small, wealthy or poor, *can* escape the impact of climate change.

(23) We *can* embrace this accord, take a substantial step forward...

(24) Or we *can* choose delay...

(25) And yet, we *can* reverse it.

In our American sample transcripts, the modal operator *can* indicates ability and possibility, which associates with epistemic modality and deontic modality. In fact, it is difficult to identify whether the modal operator *can* in the examples is epistemic or deontic or both. However, it helps us to find out the speaker's deontic modality. In example (22), the speaker uses *can* to make a judgment on what scale climate change would inflict impact to the world. If no measures were taken, there will be no exceptions. Therefore, here *can* indicates both ability and possibility. The same thing happens in example (23) and (24), here *can* involves ability, possibility and weak necessity. In example (25), *can* only indicates ability. All these modal operators involve the inclination and attitude of the political speakers. Therefore, they embody the speakers' deontic modality to some degree. Except for *can*, low value modal operators such as *might*, *could*, *would* and *may* are also used to estrange the speaker from his assessment, conveying low commitment to the proposition. The examples in American samples can be seen below:

(26) Our problems are man-made; therefore they *may* be solved by man.

(27) These measures *need not* be intrusive, or infringe upon sovereignty.

In example (26), the American leader tells a potential possibility for the solution to climate change by using the low value modal operator *may*. The sentence bears great resemblance to a Chinese old saying "jie ling haixu xi ling ren". However, it shows a slightly different opinion by using modal operator "xu" (have to), thus bearing more explicit deontic modality than its American equivalent. In example (27), American leader makes assessment on the quality of the common mechanism where the measures are negotiated. Through low-valued deontic modality, the speaker weakens the force of assertion and shows his politeness to the audience.

By contrast, just a few low value modal verbs were found in our Chinese sample transcripts.

(28)哥本哈根大会就会成为国际社会合作应对气候变化新的里程碑。

"会" shares the semantic meaning of *can* in English and they perform as low value modal operators. In the example above, it indicates the ability and possibility of the effectiveness of an international summit. Chinese political speaker shows implicitly subjective deontic modality by using of those low value operators.

B. Median Value Modal Operators

Median value modal operators convey deontic modality of a median degree. In American sample transcripts, they are mainly presented as *will*, *would*, *should*. In Chinese transcripts, they appear with the form such as "愿", "将", "会", "值得". "will" and "将" can be conceptualized as modalization, conveying implicitly subjective deontic modality which is higher than "might" with the speaker's assessment on how likely something will happen.

(29)... and everyone who is in this room *will* be part of a historic endeavor...

(30) And we *will* continue doing so.

(31)我们*将*进一步完善国内统计、监测、考核办法……

(32)中国*愿*同各国携手努力,共同为子孙后代创造更加美好的未来!

"Will" in example (29) shows a strong possibility and manifests a prediction. The American speaker makes his statement based on his beliefs, predications or intentions, rather than on his knowledge of "fact". By using the predictive *will*, the speaker shows a relatively strong confidence in his subjective assessment. More often than not, *will* and its Chinese equivalent "将" in our samples are used to express promissive attitude and willingness of the speaker. The last three examples above are good cases in point. In those three examples, median modal operators *will*, "将", and "愿" follow the subjects that are willing to offer services, conveying relatively strong inclination to take actions. By employing these operators, the speaker is affirming his deontic modality. The tone becomes sincere and cordial, hence improving the efficiency of communication on such universal occasion.

C. High Value Modal Operators

High value modal operators indicate addresser's subjectively explicit deontic modality which would create an absolute and pushy tone to the addressees. The strong interpersonal meaning embodied by deontic modality makes high value modal operators a necessity on such serious occasion. We can find a number of examples in Chinese and American sample transcripts.

(33) We also *cannot* allow the old divisions that have characterized the climate debate for so many years to block our progress (A1).

(34) We *must* have a mechanism to review whether we are keeping our commitments... (A2)

(35)*不能*要求发展中国家承担超越发展阶段、应负责任、实际能力的义务(C1)!

(36) 国际社会*应该*重视发展中国家特别是小岛屿国家(C1)!

Previously, we present the classifications of English and Chinese modal operators. According to Halliday (2000), the italic modal operators above are high value modal operators. They are used to manifest deontic modality of a high degree which evokes deontic sense and some beliefs shared by the majority of people. In example (33), the American leader shows his subjective certainty for the significance of coming to agreement on the issue. In example (34), "must" expresses the necessity to have a common mechanism to keep the commitment. In example (35) and (36), the Chinese leader firmly advocates to differentiate responsibility that developing countries should assume and the recognition of that concept could be skillfully achieved by employing high valued modal operators which have easy access to people's deontic morality.

The analysis above has roughly covered the three value modal operators in our sample transcripts. Next, we will summarize their distributions in the following table.

Table 11.3 Distribution of Modal Operators in Chinese and American Leaders' Speeches

speech / values	Chinese leaders' speeches			American leader's speeches		
	modal operators	occurrence	percentage	modal operators	occurrence	percentage
low	会	1	3.8%	can	15	30.3%
	可以	1		may	2	
				have to	5	
				need not	1	
median	将	5	11.6%	will	29	48.7%
	愿	1		would	29	
high	(需)要	9	84.6%	must	11	21.0%
	(必)须	11		can't	3	
	应(该)	20		need	2	
	不(可)能	4				
total		52	100%		76	100%

According to the distribution of modal operators in Chinese and American samples presented above, we can see modal operators are important tools to express their deontic modality, because the leaders of the two countries tend to use them a lot. However, it seems that modal operators occur more frequently in American speeches than in Chinese ones in general. In addition, there are disparities in the distribution of values. Firstly, low value modal operators employed in Chinese speeches are so scarcely distributed compared with those in American speeches, with the percentages of 3.8% and 30.3%. Secondly, in Chinese speeches, high value modal operators predominate the others with 84.6%, while American speeches give priority to median value operators, covering 48.7%, in which "will" predominates the others.

2. Different Effects of Deontic Modality Achieved by Two Orientations

Except for modal verbs, modal meanings can also be expressed in the form of projections (*I think/believe, I'm sure...*) or propositions (*it is possible/ (un) likely/certain...*). The former highlights the speaker's deontic modality to a proposal/proposition, that is, making the statement more subjective; the latter masks the speaker's deontic modality to a proposal/proposition, and making the statement more objective. (Yang Caiying, 2006:3)

The subjectivity in Chinese speeches can be found through high frequency occurrence of high value modal operators, while it is not easy to be detected in the use of modal clause. By contrast, orientation embodied by modal clause in American speeches is quite obvious. For example:

(37) *It is true that* for too many years, mankind has been slow to respond or even recognize the magnitude of the climate threat. *It is true of* my country, as well. *We recognize it.*

The demonstration of Obama above explains the attitude of mankind toward the issue of climate change. He begins with explicitly objective orientation—*it's true* to present audience an indisputable fact that mankind has made a universal mistake. The repetition of that modal projection functions as a prelude to his explicit subjective statement—I *recognize it* (I think America makes this mistake, too). We can see that those objective modal clauses function to leave space for speaker's statements and the appropriate configuration of deontic modality is an important method for mitigating effect. The cohesion of weak and strong deontic modality wins the understanding of the audience, thus the expected interpersonal meaning is achieved. Other modal projections can be seen in the examples below:

(38) All of you would not be here unless you—like me—*were convinced* that this danger is real.

(39) *I believe that* the pieces of that accord *should* now be clear(A2).

Example (38) is a typical implicitly objective structure to weaken deontic modality. It emphasizes that it is not "me" to impel you to believe something, but objective facts make you feel so. In example (39), Obama is making his deontic modality apparent through explicit subjective orientation.

In this section, we discuss deontic modality in Chinese and American political speeches from the view of modality which includes modal operators and orientations. Through the analysis of modal operators, we find similarities and differences between these two types of political speeches. In terms of similarity, both of them employ a wealth of modal operators to manipulate their deontic modality. As for differences, Chinese leaders tend to use modal operators with high values while the American leader prefers those with median values. In addition, the property of language enables English speaker to use modal projections to enrich means of expressing his deontic modality. In general, American leaders seem less subjective than their Chinese counterparts. The reason of it can be explained in the following aspects: Firstly, it associates with historical connexion. America is influenced by Cartesian Rationalism (Lyons, 1997: 336-339), which can account for the pejorative associations of the term "subjective". "Subjective" in the empiricist tradition was associated with a certain kind of unscientific and untestable mentalism; and "objectivity", with a sturdy nineteenth-century scientific materialism. For historical and ultimate social reasons, the English language is less imbued with subjectivity than others. Secondly, attitudinal involvement counts. Whether an economic power would slow her economic development out of environmental concern is still in question. Chinese culture attaches great importance to deontic morality. On such an urgent occasion, its national character of tenacity will be found. Besides, With China's increasing influence upon the world, resorting to deontic modality of a high degree is undoubtedly a natural and undisguised way to manifest Chinese leaders' stance.

11.3.4.3 Deontic Modality Based on Deixis Switch

Halliday (2000) holds that interpersonal meanings are embodied in the person system, both as pronoun (person as *thing*, e. g. *she*, *you*) and as possessive (person as deictic, e. g. *her*, *your*) (2000: 191). Li Zhanzi indicates that the switch of deixis draws the addressees' attention to different aspects (2002: 173). The speaker lowers down the release of addressing contents through deixis switch, conveying the implied assessment. Next we will take a look at the excerpt when the leaders of the two countries address the principle of common but differentiated responses and respective capabilities.

(40) But *those* rapidly growing *developing nations* that will produce nearly all the growth in global carbon emissions in the decades ahead must do *their* part, as well. Some of *these* nations have already made great strides with the development and deployment of clean energy. Still, *they* need to commit to strong measures at home and agree to stand behind *those* commitments just as the *developed nations* must stand behind *their* own. *We* cannot meet this challenge unless *all the largest emitters* of greenhouse gas pollution act together.

In the excerpt above, the virtual objects to describe are mainly developing nations and developed ones. However, they are endowed with different modal meanings. The American leader Obama tactically employs a variety of deixis to make information unfolded according to certain deontic modality. Deixis like "those", "their" and "they" are showing a hint of impersonality. The beginning of this excerpt expresses the speaker's assessment about the responsibility that developing nations should account for in a subjective explicit way. Personal reference "these" comes on top of the first sentence to weaken the tone based on the affirmation of contributions some developing nations have done for climate change. What follows next again is a series of impersonal deixis to reiterate his point of respective responsibilities. In addition, the use of impersonal deixis—"those" commitments, implicates the low degree of American leader's advocacy. In Obama's speeches, the switch of deixis assists the configuration of deontic modality which presents us as a fluctuated line. Through observing modal meanings achieved by deixis switch, we can find that the excerpt tends to express the interpersonal meanings that "they" (the developing nations) are modally responsible. However, in the excerpt of Chinese leader's speeches, the embodiment of deontic modality is quite crystal.

(41)*发达国家* 和*发展中国家* 都应该积极采取行动应对气候变化。根据《联合国气候变化框架公约》及其《京都议定书》的要求,积极落实"巴厘路线图"谈判。*发达国家* 应该完成《京都议定书》确定的减排任务,继续承担中期大幅量化减排指标,并为*发展中国家* 应对气候变化提供支持。*发展中国家* 应该根据本国国情,在*发达国家* 资金和技术转让支持下,努力适应气候变化,尽可能减缓温室气体排放。

Compared with his American counterpart, the Chinese leader displays preference for proper nouns like "中国", "发达国家", "发展中国家". Deixis appears in Chinese speeches tend to be simple and straightforward, which are far less circuitous than Obama's speeches achieved by deixis switch. The coherent impersonality helps him clear his deontic modality. And the excerpt above is conveying the information that the developed and developing countries are both modally responsible.

It is acceptable to attribute those differences to different ideologies. American people are influenced by Utilitarianism (Ron Scollon 2000:102), a concept coined by Bentham. It grows out of the Enlightment. One of the central principles is that progress (toward greater happiness, wealth, and individuality) is the goal of society (Ron Scollon, 2000:104). That may account for why successive American presidents take a negative attitude toward mitigation commitment. Though Obama's attitude takes a favorable turn towards this issue, we can see the economic power's reluctance of being a virtually generous model. As we know, mitigation action has an impact on the economic development of a country, and it is not in accordance with the concept of Utilitarianism. By contrast, as the mainstream of traditional Chinese culture, Confucianism has profound connotation of the human spirit, in which the view of humane, justice, responsibility, and integrity has great influence on people's life. Such ideology has been used in all aspects of modern society. On such an occasion concerning to the benefit of the whole world, it is obvious that the spirit of collectivism gets more emphasis in Chinese leaders' speeches than that of their American counterpart.

11.3.5 A Broadened Understanding on Deontic Modality at Appraisal Theoretic Level

In the 2004 version of *Introduction to Functional Grammar*, Halliday goes beyond the former modality system and puts forward a new system called "Modal Assessment" (2000:608-612). That indicates that Halliday has concerned about the Appraisal Theory and intended to bring it into the previous Systemic Functional Framework. Therefore, after the discussion about deontic modality in Chinese and American political speeches at Halliday's Systemic Functional Level, we will continue to make analysis at Appraisal Theoretic Level. The focus is mainly fixed on engagement and graduation due to the following reasons. Firstly, the two sub-types we present here are mainly concerned with potential effects with respect to putative audience construal, alignment and sodality (Martin, 2005: 97). Secondly, the resources of attitude are inherently gradable, graduation has to do with adjusting the degree of an evaluation—how strong and weak the feeling is (Martin, 2005: 37). Therefore, the analysis of deontic modality in terms of attitude can be incorporated into the graduation system. The two systems—engagement and graduation can provide us a broader view to further analyze deontic modality within our speech samples.

11.3.5.1 Construction of Deontic Modality with Engagement System

Engagement is concerned with the linguistic resources by which speakers/writers adopt a stance towards the value positions being referenced by the text and with respect to those they address. The vital choice in the system of engagement is between what might be termed monoglossic option and the network of responsibility by the possibility of social heterogeneity inscribed in the text (Martin, 2005: 92). In the context of political speech, it is common that there are a great number of bare assertions to present factual information about their devotion to mitigation action. Nevertheless, heteglossia and dialogism have its delicate influence upon deontic modality. Next we will take a close look at the two subtypes that obviously appear in our sample speeches—Contraction and Expansion.

1. Contraction as Means to Heighten Deontic Modality

Contraction acts to "close down the space for dialogic alternatives" (Martin, 2005: 103). Denial is a typical sub-class of contraction which is frequently used in Chinese and American speech samples. It is a source for introducing the alternative position into the dialogue, and hence acknowledging it, so as to reject it (Martin, 2005: 118). In political speeches, leaders prefer to employ denial resources to convince the audience their views. In Obama's speeches, we have identified denial resources like *no*, *not*, *without*, while in Chinese leaders' speeches, indicators for denial resources are words such as "不", "没有", "无". Now we will see how denial resources are used to realize deontic modality by analyzing cases in our samples.

(42) *Without* such accountability, any agreement would be empty words on a page.

(43) It is *not* fiction, it is science.

(44)*无*视历史责任,*无*视人均排放和各国的发展水平,要求近几十年才开始工业化、还有大量人口处于绝对贫困状态的发展中国家承担超出其应尽义务和能力范围的减排目标,是毫*无*道理的。

(45)中国政府确定减缓温室气体排放的目标是中国根据国情采取的自主行动,是对中国人民和全人类负责的,*不*附加任何条件,*不*与任何国家的减排目标挂钩。

Examples above are "denial resources" in dialogic Contraction. In example (42), Obama uses denial resources to respond to the belief that there must be accountability in this international agreement, thus aligns with audience who hold the same view. Example (43) is a denial resource against the claim that the climate emergency is non-factual, and various scientific facts have convinced us what the current situation is like. Denial in example (44) is a response to the justifiability of taking conditions of different countries into consideration. Besides, he accuses the putative audience of the past deeds and aligns with the audience who feel the same. In example (45), by employing "不" (does not), Chinese rejects the belief that the participation of mitigation action should contain certain additional conditions, dwindling the putative audience who advocate additional conditions.

From the analysis above, we may infer that by denial resources both American and Chinese leaders directly position themselves towards the issue they address. In this respect, denial is a variable mechanism with respect to alignment and putative audience positioning. In other cases like example (44), denial resources will also be against the putative addressee, especially against the beliefs which the speaker assumes that at least some members of his mass audience will be subject to. Thus, those statements are objective with explicit and implicit features, and denial is another method to adjust deontic modality. As for differences, denial effect conveyed by deontic modality in the two cultures is not much the same. Most denial resources used in American speeches are for logical purpose while in Chinese speeches many cases with repeated denial resources for emphasizing purpose are found. In this respect, Chinese leaders present themselves as more modally responsible than their American counterpart.

Counter is another sub-type of contraction which is widely seen in our samples. Counters are formulations which represent the current proposition as replacing or supplanting, and thereby "countering", a proposition which would have been expected in its place. The countering is typically conveyed via conjunctions and connectives such as *although*, *however*, *yet*, *but* and some comment adjuncts/adverbials, such as *even*, *only*, *just* and *still* (Martin, 2005: 120). Correspondingly, we identify a number of counters such as "且" (furthermore), "只" (only), "更" (even) in Chinese speeches.

(46) *Still*, they need to commit to strong measures at home and agree to stand behind those commitments just as the developed nations must stand behind their own.

(47) ... if—and *only* if—it is part of a broader accord that I have just described (A2).

(48)我们言必信、行必果,无论本次会议达成什么成果,都将坚定不移地为实现、*甚至*超过这个目标而努力。

The application of counter resources in American speeches bears great resemblance to that in Chinese ones. "Still" in example (46) is aligning rather than disaligning in that they construe the speaker as sharing his values with the audience, asking for the efforts of developing countries. In the other three examples, the speaker is presented in such a way—just as surprised by the "exceptional" case as it is assumed the reader will be. In this way, counter resources highlight addresser's deontic modality, making the embodiment of deontic modality more psychologically tactically.

2. Expansion: Heterogolssic Backdrop for Deontic Modality

The effect of expansion is to "invite or at least entertain dialogic alternatives and thereby to lower the interpersonal cost for any who would advance such an alternative" (Martin, 2005: 103). In this sense, it serves as a means to detach from the speaker's deontic modality.

Entertain is subordinate to expansion. Martin terms *entertain* as "those wordings by which the authorial voice indicates that its position is but one of a number of possible positions and thereby, to greater or lesser degrees, makes dialogic space for possibilities" (Martin, 2005: 103-105). It encompasses meanings by which a speaker/writer makes assessments of likelihood via modal auxiliaries (*may*, *might*, *could*, *must*, etc.) via modal adjuncts (*perhaps*, *probably*, *definitely*, etc.), and via certain mental verb/attribute projections (*I believe*, *I think*... etc.) (103-105). As we have made a large amount of analysis about modal auxiliaries in the last section, here we will focus on mental verb/attribute protection. And the examination of the realization of deontic modality in expansion will be displayed as follows:

(49) *I believe* that the pieces of that accord *should* now be clear.

(50) *There are those* developing countries that want aid with no strings attached, and no obligations with respect to transparency. *They think* that the most advanced nations should pay a higher price; I understand that. *There are those* advanced nations who *think* that developing countries either cannot absorb this assistance, or that will not be held accountable effectively...

In example (49), Obama employs the mental-verb projection *I believe that*. Here, the maximally explicit grounding of the value position in his own subjectivity acts to construe a heteroglossic backdrop by which Obama can be strongly committed to a viewpoint, nevertheless, being prepared to signify a recognition that others may not share his value position. Hence, Obama makes very explicit assessment and give the chance to the audience to challenge. Meanwhile, he is not modally responsible for external voice. The italic words in example (50) act to disassociate the speaker's voice from current proposition by entertaining dialogistic alternatives. In the meantime, Obama tries to align with the audience of both sides, tactically arousing the interest of the audience towards his views. In Chinese speeches, there are just a few *entertain* resources realized via modal auxiliaries while *entertain* resources realized by other means can be scarcely found.

(51)*我相信*，只要我们本着对各自国家和人类社会负责任的态度……

Like the English equivalents in Obama's speeches,"我相信" (I believe) in example (51) performs the function to acknowledge a heteroglossic backdrop for the proposition by presenting them as potentially at odds with certain dialogistic alternatives, weakening deontic modality to some degree.

From the cases in Chinese speeches and American ones, we can draw a conclusion that *entertain resources* function well in constructing a heteroglossic backdrop for subjective views, hence downplaying the speaker's deontic modality. In addition, heteroglossic diversity broadens the semantic potentiality of the speech, acknowledging the heteroglossic negotiable possibility of different stances. In our samples, American leaders adopt *entertain* resources much more frequent than his Chinese counterparts. That is to say, less negotiable meaning with the audience can be found in Chinese speech transcripts because it tends to disclaim or neglect of the heteroglossia. Different cultural contexts might account for this. In China, advanced class and political party are responsible for correct "Media Direct" as to promote the progress of the whole society. Therefore, Media Direct plays an important role in social functions. While in western world, Direct is considered as an infringement to individualism. People must live by rationality rather than accept findings of others passively. Consequently, media impact on individual is achieved by taking form of suggestions, which also contributes to relatively down-scaled deontic modality presented by American leaders.

As another sub-category within expansion which is used in our speech samples, *acknowledge* can be realized by "the locutions where there is no overt indication, at least via the choice of framer, as to where the authorial voice stands with respect to the proposition" (Martin, 2005: 112). In our speech samples, we have identified the employment of *acknowledge* in American speeches. By contrast, no such cases are found in Chinese speeches.

(52) And yesterday, Secretary Hillary Clinton, my Secretary of State, *made it clear that* we will engage in a global effort to mobilize $ 100 billion in financing by 2020, if—and only if—it is part of a broader accord that I have just described.

In the example above, Obama uses the reporting verbs "make clear that" to associate the proposition being advanced voices which are external to that of the transcript itself and present his own voice as engaging interactively with Secretary Hillary Clinton's voice. By detaching himself from deontic modality for what is being said, Obama adds extra conditions to American financing effort. Furthermore, the vague word "broader" blurs the property of those extra conditions, which further obscure Obama's deontic modality. In addition, the *acknowledge* resources serve the purpose of aligning or disaligning with certain audience.

11.3.5.2 Interpretations of Deontic Modality with *Graduation* System

Graduation concerns about the gradability of the attitudes. It shows the degree of the speaker's attitude which also closely associates with deontic modality. According to Martin, *graduation* can be divided into force and focus. Force adjusts gradable items by the approach of raising or lowering whereas focus makes non-gradable words gradable by the approach of sharpening or softening (Martin,2005:137).

This section will provide resources by which *graduation* is realized and a discussion of the key dialogistic effects concerned with the up-scaling and down-scaling. As there are few occurrences of focus resources in both Chinese samples and English ones, we will devote to the comparative analysis of deontic modality in term of force. Force covers assessment as the degree of intensity and quantification. The former can operate over qualities, processes and the verbal modalities, which can be classified into intensification whereas the latter is applied to entities, which involve scaling with respect to amount, extent and proximity in time of space and can be categorized into quantification (Martin,2005:137).

1. Up-scaling Force: Lexical Scalability in Deontic Modality

Up-scaling force acts to "construe the speaker as maximally committed to the value position being advanced and hence as strongly aligning the reader into that value position" (Martin,2005:152). In our samples, it is found that a wealth of resources represent heightened deontic modality by employing up-scaling force in both Chinese and American speeches.

(53)……在如此长时间内这样大规模降低二氧化碳排放,需要付出*艰苦卓绝*的努力。

(54)中国是近年来节能减排力度*最*大的国家。

(55) We risk consigning future generations to an *irreversible catastrophe*.

(56)... it is *better* for us to act than to talk; it's *better* for us to choose action over inaction (A2).

Example (53) intensifies evaluation by isolated item "卓绝"(extremely) to perform the function of setting the level of intensity. Example (55) is realized by infused item in which there are no lexical forms conveying the sense of up-scaling or down-scaling. Specificly speaking, "irreversible" bears stronger degree than the word "severe", and "catastrophe" overweighs "disaster". Similar usage like "dramatically", "historic" and etc. also appears in American speech samples. By contrast, Chinese leaders prefer isolated item by using "最", "很", "尽可能", "都" and "更" as pre-modifications to realize intensification. Furthermore, in Chinese samples, force is realized by comparatives and superlatives (6 occurrences) are fewer than maximization (11 occurrences). While in American samples, comparatives and superlatives (20 occurrences) obviously outnumber maximization (8 occurrences). As for repetitions, both the leaders of two countries apply a number of repetitions by repeating the same lexical item to stress their points. However, repetitions with semantic relations like "... is *serious*, it is *urgent*, and it is *growing*" also appear in American samples while no such use is found in Chinese ones.

From the analysis above, we can see that the judgment for deontic modality can be extended to the observation to the lexical scalability. In this sense, Obama expresses his deontic modality more implicitly and diversified than Chinese leaders.

2. Down-scaling Force as Means to Realize Implicit Deontic Modality

Down-scaling frequently has the obverse effect of construing the speaker as having only a partial or an attenuated affiliation with the value position being referenced (Martin, 2005:153). Therefore, sometimes, down-scaling force acts to a way to weaken speaker's deontic modality. In general, down-scaling resources are much fewer than up-scaling ones in both Chinese and American samples due to the characteristics of this kind of political speech. Still, we have identified some down-scaling resources which would be presented as follows:

(57) *仅*通过降低能耗一项，中国 5 年内*可以*节省能源 6.2 亿吨标准煤，相当于少排放 15 亿吨二氧化碳。

(58) *I think* our ability to take collective action is in doubt right now, and it hangs in the balance.

(59) We are convinced, as *some* of you *may* be convinced...

(60) That's why it is in our mutual interest to achieve a global accord in which we agree to *certain* steps, and to hold each other accountable to *certain* commitments.

In the first excerpt, Chinese leader employs the down-scaling intensification "仅" (just/only) to minimize the energy-saving measures. The use of "可以", which can also be seen in the third excerpt, function to lessen the commitment in this proposition. The combination use of "仅" and "可以" actually indicates the superb capability of China to deal with mitigation by displaying implicit deontic modality. In example (58), Obama uses "I think" to reduce his investment into the proposition he makes. Meanwhile, he invites the alternatives to align with the audience who hold the same view as well as who hold the other views since he frames the thought into the subjectivity. In the last two excerpts, Obama employs the down-scaling force resources "some" and "certain" to weaken the degree of the amount they modified. The fact that Obama detaches his deontic modality can be more easily observed in the last excerpt. While in Chinese samples, the employment of qualifications as down-scaling resources is scarcely found.

11.4 Summary

Taking American and Chinese leaders' speeches on climate summit as samples to demonstrate how deontic modality is realized to fulfill the function of public political speeches, we summarize the findings of the present study as follows:

Firstly, deontic modality can be embodied by various modal resources other than modal orientations. By investigating the mood system in our speech samples, we found that the leaders of the two countries bear resemblance in the use of declarative mood and interrogative mood. Both the Chinese and the American sample transcripts employ declarative mood in abundance to address the issue of climate change, with no occurrence of interrogative mood. However, Chinese leaders are more inclined to use imperatives and exclamatives to clarify his stance. In that way, deontic modality reaches a high degree, consequently, possessing more power to appeal and evoke people's awareness. Besides, American leaders use "dialogue" and passive structures in their speeches, which rarely appear in Chinese speech samples. In terms of deontic modality embodied by modality, it is discovered that American and Chinese leaders all employ a number of modal operators to manipulate their deontic modality. However, Chinese leaders tend to use modal operators with high values while American leaders prefer those with median values. In addition, the property of language enables English speakers to use modal projections to vary the orientations. And American leaders seem less subjective than their Chinese counterparts. When it comes to deontic modality embodied by deixis switch, the frequent appearance and switch of deixis assists the tactical configuration of American leaders' deontic modality, which makes their statement more devious and less sharp. While deixis switch Chinese leaders' speeches tends to be monotonous, but make the embodiment of deontic modality more crystallized.

Secondly, appraisal resources can provide us a more profound view for the study of deontic modality. We mainly focus on the systems of engagement and graduation which conceptually related to deontic modality. With regard to engagement, the most frequently used heteroglossic resources are "denial" and "counter" in both Chinese and American speeches. However, American leaders also employ "entertain" and "acknowledge" resources which their Chinese counterparts seldom use. In terms of graduation, up-scaling resources are abundant in both Chinese and American sample speeches to heighten speaker's deontic modality. And there is almost no occurrence of focus resources in our samples. As for difference, Chinese leaders prefer to embody their deontic modality by maximization and repetition, whereas American leaders favor comparatives, superlatives and lexicalization. Besides, down-scaling resources that appear in American speeches are far more than those in Chinese ones. In general, means to embody deontic modality in American speeches is more diversified and devious than those in Chinese ones, while less sharp and heightened in term of interpersonal effect.

Thirdly, the exploration of different ideologies helps further understand the cross-cultural disparities of deontic modality. In this chapter, we have discussed the potential ideological factors which might exert impact upon the expressing modes of deontic modality. Chinese culture is characterized by strict hierarchy and high power distance index. On the contrary, American culture is characterized by loose hierarchy and low power distance index. Furthermore, influenced by Confucianism, Chinese people have been used to putting themselves into the whole society and proposing humanity, duty and devotion to the society. In contrast, the concept of Utilitarianism is of great dominance in American ideology which might influence their virtual stance towards issue of climate change. And the tactical manipulation of deontic modality distracts the audience's attention from Obama's certain vague attitude towards the issue. All those above might also explain why the Chinese leaders display their deontic modality more heightened and exaggerated than their American counterpart.

Chapter 12 Contrastive Analysis of Expressivity of Deontic Modality—in Case of Political Speech and Business English

12.1 Background of the Research

The study of modality has a long history of more than two thousand years, which can date back to ancient Greek philosophy, and then to logic and to modern linguistics. Due to the fact that modality is widely known as one of the important semantic carriers for interpersonal function, the study on interpersonal meanings expressed by modality has drawn many scholars' attention such as Huang Guowen (1999) and Li Zhanzi (2000). Therefore, there appear a lot of studies about how modality expresses interpersonal meanings in various types of discourse based on Halliday's Systemic Functional Grammar. Later on, modality is further divided into epistemic modality and deontic modality by Lyons (1977). Although deontic modality doesn't get so much attention as epistemic modality in past decades, there are still few studies on it. Yet the few existing studies on deontic modality are merely about its interpersonal function in a certain kind of discourse rather than the different degrees of its modal meanings in various kinds of discourse. Therefore, in order to fill in this gap, the present chapter intends to conduct a study on the expressivity of deontic modality based on the two types of English discourse, that is, political speeches and business English. Besides, the reason why this chapter chooses political discourse and business English as the research materials is that these two types of discourse are the most commonly and frequently used as the object materials in previous studies about the interpersonal function of deontic modality. The present chapter attempts to study deontic modality in the same typical discourse only from a different perspective.

12.2 Purpose and Significance of the Study

The purpose and significance of the chapter can be learned from the following four aspects.

The first is to figure out the distributions and occurrence frequencies of main modal expressions of deontic modality, that is, finite modal operators and expansions of the predicator, along with their modality value and modal orientation allocation in the forty pieces of discourse.

The second is to define the expressivity of deontic modality and mainly illustrate the scales of modal meanings including modal responsibility (obligation) and modal commitment (inclination) expressed by deontic modality in political speeches and business English discourse through analyzing its embodiments, that is, modality values and modal orientations.

The third is to display to what extent the deontic modality expressivity is similar to or different from each other between the selected two types of discourse and try to figure out the reasons for that.

Last but not least, this chapter aims to help readers and listeners, especially Chinese English learners, have a better understanding of the degree of the speakers' responsibility and obligation and the scale of their commitment and permission conveyed by deontic modality in different types of discourse with the knowledge of deontic modality expressivity in them.

12.3 Definition of Deontic Modality Expressivity

As discussed above, modality involves degrees and scales, so does deontic modality. The speaker may, for instance, signal a higher or lower degree of certainty about the validity of a proposition, or a higher or lower degree of pressure on the other person to carry out a command. However, although Halliday has attributed three basic values or points on the scale: high, median and low, we must keep in mind that this is an idealization, and that the three labels represent areas on a scale rather than absolute categories, with more delicate distinctions possible. Here we use the expressivity of deontic modality to refer to the degree of the specific modal meanings such as commitment and obligation expressed by deontic modality in different types of discourse. And it is mainly embodied by modality value and modal orientation.

12.4 Research Methodology

This chapter mainly aims to analyze to what degree the deontic modality has conveyed commissive and obligative meanings based on political speeches, business English letters and business negotiation conversations. Then, a contrastive analysis of deontic modality expressivity between political speeches and business English discourse will be made. Through comparison, we attempt to find out the similarities and differences of deontic modality realizations and expressivity of deontic modality in various types of discourse. Finally, the chapter tries to interpret the causal factors for the expressivity similarities and differences from the perspectives of discourse style and pragmatic effect.

In this chapter, on the basis of the research purpose mentioned above, research questions and target materials will be introduced. And then the data analysis methods will be further explained.

12.4.1 Research Questions

With the purpose mentioned above, these following questions shall be concerned in this chapter:

1. What is the expressivity of deontic modality and how is it embodied in political speeches and business English discourse?

2. To what extent is the deontic modality expressivity similar to or different from each other between political speeches and business English discourse?

3. What are the causal factors for the similarities and differences of deontic modality expressivity in selected discourse?

Since modality is usually regarded as a whole concept in most of the previous studies and interpersonal meaning of modality as the study focus, the present study takes deontic modality, a specific aspect of modality, as the main subject and aims to analyze to what extent it expresses inclination, obligation, modal responsibility and modal commitment in political speeches and business English discourse.

12.4.2 Data Collection

As for the research data, this chapter collects political speeches, business English letters and business negotiation conversations as the target subject, altogether including 40 texts from both the internet and books. And in each type, we will collect 20 texts to analyze the expressivity of deontic modality in them respectively and contrastively.

In terms of the political discourse, it takes the presidential speeches and debates delivered by the President Barack Obama and Republican Party's presidential candidate Mitt Romney in the 2012 presidential election of the United States. And business English includes business letters and business negotiation conversations selected from several books.

Among these political speeches, samples from 1 to 7 are selected from Barack Obama's speech at the Democratic National Convention to accept the Democratic Party's presidential nomination on Sept. 6, 2012. Sample 8, 9, 10, 11 and 12 are cited from Mitt Romney's speech at the Republican National Convention to accept the Republic Party's presidential nomination on August 30, 2012. And samples from 13 to 17 are selected from the first of the 2012 presidential debates on Wednesday and the last three samples are chosen from the third presidential debate. All of these speech transcripts are selected from the internet.

The first presidential debate which took place on Wednesday, October 3rd at Colorado's University of Denver is mainly on the economy and job creation, the federal deficit, entitlements and differences between the candidates on Social Security, health care and the Affordable Care Act, the role and mission of the federal government of the United States, and governing in a presidential system and dealing with gridlock.

The third presidential debate which took place on Monday, October 22 at Florida's Lynn University is mainly on American foreign policy. And the topics include discussions of the recent attack on the U. S. consulate in Benghazi, Libya, Iran's nuclear program, the Arab Spring, especially the Syrian civil war, relations with Israel and Pakistan, the War on Terror, the withdrawal of U. S. troops from Afghanistan, the size and scope of the U. S. military, and relations and trade with China, as well as the rise of China. Governor Romney also briefly broached the subject of the ongoing insurgency in Mali. Although the debate was supposed to strictly concern only foreign policy, the candidates did manage to fit a few domestic policy issues, such as job creation, the federal deficit and education into the discussion.

Therefore, through studying the modality value and modal orientations of the deontic modality in the above political speeches, the strategies for both domestic issues and foreign policy of Obama and Romney can be seen clearly. Furthermore, the difference of the strategy between these two parties will also be learned obviously.

With the rapid growth of global economy, business English letters and business negotiation conversations, which are the most popular approaches in international business trade, have played an important role in economic exchange. Therefore, to some extent, the language used by the two business parties determines the success and failure of the establishment of business relations. The analysis of deontic modality expressivity in business English letters and negotiation conversations from the perspective of Systemic Functional Grammar is conducive to a better understanding of the other party's purpose and demand, and thus establishing good trade relations of cooperation. Meanwhile, the detailed analysis of modality value and modal orientation of deontic modality contributes to have a deep knowledge of the modal meanings in business English letters and negotiation conversations, hence enabling the letter writers and negotiators to exactly deliver their true meaning and avoid producing international trade disputes.

12.4.3 Research Procedures

Based on the research questions listed above, the analysis of deontic modality expressivity based on the selected corpus is carried out in the following procedures.

First and foremost, the occurrence frequency for the modal expressions of deontic modality in every discourse, including the finite modal operators and expansion of the predicators, is examined one by one with the aid of computer search service. The overall frequency of modal expressions in each discourse is calculated. Through this, the general tendency of deontic modality used in different discourses is discovered. Then, these modal realizations are attributed to the following two deontic modality categories, that is, obligation and inclination. And the analysis of the frequencies of modality value of the modal expressions, especially finite modal operators, in each category will be studied.

It is worth mentioning here that some modal expressions are multi-semantic and therefore not always serve as deontic modality category. For example, *may*, *might*, *can* and *could* sometimes don't serve as deontic modality but as epistemic modality or dynamic modality with the meaning of probability or ability in the selected discourse. Therefore, modal expressions like them are not counted in this study but have been marked out in the corpus.

Since the computer search service cannot identify the deontic modality realizations correctly, it is indispensable to do some manual work to delete the irrelevant ones. For the sake of accuracy, the final outcome has been checked several times. Although it is a tough job and one hundred percent precision cannot be guaranteed, the deletion of the irrelevant modal expressions does ensure a much more accurate data for analyzing.

Apart from the above-mentioned quantitative analysis of the modal expressions and values of deontic modality in the corpus, the qualitative study of the data will be adopted. The qualitative analysis of the data focuses on the illustration of the expressivity of deontic modality mainly from the aspects of modality value, modal orientation and modal meanings in each kind of discourse. Furthermore, in order to explore the deontic modality expressivity more deeply, more detailed statistics will be listed in accordance with examples from the corpus. In the end, the similarities and differences among the selected two types of discourse will be examined as well. And then the possible causes for similarities and differences of deontic modality expressivity between political speeches and business English discourse will be explained with the ultimate purpose of obtaining a better understanding and acquiring a good knowledge of the exact modal meanings deontic modality expressed in specific discourse.

12.4.4 Results and Discussion

In this part, based on the framework of deontic modality in Systemic Functional Grammar, efforts will be devoted to the analysis about deontic modality expressivity in the corpus, namely political speeches, business English letters and business negotiation conversations. In addition, there will be a contrastive analysis between them with the purpose of trying to figure out the similarities and differences of the expressivity of deontic modality in the selected discourse. In the final part, causes for similarities and differences will be illustrated from two aspects.

To begin with, the two kinds of modal expressions of deontic modality will be calculated, namely, finite modal operators including *may*, *might*, *can*, *could*, *must*, *shall*, *should*, *will*, *would*, *ought to*, *have to*, *dare* and *need*, and expansion of the predicators, which includes adjective phrases and passive verb phrases such as *be happy to*, *be determined to*, *be expected to* and *supposed to* and the like. Next, the modality value, modal orientation and modal meanings of the deontic modality realizations in each type of discourse will be studied respectively and more detailed analysis will be presented with examples from chosen discourses. As for the contrastive study and the reasons exploration, it will be elaborately illustrated and eventually pointed out in the last section.

12.5 Deontic Modality Expressivity in Political Speeches

12.5.1 Deontic Modality Expressions Analysis

As discussed in previous parts, deontic modality expressions include finite modal operators and expansion of the predicators. Therefore, the occurrence frequency of these two kinds of modal expressions in every discourse will be studied one by one. Based on the political discourse corpus, a careful and detailed statistic analysis of realization forms of deontic modality in the twenty political speeches is conducted. And the distributions of modal expressions of deontic modality in the selected political speeches are shown in the following figure.

Table 12.1 Distributions of Deontic Modality Expressions in Political Speeches

sample number	finite modal operators & frequency	total number	percentage of total deontic modality
1	will 5		
2	can 3, will 2, should 1		
3	Can 6		
4	can 3, should 3, have to 3, must 3	47	36.43%
5	will 3, should 1, have to 1		
6	must 6		
7	will 4, should 2, have to 1		
8	can 2, will 1, have to 1		
9	can 2, will 7, would 1		27.91%
10	will 8, should 2	36	
11	will 9		
12	can 1, will 2		
13	have to 3		
14	can 3, will 2, have to 1, ought to 1		
15	can 2, will 5, would 1, have to 1		
16	can 1, would 2, should 1, have (got) to 4	46	35.66%
17	can 2, would 2, have to 2		
18	can 1, must 1, have to 3		
19	could 1, would 3		
20	should 2, have to 2		
grand total	can 26, could 1, will 48, would 9, should 12, have to 22, must 10, ought to 1	129	100%

The results in table 12.1 tell us that in all the twenty political speeches, there is no expansion of the predicators and only finite modal operators are used to express deontic modality meaning. In other words, it means that whether in the presidential nomination speech or the presidential debate, both Obama and Romney prefer to employ finite modal operators to express deontic modality meanings such as commitment, promise, obligation and responsibility in their speeches. And the word *will* and *can* are the most commonly used ones. Their modal meanings involve commitment, permission, obligation as well as responsibility.

In addition, it can be observed that modal expressions in sample speeches from 1 to 7 take the first place by accounting for 36.43% with the total number of 47. And modal expressions in selected speeches from 13 to 20 take the second largest share by occupying 35.66% with the total number of 46. The modal expressions in sample speeches from 8 to 12 make up the least proportion by taking up 27.91% with the number of 36. Based on the data collection and the above statistics, we can get that Obama, who had won his first presidential election in 2008 with his excellent speech capability and skills, is fond of and good at using finite modal operators to deliver his attitude and opinion. By comparison, Romney, a new candidate for the 2012 presidential election, seems a little unskillful at the use of modal expressions of deontic modality in his speech. However, during the presidential debate, the two of them have a tendency to adopt more modal expressions to express their point of view, obligation, commitment and strategy under the pressure of the other's query and denial as well as the intense debate atmosphere. Let us look at some typical examples from the corpus.

(1) PRESIDENT OBAMA: But when all is said and done, when you pick up that ballot to vote, you will (inclination: commitment) face the clearest choice of any time in a generation. Over the next few years, big decisions will (inclination: promise) be made in Washington, on jobs, the economy; taxes and deficits; energy, education; war and peace, decisions that will (inclination: commitment) have a huge impact on our lives and our children's lives for decades to come.

(2) PRESIDENT OBAMA: And now you have a choice: we can (inclination: promise) give more tax breaks to corporations that ship jobs overseas, or we can (inclination: promise) start rewarding companies that open new plants and train new workers and create new jobs here, in the United States of America. We can (inclination: promise) help big factories and small businesses double their exports, and if we choose this path, we can (inclination: promise) create a million new manufacturing jobs in the next four years. You can (inclination: promise) make that happen. You can (inclination: promise) choose that future.

(3) PRESIDENT OBAMA: We are forever in debt to a generation whose sacrifice has made this country safer and more respected. We will (inclination: commitment) never forget you. And so long as I'm Commander-in-Chief, we will (inclination: commitment) sustain the strongest military the world has ever known. When you take off the uniform, we will (inclination: commitment) serve you as well as you've served us.

The examples above indicate that the word *will* and *can* frequently appear in President

Obama's speech. And they are usually employed to convey inclination to voice the speaker's promise and commitment.

12.5.2 Deontic Modality Value Analysis

According to the previous discussions, it is known that modality involves degrees and scales, and so does deontic modality. Halliday (2000) considers that the third variable in modality—value, is attached to the modal judgment: high, median and low. Every modal expression can be attributed to a certain value. The frequencies and percentage of the value of modal expressions in the twenty political speeches are listed as follows:

Table 12.2 Modality Value in Political Speeches

modality	finite modal operator	frequencies	percentage	value
obligation	must (high value)	10	7.81%	33 high value 25.78%, 12 median value 9.38%, 4 low value 3.13%
	should (median value)	12	9.38%	
	have to (high value)	22	17.19%	
	can (low value)	4	3.13%	
	ought to (high value)	1	0.78%	
	total	49	38.28%	
inclination	will (median value)	48	37.5%	57 median value 44.53%, 22 low value 17.19%
	would (median value)	9	7.03%	
	can (low value)	22	17.19%	
	total	79	61.72%	

The statistics in table 12.2 displays that the value of finite modal operators in selected political speeches also falls into the three scales: high, median and low. Among them, median and high values are the major used ones. Therefore, they are regarded as the dominant deontic modality devices in political speeches. In addition, among all these finite modal operators, the median value word *will* takes the first place with the percentage of 37.5%, more than half of the total percentage in inclination category. The high value words *have to* in obligation category and the low value word *can* in inclination category also occupy an important portion with the same figure of 17.19%. Moreover, a majority of the median value word *will* and *can* convey inclination in proposals to indicate commitment, intention, expectation and permission. While most of the high value word *have* to conveys obligation in proposals to clearly express responsibility and liability. Based on the result, we can come to the conclusion that:

In terms of obligation, the speaker often uses high value deontic modality to clearly state the responsibility of the government and that of all the citizens of the United States. Take education for an example, it involves the responsibility of teachers, principals, parents as well as the students. Moreover, high value deontic modality is usually employed to claim the right of the Americans to enjoy a better life and benefit from the government. On the other hand, it is also adopted to indicate that voters are supposed to make their choices and decisions for the future of the United States.

In terms of inclination, the speaker is more likely to employ median value deontic modality to convince the voters of his ability to build a better future than his opponent from the other party, to make commitments and promises to the soldiers who have made contributions to the country to assure them that they will get serviced as well as they serve the country when they come home, and to argue that he is capable of cutting the federal deficit and creating more jobs. On the other hand, median value deontic modality is also adopted to inform voters of the negative consequence of the other party's wrongdoings, hence strengthen the speaker's credibility and reliability. Some classic examples chosen from the political speech corpus are presented as follows:

(4) PRESIDENT OBAMA: A government has a role in this. But teachers must (obligation: responsibility) inspire; principals must (obligation: responsibility) lead; parents must (obligation: responsibility) instill a thirst for learning, and students, you've gotta (obligation: responsibility) do the work. (Sample 4)

(5) PRESIDENT OBAMA: But for all the progress we've made, challenges remain. Terrorist plots must (obligation: responsibility) be disrupted. Europe's crisis must (obligation: responsibility) be contained. Our commitment to Israel's security must (obligation: responsibility) not waver, and neither must (obligation: responsibility) our pursuit of peace. (Sample 6)

(6) MR. ROMNEY: We will (inclination: commitment) give our fellow citizens the skills they need for the jobs of today and the careers of tomorrow. We will (inclination: commitment) cut the deficit and put America on track to a balanced budget. And we will (inclination: commitment) champion SMALL businesses, America's engine of job growth. (Sample 10)

(7) MR. ROMNEY: If I am elected President of these United States, I will (inclination: commitment) work with all my energy and soul to restore that America, to lift our eyes to a better future. (Sample 12)

In sample (4), the high value words *must* and *have to* convey modality obligation to clearly state the responsibility of teachers and parents as well as the duty of the students in education. In the fifth example, Obama employs the high value word *must* to express the government's obligation and resolution to meet various challenges from terrorists, financial crisis to social security. With these words, he is trying to convince all the citizens of the United States that his government has the ability to take the challenges and build a secure and powerful state.

On the other hand, in the sixth and seventh examples from Romney's speech, the median value word *will* conveys modality inclination to deliver his commitment and promise as well as intention to build a better future by reducing the federal deficit and creating more jobs for the Americans. Maybe, it is because of the less emphasis on declaring his responsibility and obligation with high value deontic modality in his speech that Mr. Romney did not obtain as much support as President Obama.

12.5.3 Deontic Modality Orientation and Meaning Analysis

Generally speaking, modal orientation has four types: subjective explicit, subjective implicit, objective explicit and objective implicit (Halliday, 2000: 357). They can be realized by many modal expressions such as finite modal operators, modal adjunct, passive verb predicator and projecting clauses. But as for deontic modality, since its modal expressions are mainly finite operators and the expansion of the predicators, the analysis of modal orientation in this thesis will focus on the two kinds of modal expressions, that is, finite modal operators and expansion of the predicators.

From the perspective of Systemic Functional Grammar, the orientation of finite modal operators is regarded as subjective implicit. Therefore, the modal orientation of deontic modality in political speeches is mainly subjective implicit. By employing subjective implicit orientation, the speaker in political speeches intends to make his/her point of view and attitude objective and apt to embrace, thus avoiding unnecessary arguments and winning more support.

In terms of the modal meanings of deontic modality, there are two categories: inclination and obligation. In other words, it can be called commissive and obligative. From the statistics in table 12.2, it can be learned that the inclination or commissive takes the dominant part with a percentage of 61.72%, over half of the total deontic modality. The obligation only accounts for 38.28%. That means the principal meaning of deontic modality used in political speeches is inclination or commissive. In addition, it is in accord with the pragmatic function of deontic modality in political speeches. That is to say, speakers are mainly inclined to express their commitment and promise in political speeches.

In light of the result, it can be observed that on the one hand, the speaker tends to express inclination and obligation with subjective implicit orientation in an indirect way in the political speeches. On the other hand, compared with obligation, inclination and commissive are the major modal meanings the speaker intends to convey in political speeches.

12.6 Deontic Modality Expressivity in Business English

12.6.1 Deontic Modality Expressions Analysis

In terms of business English, there are mainly two types of discourse, namely business English letters and business negotiation conversations, selected by different business issues and negotiation stages from several business English books published in recent years.

Among business English Letters, sample letter 1 to 3 are selected from the book *International Business Correspondence* written by Han Qin and Bian Jieying (2007), sample letter 4 to 7 are chosen from the book *English for International Business Communication* written by Hou Fangmiao (2010) and sample letter 8 to 10 are selected from the book *English Business Letters* by Cao Ling (2000). All of them are the real letters used in Business English.

In accordance with the business English corpus, a careful and detailed statistic analysis of the realization forms of deontic modality in the twenty pieces of business English discourse is conducted. And the allocations of modal expressions of deontic modality in the sample business letters and negotiation conversations are shown in the following table.

Table 12.3 Distributions of Deontic Modality Expressions in Business English Letters

sample letter number	modal expressions & frequency	total number	percentage of total deontic modality
1	could 1, would 2, should 1, be interested in 1	5	10%
2	can 1, will 2, be willing to1, be pleased to 1	5	10%
3	will 2, would 1, have to 1, be interested in 1, be pleased to 1	6	12%
4	cculd 1, will 2, would 1, be interested in 1	5	10%
5	can 2, will 3, would 1, be happy to 1, be to be made 1	8	16%

Table 12.3 (continued)

sample letter number	modal expressions & frequency	total number	percentage of total deontic modality
6	can 1, would 1, should 1	3	6%
7	can 1, will 1, have to 2, may 1	5	10%
8	could 1, would 2, shall 1	4	8%
9	would 2, should 1, must 1, have pleasure in 1, be pleased to 1	6	12%
10	can 1, could 1, be willing to 1	3	6%
grand total	can 6, could 4, will 10, would 10, shall 1, should 3, have to 3, must 1, may 1, be willing to 2, be pleased to 3, have pleasure in 1, be happy to 1, be interested in 3, to be made 1	50	finite modal operators 39, 78%; expansion of predicators 11, 22%

The statistics in table 12.3 shows that finite modal operators take a large proportion with the figure of 78% in number of 39 in the sample letters. Expansion of the predicators only takes up a small part with the percentage of 22% in total number of 11. In other words, in business English letters, whether in inquiries, offers or replies, the businessmen prefer to employ finite modal operators, the major realization form of deontic modality, to express their willingness and commitment as well as obligation and responsibility.

In addition, among all the finite modal operators, the word *will* and *would* are the most frequently used to deliver the writers' intention, expectation and commitment. And among the expansion of the predicators, the adjective phrases *be pleased to* and *be interested in* are commonly used to show the writer's interest in the other party's products and the inclination and willingness to place an order and do business with the other party. On the other hand, in order to make the business work out smoothly, deontic modality is less employed to directly require the other party to do what the writer wants unless when it comes to payment which may affect the writer's interests if not handled properly.

Furthermore, table 12.3 shows that modal realizations in sample letter 5 and 9, which are reply letters, rank the first place with the percentage of 16% and 12% respectively. And those in sample letter 3 and 7, which are declining letters, take the second position with the figure of 12% and 10%. In light of these statistics, it can be learned that businessmen tend to employ more modal expressions to show their interest, commitment, request, obligation, requirement as well as expectation in reply letters and declining letters. The following examples can provide more detailed explanations for the points discussed above.

(8) After careful consideration, we do not deny that we are interested in (inclination to express interest) your products, as you know. However, we find that we can (ability or probability) obtain from another firm at a price of 10% lower than that of yours. If you would (inclination to express request) reduce your price to that extent, we will (inclination to express commitment) be pleased to (willingness) place with you an order that will (inclination to express commitment) carry us for the rest of this year. Otherwise, we have to (obligation) turn to other resources. (Sample letter 3)

(9) Our prices on the price list are on CIF basis. If you purchase not less than 100 dozen of individual items, we would (inclination to express commitment) grant you a discount of 3%. Payment is to be made (obligation to express requirement) by irrevocable and confirmed L/C. We hope you will (inclination to express expectation) let us have your order before costs rise further. (Sample letter 5)

In the aspect of business negotiation conversations, dialogues 1 to 6 are chosen from the book *Spoken English for Business Negotiation* written by Qin Chuan (2003), dialogue 7 to 10 are cited from the book *Business Negotiation* written by Ma Shaoming et al (2005). All of them are the actual conversations in business negotiation. In the following figure, the occurrence frequency of each finite modal operator in the selected negotiation conversations is demonstrated.

Table 12.4 Distributions of Modal Expressions in Business English Negotiation

dialogue number	modal expressions & frequency	total number	percentage of total deontic modality
1	can 1, could 1, will 2, would 2, ought to 1, have to 1	8	11.11%
2	can 2, could 1, will 4, shall 1, should 1	9	12.50%
3	must 2, will 3, would 1	6	8.33%
4	must 1, could 1, will 1, should 1, may 1, be pleased to 1	6	8.33%
5	shall 1, should 1, ought to 1	3	4.17%

Table 12.4 (continued)

dialogue number	modal expressions & frequency	total number	percentage of total deontic modality
6	can 1, will 3, would 1, shall 1	6	8.33%
7	could 1, will 3, should 3	7	9.72%
8	can 1, could 1, will 5, should 1, have to 2	10	13.89%
9	can 2, will 3, would 1, have to 1, be willing to 1	8	11.11%
10	can 1, will 5, would 2, has to 1	9	12.50%
grand total	can 8, could 5, will 29, would 7, ought to 2, have(s) to 5, shall 3, should 7, must 3, may 1, be pleased to 1, be willing to 1	72	Finite modal operators 70, 97.22%; expansions of predicator 2, 2.78%

In light of the above table, it could be seen that finite modal operators take the prevailing position by occupying 97.22% with the number of 70 out of the total figure 72 in the ten business negotiation conversations; while the expansion of the predicators only takes up a very tiny part of all the modal expressions of deontic modality in the corpus. Besides, modal expressions in conversation 1, 2, 8, 9 and 10 take a large proportion with the figure of 11.11%, 12.50%, and 13.89%, 11.11% and 12.50% respectively. That means when it comes to payment (dialogue 1, 2, 9), package (dialogue 7, 8) and shipment (dialogue 10) the two parties in negotiation have tendency to use more deontic modality than on other occasions like the final stage of negotiation, that is, to sign the contract (dialogue 3, 4, 5, 6). Among all of the finite modal operators, the word *will* is the most commonly used one conveying inclination to express commitment. Some typical examples selected from the corpus are listed below.

(10) Well, we will (inclination to express commitment), as a special case, accept D/P at sight for this sample order. (Dialogue 2)

(11) If you insist, we'll (inclination to express commitment) use plastic boxes instead. But the cost will (inclination) be much higher. (Dialogue 8)

(12) I'm sure our visits will (inclination to express commitment) contribute a lot to the setting of the payment problem that concerns both of us. (Dialogue 9)

(13) I fully agree with you. I'll (inclination to express commitment) ask my shipping manager to find out the possibility of transshipment via Pusan. (Dialogue 10)

Obviously, all of the finite modal operator *will* in the above examples deliver deontic modality inclination and clearly express the negotiator's firm commitment and determination.

12.6.2 Deontic Modality Value Analysis

According to the discussion in previous sections, we know that deontic modality involves degrees or scales. In general, it is finite modal operators that are used to realize the value of deontic modality for the fact that they can clearly show the speaker's attitude and willingness in the chosen discourses. The following table 12.5 and 12.6 displays the different scales of finite modal operators in business English letters and business negotiation conversations respectively.

Table 12.5 Modality Value in Business English Letters

modality	finite modal operator	frequencies	percentage	value
obligation	must (high value)	1	2.56%	4 high value 10.26%, 1 median value 2.56%, 1 low value 2.56%
	should (median value)	1	2.56%	
	have to (high value)	3	7.69%	
	can (low value)	1	2.56%	
	total	6	15.38%	
inclination	will (median value)	10	25.64%	24 median value 61.54%, 9 low value 23.08%
	would (median value)	10	25.64%	
	can (low value)	5	12.82%	
	could (low value)	4	10.26%	
	shall (median value)	1	2.56%	
	should (median value)	2	5.13%	
	care to (median value)	1	2.56%	
	total	33	84.62%	

Table 12.6 Modality Value in Business English Negotiation

modality	finite modal operator	frequencies	percentage	value
obligation	must (high value)	3	4.29%	10 high value 14.29%, 7 median value 10%, 2 low value 2.86%
	should (median value)	6	8.57%	
	have(s) to (high value)	5	7.14%	
	can (low value)	2	2.86%	
	ought to (high value)	2	2.86%	
	shall (median value)	1	1.43%	
	Total	19	27.14%	
inclination	will (median value)	29	41.43%	39 median value 55.71%, 12 low value 17.14%
	would (median value)	7	10%	
	can (low value)	6	8.57%	
	could (low value)	5	7.14%	
	shall (median value)	2	2.86%	
	should (median value)	1	1.43%	
	may (low value)	1	1.43%	
	Total	51	72.86%	

The statistics in table 12.5 and 12.6 indicate that the scales of finite modal operators both in business English letters and negotiation conversations are attributed to high value, median value and low value respectively. Among them, median and low are the most commonly used ones. Therefore, they are thought of as the dominant deontic modality value in business English discourse. Moreover, among all these finite modal operators, the median value word *will* and *would* are playing the major role with the percentage of 25.64% in business English letters and 41.43% in business negotiation conversations. In addition, most median value word *will* conveys inclination to express the speakers' requests for an easier payment terms and expectations for the reduction of the quoted price as well as for the future business relations. Also a majority of the median value operator *would* delivers the writers' and speakers' requests and commitments to the other party. Among all the low value modal operators, the word *can* is frequently adopted to convey commitment and obligation. In view of the results reflected from the table 12. 3 to 12. 6, we can make a summary as follows:

In sample letter 1, 4 and 8 about inquiries, the buyers usually use median value deontic modality to show their interest in the products and their polite request for more information about quotations and samples. Also, they employ median value deontic modality to voice their commitment and promise to pay prompt attention to newly information and express their willingness to place an order and their best wishes for future friendly business cooperation relations.

In both firm offers and non-firm offers such as sample letter 2 and 6, the sellers often adopt median value deontic modality to deliver their willingness and commitment to establish business relations with the buyer and hope for the coming order. But on the other hand, in firm offers, the sellers usually put forward their specific trade price and employ low value deontic modality to express the present increasing market demand and expect the buyer to place an order as soon as possible.

In sample letter 3, which is about declining an offer, the buyers prefer to employ median value deontic modality to express their request to sellers for reducing price and high value deontic modality to convey that if the price is not lowered, they will have no choice but to get the products from other suppliers.

In sample letter 5 and 9, which are about a reply to an inquiry, sellers tend to use median and low value deontic modality to make the commitment for what they can do to the most under the current conditions, to deliver their willingness and pleasure to do business with the buyer and to show their expectations for coming orders at the same time. In addition, when it comes to payment, the sellers prefer to employ high value deontic modality to express their requirement for the payment terms due to the fact that payment terms affect their interests, so they have to make sure that the payment terms are secure and effective.

Different from other issues of business letters, in the declining order letter such as sample letter 7, the sellers tend to use high value deontic modality to express their responsibility and obligation to explain that their quotation is reasonable and is in line with the price ruling in the present market. Also, they adopt high value deontic modality to show their appology and regret for not meeting the buyer's demand.

Finally, in sample letter 10, which concerns declining the counteroffer, sellers prefer using low value deontic modality to signify that they have done their best at price aspect and hope that the buyer can take the excellent product quality and highly competitive market into consideration and ultimately make a concession and accept the reasonable quotation.

On the other hand, during the negotiation about payment, the sellers try to persuade the buyers to use the payment by letters of credit in order to reduce the risk of taking delivery of goods without payment. And sellers usually employ median value and low value deontic modality to clearly state their payment requirement without hurting the buyers' feelings and destroying the business relations between them. Meanwhile, the buyers, who want to get the permission for easier payment terms, also use median value and low value deontic modality to make a request for their goal. The only difference of the behaviors between buyers and sellers is that apart from median and low value deontic modality, buyers also use high value deontic modality such as *have to* and *should* to show their difficulties in payment and expect sellers to understand them so that they can get the permission for easier payment terms.

In negotiation about package and shipment, since both of them can affect the quality and quantity of the goods and as well as the arrival time of seasonal goods, so the buyers try to make sure that sellers can handle properly at these two aspects. And they often employ median value and low value deontic modality, such as *will*, *could* and *would*, to politely suggest the sellers to use the safest and most effective package and mode of shipment.

Finally, in the last stage of negotiation, before the two parties are going to sign the contract, they always tend to go over it just in case of any mistakes and to avoid future disputes or troubles about the contract. In this case, the party who has drafted the contract often uses median value deontic modality such as *will* or *would* to show his/her politeness and consideration. However, when concerning details that need to be corrected or added, the two parties will adopt high value deontic modality to show their determination to improve and perfect the contract. In addition, they also employ high value deontic modality to state their responsibility and commitment to follow the business practice and abide by the approved contract. Some typical examples can demonstrate this as follows:

(14) We are interested in (inclination to express interest) buying large quantities of *White Cat Shampoo* and should (obligation) be obliged if you would (inclination to express request) give us a quotation per bottle CIF Lagos Nigeria. (Sample letter 1 A special inquiry)

(15) Our machines are of top quality and reasonable price. All machines are guaranteed for one year free, and we can (inclination to express commitment) also provide spare components and after-sales services to customers. We hope that the above quotations will (inclination or willingness to express expectation) be accepted and assure you of our best services at any time. (Sample letter 2 A Non-firm Offer)

(16) We are large dealers in textiles and believe there is a promising market in our area for

moderately priced goods mentioned above. We hope this will (inclination to express expectation) be a good beginning of our long and mutually beneficial business relations. Your prompt attention will (inclination to express commitment) be much appreciated. (Sample letter 4 A general inquiry)

(17) Taylor: You see, our government is reluctant to approve of credit. If D/A is possible, it will (inclination) help ease the licensing problem. Or, would (inclination to express request as well as a suggestion) you consider documents against payment? It is unwise to insist on one's own views. (Dialogue 1 Discussing the payment terms)

(18) Taylor: All right, it seems I have to (obligation to express have no choice) take things as they are. But I hope you would (inclination to express expectation) leave us some leeway in future terms of payment. (Dialogue 1 Discussing the payment terms)

(19) Wen: Don't you think this clause should (obligation, is supposed to change) be improved? You see, it's stipulated in the contract that all the blouses shall (obligation to express requirement) be packed each in a paper box and then in cardboard cartons. It's all right for blouses, but it is not necessary for accessories, is it?

Owen: No, it's not. Accessories ought to (obligation to express requirement) be packed separately. (Dialogue 5 Discussing about signing the contract)

12.6.3 Deontic Modality Orientation and Meaning Analysis

According to the fact that finite modal operators are usually regarded as subjective implicit and the expansion of the predicators is objective explicit, it is obvious that most of the deontic modality expressions in business English letters and negotiation conversations are subjective implicit orientation. In effect, both subjective implicit and objective explicit indicate objectivity. Therefore, it can be learned that in business English discourse, the writer and the negotiator tend to express his or her attitude and opinion in an euphemistic and wild way rather than with a direct tone. The letter writers and negotiators apply subjective implicit and objective explicit orientation to show their inclination and obligation in an objective way so that their points of view seem to be tendered and make the other party feel that the liability is from other sources rather than the speakers themselves.

The modal meanings of deontic modality in business English discourse also fall into these two categories: inclination and obligation, or commissive and obligative. In business English discourse, whether in business letters or negotiation conversations, modality inclination or willingness takes up the largest portion with the percentage of 84.62% and 72.86% in the two types of business English discourse respectively, while modality obligation and responsibility only occupy 15.38% and 27.14% respectively. Consequently, inclination, which is usually conveyed by median value operators, is the dominant modal meaning of deontic modality in business English discourse, that is, to express request, willingness, commitment and expectation.

What's more, in the aspect of obligation, the writers and negotiators often use high value deontic modality to clearly indicate their responsibility, show their helplessness and apology in a euphemistic way, and also to demand or require the other party to undertake the due responsibility and obligation. Meanwhile, they are used to employing median value deontic modality to convey inclination to express their intention to make promises and commitments as well as their best wishes and expectations for the future business relations.

12.7 Contrastive Analysis of Deontic Modality Expressivity in Political Speeches and Business English

Based on the discussions and statistics in previous chapters, we can get the following two tables about the distributions of deontic modality values and modal meanings in the whole corpus.

Table 12.7 Modality Values in the Corpus

discourse type	value	finite modal operators	frequencies	percentage
political speeches	high	must	10	25.78%
		have to	22	
		ought to	1	
	median	should	12	53.91%
		will	48	
		would	9	
	low	can	26	20.31%
	total		128	100%

Table 12.7 (continued)

discourse type	value	finite modal operators	frequencies	percentage
business English	high	must	4	12.84%
		have to	8	
		ought to	2	
	median	should	10	65.14%
		will	39	
		would	17	
		shall	4	
		care to	1	
	low	can	14	22.02%
		could	9	
		may	1	
	total		109	100%

Table 12.8 Modal Meanings in the Corpus

discourse type	deontic modality	number of modal operators	percentage
political speeches	obligation	49	38.28%
	inclination	79	61.72%
	total	128	100%
business English	obligation	25	22.94%
	inclination	84	77.06%
	total	109	100%

In accordance with the statistics and results above, it can be obviously observed that there exist some similarities and differences between political speeches and business English discourse. The following section will give a detailed analysis about this and try to interpret it from these two aspects of discourse style and pragmatic function.

12.7.1 Expressivity Similarities

By comparing the statistics and results displayed in previous sections, we find that there are several similar aspects of the expressivity of deontic modality between political speeches and business English discourse.

First, as shown in table 12.4, 12.5 and 12.6 the distributions of modal expressions of deontic modality in political speeches, business English letters and business negotiation conversations, finite modal operators are the dominant modality device in the whole corpus. On the other hand, due to the fact that finite modal operators are regarded as subjective implicit, so the political speeches and business English discourse have the same modal orientation, namely subjective implicit orientation, to indicate objectivity. In consequence, we can easily get the idea that all the speakers, the letter writers and the negotiators have the tendency to employ subjective implicit expressions to convey obligation and inclination in a temperate and euphemistic way.

Second, as the table 12.7 displays that both in political speeches and business English discourse, the median value modal expressions take the first position among the three values, hence we can learn that the speakers, writers and negotiators have a preference to adopt median value deontic modality to express their point of view and attitudes. It implies that the speakers try to express themselves not too arbitrary or absolute. And sometimes, the speakers' choice of median value modal expressions is out of politeness. They want to avoid any argument or disagreement and make their opinions more acceptable and less controversial.

Third, as the statistics in table 12.8 indicate that modality inclination is the major modal meaning both in political speeches and business English, that is to say, the speakers, letter writers and negotiators prefer employing deontic modality to underline their commitment, willingness, request and expectation rather than their obligation, responsibility and liability.

Last but not least, both in political speeches and business English, when speakers intend to convey obligation and responsibility, they all have the tendency to adopt high value modal expressions to strengthen their resolution. On the contrary, the speakers usually tend to employ median value modal expressions to take on a tender attitude, make firm commitment and display strong intentions when they want to convey inclination.

12.7.2 Expressivity Differences

However, apart from similarities, we also figure out the differences of the deontic modality expressivity between the two types of discourse. Let us focus on table 12.7 and 12.8.

According to table 12.7, it can be observed that in political speeches, high value modal expressions occupy a larger percentage than the low value ones, while in business English the percentage of high value is smaller than that of low value. In other words, high value deontic modality is more frequently used in political speeches to express obligation and responsibility and low value deontic modality is more commonly used in business English to convey permission, request, commitment and expectation. During the presidential election, the two candidates need to establish their authority and openly assume their due responsibility so as to persuade the audience to share the same viewpoint and embrace their policy. By comparison, the letter writers and negotiators in business English are inclined to make use of low and median value expressions like *could*, *would* and *will* to express their firm commitment, strong request or suggestion and insistent expectation and hope for future business cooperation relations. By applying these expressions, their requests and suggestions will be easily got approved.

In addition to that, the statistics in table 12.8 shows that modality obligation is comparatively more widely employed in political speeches, although modality inclination is the most commonly used among all the selected two types of discourse. That is to say, the speakers are more inclined to emphasize responsibility and liability in political speeches than in business English discourse. On the contrary, the business English letter writers and negotiators tend to focus on conveying inclination to express their requests or suggestions for trade activities and their commitment to properly reduce price in line with the order quantity and expectation for the acceptance of quotations and quick orders.

12.7.3 Causes for Similarities and Differences

In connection with the similarities and differences of deontic modality expressivity between political speeches and business English discourse discussed above, this section attempts to figure out the possible causal factors for them from the perspectives of discourse style and pragmatic effect.

12.7.3.1 Discourse Style Factors

It is discourse style that determines the discourse language. And language is made up of various utterance expressions. In terms of deontic modality, it is widely used in different types of discourse and can be realized by many expressions. But finite modal operators are the most frequently used among all of the deontic modality realizations. Therefore, there is no doubt that finite modal operators play a dominant role both in political speeches and business English discourse.

Besides, although political speeches, business English letters and negotiation conversations belong to different specific discourse type, they can be regarded as the same discourse style from another perspective. To be more accurate, both of them can be identified as persuasive discourse on the whole. And speakers in persuasive discourse prefer to deliver their statements in a tender way. Hence, it is reasonable to see both the speakers in political speeches and the letter writers and negotiators in business English have the tendency to use median value deontic modality to voice their commitment, promise and permission with the subjective implicit orientation. All of them intend to make their attitudes objective and opinions easier to accept.

However, it is the discourse style distinction that leads to the distribution differences of high value and low value deontic modality as well as the modality obligation between political speeches and business English discourse. And this will be elaborately explained in the next section.

12.7.3.2 Pragmatic Factors

The reason why it is the discourse style distinction that leads to the differences in the distribution of high value and low value deontic modality as well as the obligation meaning among the whole discourse corpus is that discourse style distinction determines the different pragmatic meanings. And in this chapter, the distinct pragmatic meanings need to be realized by different deontic modality values and modal meanings.

In political speeches which are selected from the 2012 Presidential Election of the United States, the candidate, whether President Obama or Governor Romney, needs to try to convince the audience to believe that he has the capability of and can do better than the other in resolving domestic problems, such as federal deficit and employment issue, and eliminating the outside threats to the United State and finally leading the country to a better future.

Due to the fact that electing the President is a big decision, the voters not only want to see the determination and resolution as well as commitment of the candidate, but also would like to know the extent to which the candidate overtly takes his due obligation and responsibility. That is to say, it is necessary for the speakers to clearly state their obligation and openly assume their due responsibility in their speech. So undoubtedly, high value deontic modality expressions are more frequently used to convey modality obligation and modal responsibility in political speeches.

On the other hand, the main purpose of the business English letters and negotiations is to contribute to establishing business cooperation relations and signing the contract. In view of this goal, the letter writers and negotiators not only need to show their keen interest in the other party's products and request for detailed product information politely, but also should indicate their willingness to place an order with the other party and commitment to properly lower price based on the order quantity as well as the ardent expectation for future friendly cooperation in a euphemistic way. Therefore, it is obviously that low value and median value deontic modality is more commonly employed to convey modality inclination or modal commitment in business English discourse.

12.8 Summary

In view of Halliday's Systemic Functional Grammar, this chapter mainly analyzes the expressivity of deontic modality in twenty political speeches selected from the 2012 presidential election in the United States and twenty pieces of business English discourse including ten business letters and ten business negotiation conversations. The major findings of the study can be summarized as follows:

Firstly, the expressivity of deontic modality in political speeches is on the whole comparatively higher than that in business English discourse. And the reason is that speakers are more likely to employ high value deontic modality to overtly deliver their opinions and attitudes and explicitly state their responsibilities and obligation in political speeches, while the letter writers and negotiators tend to adopt median and low value deontic modality to implicitly express their requests, willingness and promises and indirectly convey their expectations in business English discourse.

Secondly, in terms of the expressivity of deontic modality, there exist both similarities and differences between political speeches and business English discourse. Specifically speaking, in the aspect of obligative deontic modality, since its expressivity is in line with the modal orientation and the fact that modal orientation is subjective implicit in political speeches and business English discourse, the expressivity of obligative deontic modality is similar to each other in the two types of discourse. Whereas, in the aspect of inclination deontic modality, due to the fact that its expressivity is mainly in accordance with modality values and that high value deontic modality takes the second largest proportion in political speeches while low value deontic modality takes larger percentage than high value deontic modality in business English, therefore, the expressivity of inclination deontic modality is different between the two types of discourse.

Thirdly, some factors contribute for the similarities and differences of deontic modality expressivity between the selected two types of discourse. On the one hand, it is the common discourse style, i. e. persuasive discourse, that makes political speeches and business English discourse have similar, subjective and implicit modal orientation. To be more specific, speakers in persuasive discourse have the tendency to deliver their statements in a tender and indirect way. Therefore, both speakers in political speeches and letter writers and negotiators in business English prefer to use median value deontic modality to express their opinions and comments with subjective implicit orientation, and thus making their attitudes appear more objective and easy to accept.

On the other hand, it is the different pragmatic effects that enable the distinct distributions of high value deontic modality and low value deontic modality in political speeches and business English. Specifically speaking, communication purpose and pragmatic effect vary with different discourse occasions. In political speeches, especially the presidential election occasion, speakers are supposed to clearly state their attitudes and comments and overtly take on their due responsibility and obligation in public. While in business English, letter writers and negotiators are supposed to implicitly voice their request, interest and willingness, as well as good expectations. Consequently, high value deontic modality is more often used in political speeches to explicitly claim obligation and responsibility and low value deontic modality is quite frequently employed in business English to show request and inclination in a tender way.

Last but not least, the interpretation for the similarities and differences of the expressivity of deontic modality from the aspects of discourse style and pragmatic effect based on the selected English discourse presents a reasonable and detailed illustration in the last section of this chapter. The study not only testifies the practical applicability of the Systemic Functional Theory in specific discourse analysis, but also further deepens our understanding of the allocations and pragmatic meanings of deontic modality in political speeches and business English. What's more, we hope this chapter can be conducive for English learners to gain a better knowledge and understanding of how to appropriately express commitment, permission, responsibility and obligation to achieve their communicative purpose and intention in different types of discourse, thus enhancing communicative competence.

However, we have to acknowledge that there are some limitations in this part. First of all, although forty pieces of discourse altogether selected for this study is up to a certain scale, the analysis would be more comprehensive if more data could be selected. The size of the corpus should be searched in a larger range, so that the findings could be more representative and persuasive. Second, the present study mainly focuses on the finite modal operators and expansion of the predicators of deontic modality, but the modal adjuncts and metaphors of modality are not examined in detail. In addition, the feature revealed in this chapter is just one of the components of political speeches and business English discourse, and it is essential to further study the other features and levels in such corpus to make the result more convincing. Since the writer's knowledge and experience is limited, this research and its conclusion are definitely welcome to criticism and correction.

References

[1] Albert E. Value System. In D. L. Sills (Ed.), International Encyclopedia of the Social Sciences[M]. New York: Macmillan, 1968, 17: 32.

[2] Asher E A, ed. The Encyclopedia of Language & Linguistics[M]. Oxford: Pergamon, 1994.

[3] Bex T. Varieties in Written English—Texts in Society: Societies in Text[M]. London: Rourledge, 1996.

[4] Biber D, et al. Longman Grammar of Written English[M]. London: Pearson Education Limited, 1999.

[5] Bussmann H. Routledge Dictionary of Language and Linguistics[M]. Beijing: Foreign Language Teaching and Research Press, 2000.

[6] Bybee J, et al. The Evolution of Grammar[M]. Chicago and London: The University of Chicago Press, 1994.

[7] Bybee Joah L. Modality in Discourse: An Introduction Essay[M]. Amsterdam: John Benjamins, 1995.

[8] Coates, J. The Semantics of the Modal Auxiliaries[M]. Beckenham: Croom Helm, 1983.

[9] Donald W Hendon, Rebecca Angeles Hendon, Paul Herbig. Cross-cultural Business Negotiations[M]. Westport, Conn: Quorum, 1996.

[10] Downing A, Locke P. A University Course in English Grammar[M]. Hemel Hempstead: Phonix ELT, 1992: 382.

[11] Eggins S. An Introduction to Systemic Functional Linguistics[M]. London: Printer, 1994.

[12] Eggins S, Slade D. Analyzing Causal Conversation[M]. London: Cassel, 1997.

[13] Facchinetti R, Krug M, Palmer F R. Modality in Contemporary English[M]. Berlin and New York: Mouton de Gruyter, 2003.

[14] Fowler R. Language in the News[M]. London: Routledge, 1993.

[15] Fowler R, et al. Language and Control[M]. London: Routledge & Kegan Paul, 1979.

[16] Givon T. Functionalism and Grammar[M]. Amsterdam: J. Benjamins, 1995.

[17] Halliday M A K. An Introduction to Functional Grammar[M]. Beijing: Foreign Language Teaching and Research Press, 2000.

[18] Halliday M A K, Hasan R. Cohesion in English[M]. Beijing: Foreign Language Teaching

and Research Press, 2001.
[19] Halliday M A K, Mathiessen. Construing Experience through Meaning: A Language-based Approach to Cognition[M]. London: Continuum, 1999.
[20] Halliday M A K, Hasan R. Language, Context and Text: Aspects of Language in a Social-Semiotic Perspective[M]. Vivtoria: Deakin University Press. 1985.
[21] Hoye L. Adverbs and Modality in English[M]. London & New York: Longman, 1997
[22] Geert H. Culture's Consequences: Comparing Values, Behaviors Institutions, and Organizations across Nations[M]. Thousand Oaks, CA: Sage, 2001
[23] Geert H. Culture's Consequences: International Differences in Work-related Values[M]. Berverly Hills, CA: Sage, 1980.
[24] Jesperson Otto. Essentials of English Grammar[M]. London: George Allen & Unwin Ltd., 1933.
[25] Langacker R. Foundations of Cognitive Grammar[M]. Stanford: Stanford University, 1991, 2.
[26] Leech G. Principles of Pragmatics[M]. New York: Longman, 1983.
[27] Levinson S. Pragmatics[M]. Cambridge: Cambridge University Press, 1986.
[28] Lucy John A. Reflective Language — Reported Speech and Metapragmatics[M]. Cambridge: Cambridge University Press, 1993.
[29] Lyons J. Semantics[M]. Cambridge: Cambridge University Press, 1997.
[30] Martin J R. English Text: System and Structure[M]. Amsterndam: John Benjamins Publishing Company, 1992.
[31] Martin J R, Matthiessen C M I M, Painter C. Working with Functional Grammar[M]. London: Arnold, 1997
[32] Martin J R, Rose D. Working with Discourse: Meaning beyond the Clause[M]. London: Continuum, 2003.
[33] Martin J R, White P R R. The Language of Evaluation: Appraisal in English[M]. London: Macmillan Publishers, 2005.
[34] Nuyts Jan. Epistemic Modality, Language and Conceptualization: A Cognitive-Pragmatic Perspective[M]. Amsterdem: John Benjamins, 2001.
[35] Palmer F R. Mood and Modality[M]. Cambridge: Cambridge University Press, 2007.
[36] Palmer F R. The English Verb[M]. New York: Longman World Publishing Corp, 1989.
[37] Palmer F R. Modality and the English Modals[M]. New York: Longman, 1979.
[38] Papafragou A. Modality: Issues in the Semantics-Pragmatics Interface. Current Research in the Semantics/Pragmatics Interface[M]. Oxford: Oxford University Press, 2003.
[39] Papafragou A. Modality: Issues in the Semantic and Pragmatic Interface[M]. New York:

Elsevier, 2000.
[40] Perkins M R. Modal Expressions in English[M]. London: Pinter, 1983.
[41] Peter Collins. Modals and Quasi-modals in English[M]. Amsterdam-New York, 2009.
[42] Radford A. Transformational Grammar: A First Course [M]. Beijing: Foreign Language Teaching and Research Press, 1988.
[43] Rescher N. Topics in Philosopgical Logic[M]. Dortrecht: Reidel, 1968.
[44] Rokeach Milton. The Nature of Human Values[M]. New York: Free Press, 1973.
[45] Saeed J I. Semantics[M]. Malden: Blackwell Publishers, 1997.
[46] Scollon Ron, Suzanne Wong Scollon. Intercultural Communication: A Discourse Approach [M]. Beijing: Foreign Language Teaching and Research Press, 2000.
[47] Samovar Larry A, Porter Richard E, Stefano Lisa A. Communication between Culture[M]. Beijing: Foreign Language Teaching and Research Press, 2000.
[48] Searle J R. Intentionality[M]. Cambridge: Cambridge University Press, 1983.
[49] Sweetser Eve. From Etymology to Pragmatics: Metaphorical and Cultural Aspects of Semantic Structure[M]. Cambridge: Cambridge University Press, 1990.
[50] Thompson G. Introducing Functional Grammar[M]. Beijing: Foreign Language Teaching and Research Press, 2000.
[51] White P R R. Telling Media Tales: The News Story as Rhetoric[M]. Sydney: University of Sydney, 1998.
[52] Von Wright G H. An Essay in Modal Logic[M]. Amsterdam: North-Holland Publishing Co., 1951.
[53] United States. The White House. Remarks by President Obama at United Nations Secretary General Ban Ki-moon's Climate Change Summit. By ObamaBarack. (2009-09-22). http://www.whitehouse.gov/briefing-room/speeches-and-remarks.
[54] United States. The White House. Remarks by President Obama at the Morning Plenary Session of the United Nations Climate Change Conference[C/OL]. By ObamaBarack. (2009-12-18). http://www.whitehouse.gov/briefing-room/speeches-and-remarks.
[55] United States. The CNN Political Unit. Transcript of Wednesday's Presidential Debate[C/OL]. CNN. (2012-10-04). http://edition.cnn.com/2012/10/03/politics/debate-transcript/index.html.
[56] United States. The CNN Political Unit. Transcript: Third Presidential Debate[C/OL]. CNN Politics. (2012-10-22). http://politicalticker.blogs.cnn.com/2012/10/22/transcript-third.presidential-debate/iref = allsearch.
[57] United States. Fox News. Transcript of Obama's Speech at the Democratic National

Convention[C/OL]. Fox News. (2012-09-06). http://www. foxnews. com/politics/2012/09/06/transcript-obama-speech-at-dnc/.

[58] United States. ABC News. Mitt Romney's Speech at the Republican National Convention[C/OL]. ABC News. (2012-08-30). http://abcnews. go. com/Politics/previewed-excerpts-mitt-romneys-speech-republican-national-convention/storyid = 17120765.

[59]陈洁燕. 从系统功能语法角度研究商品广告的人际意义[D]. 广州:广东外语外贸大学,2005.

[60]陈治安,蒋宇红. 情态系统在话语中的人际意义研究——从语言的多维角度[C]. 八届全国功能语言学研讨会论文集. 秦皇岛:中国高校功能语法教学研究会,2003:77-79.

[61]陈治安,彭宣维. 人称指示语研究[C]. 束定芳. 中国语用学研究论文精选. 上海:上海外语教育出版社,2001:565-579.

[62]常晨光. 英语中的人际语法隐喻[J]. 外语与外语教学,2001(7):6-8.

[63]崔希亮. 事件的情态和汉语表态系统[J]. 语法研究与探索,2003 (12):23-28.

[64]范文芳. 语法隐喻理论研究[M]. 北京:外语教学与研究出版社,2001.

[65]贺阳. 试论汉语书面语的语气系统[J]. 中国人民大学学报,1992 (5):59-63.

[66]韩芹,边洁英. 国际商务英语函电[M]. 北京:北京大学出版社,2007.

[67]河江海. 中美电视访谈节目中的情态对比研究[D]. 长春:东北师范大学,2011.

[68]何自然. 语用学与英语学习[M]. 上海:上海外语教育出版社,1997.

[69]何兆熊. 新编语用学概要[M]. 上海:上海外语教育出版社,2000.

[70]侯芳淼. 外贸英语函电[M]. 北京:电子工业出版社,2010.

[71]胡壮麟,等. 系统功能语言学概论[M]. 北京:北京大学出版社,2008.

[72]胡壮麟. 功能语言学导论[M]. 北京:外语教学与研究出版社,2000.

[73]胡壮麟. 功能主义纵横谈[M]. 北京:外语教学与研究出版社,2000.

[74]胡壮麟. 语篇的衔接与连贯[M]. 上海:上海外语教育出版社,1994.

[75]黄国文.《清明》一诗英译文的人际功能探讨[J]. 外语教学,2002(3):34-38.

[76]黄国文. 英语语言问题研究[M]. 广州:中山大学出版社,1999.

[77]黄国文. 言语交际中的指示人称代词[J]. 四川外语学院学报,1999(1):47-49.

[78]黄俊杰. 传统中华文化与现代价值激荡[M]. 北京:社会科学文献出版社,2002.

[79]李芳.《傲慢与偏见》中语气及情态系统的人际意义[D]. 保定:河北大学,2003.

[80]李丰. 政治演讲语篇中语气及情态系统的人际功能分析[J]. 长春理工大学学报,2011(12):80-81.

[81]李阔. 英语中的道义情态研究[D]. 哈尔滨:黑龙江大学,2007.

[82]李杰. 情态的表达与意识形态的体现[J]. 外语学刊,2005(4).

[83]李杰,钟永平. 论英语的情态系统及其功能[J]. 外语教学,2002,23(1).

[84]李留. 英汉情态隐喻对比研究[J]. 华南理工大学学报,2005(5).
[85]李文梅,王雯. 论冲突类外贸英语信函的人际功能实现[J]. US-China Foreign Language, 2008 (8).
[86]李战子. 从语气、情态到评价[J]. 外语研究,2005,(6):14-19.
[87]李战子. 话语的人际意义研究[M]. 上海:上海外语教育出版社,2002.
[88]李战子. 学术话语中认知型情态的多重人际意义[J]. 外语教学与研究,2001 (5).
[89]李战子. 情态——从句子到语篇的推广[J]. 外语学刊,2000 (4).
[90]梁晓波. 情态的认知阐释[J]. 山东外语教学,2001(4).
[91]刘利. 中美新闻个人评论语篇中情态的对比研究[D]. 济南:山东大学,2011.
[92]刘世生. 西方文体学论纲[M]. 济南:山东教育出版社,1998.
[93]刘燕芹,英汉限定情态功能词的共性和个性[J]. 安庆师范学院学报,2008(11).
[94]刘源. 责任型情态隐喻在商务英语谈判中的人际意义研究[D]. 哈尔滨:哈尔滨工程大学,2011.
[95]鲁川. 立足汉语实际的信息语言学[J]. 语言科学,2003 (4).
[96]马庆株. 汉语动词和动词性结构[M]. 北京:北京语言学院出版社,1992.
[97]马绍明. 商务谈判英语口语 Business Negotiation[M]. 大连:大连理工大学出版社,2005.
[98]苗兴伟. 人际意义与语篇的建构[J]. 山东外语教学,2004(1).
[99]彭宣维. 英汉语篇综合对比[M]. 上海:上海外语教育出版社,2000.
[100]齐沪扬. 论现代汉语语气系统的建立[J]. 汉语学习,2002 (2):1-12.
[101]秦川. 商务英语谈判 Spoken English for Business Negotiation[M]. 北京:中国对外经济贸易出版社,2003.
[102]曲家丹. 论英语情态意义的表达[J]. 沈阳大学学报,2005 (1).
[103]孙启耀,董欣荣. 责任型情态在语篇中人际意义的分析[J]. 哈尔滨学院学报,2010 (7).
[104]孙启耀,嵩贺. 中英文广告中责任情态人际意义的分析对比[J]. 四川文理学院学报,2012 (1).
[105]王镭. WTO 与中国涉外企业所得税收制度改革[M]. 北京:社会科学文献出版社,2004.
[106]王力. 中国语法理论[M]. 济南:山东教育出版社,1984.
[107]王晓朝,杨熙楠. 沟通中西文化[M]. 南宁:广西师范大学出版社,2006.
[108]魏本力. 情态动词的量值取向[J]. 外语学刊,2005 (6).
[109]杨才英. 论语篇中的人际意义衔接[J]. 西安外国语学院学报,2006(3).
[110]杨海虹. 英语公益广告语篇中情态的人际意义[D]. 临汾:山西师范大学,2011.
[111]杨曙. 英语公益广告语篇的情态分析[J]. 外语与外语教学,2006 (1).

[112]杨燕. 浅谈新闻的讽刺美[J]. 新闻爱好者,1990(10).
[113]应巧君. 冷战期间美国总统就职演讲中情态系统的人际意义研究(1945—1991)[D]. 金华:浙江师范大学,2010.
[114]曾文雄. 商务英语谈判的语用策略[J]. 遵义师范学院学报,2002(1).
[115]张德禄. 功能文体学[M]. 济南:山东教育出版社,1998.
[116]张曼. 摘要中情态承诺和情态责任的配置[J]. 中国外语,2008(6).
[117]张珊珊. 社会科学学术论文人际意义研究[D]. 曲阜:曲阜师范大学,2004.
[118]赵楠. 英汉情态取向在新闻语篇中的对比分析[J]. 长春:东北师范大学,2004.5.
[119]郑元会. 翻译中人际意义的跨文化建构[M]. 北京:中国社会科学出版社,2009(1).
[120]郑元会. 话语人际意义的跨文化建构——评《红楼梦》中王熙凤一段会话的英译[J]. 解放军外国语学院学报,2005(3).
[121]郑元会. 情态与汉语情态动词[J]. 山东外语教学,2005(2).
[122]周大军. 英语的情态隐喻及其语篇解释力[J]. 四川外语学院学报,2003,19(5).
[123]朱永生. 功能语言学导论[M]. 上海:上海外语教育出版社,2004.
[124]朱永生,严世清. 系统功能语言学多维思考[M]. 上海:上海外语教育出版社,2001.
[125]中华人民共和国. 外交部. 携手应对气候变化挑战[C/OL]. 胡锦涛.(2009-09-22). http://www.fmprc.gov.cn/chn/pds/ziliao/zyjh/t646509.htm.
[126]中华人民共和国. 外交部. 凝聚共识加强合作推进应对气候变化历史进程[C/OL]. 温家宝.(2009-12-18). http://www.fmprc.gov.cn/chn/pds/ziliao/zyjh/t646509.htm.